TRAILS OF THE FEATHER RIVER REGION

A TREASURE TROVE OF NORTHEASTERN CALIFORNIA TRAILS.

Over 200 Trails Anyone Can Hike.

SCOTT J. LAWSON

Valderi Valdera
Publishing
Blairsden, California

Copyright ©2003
by Scott J. Lawson
First Edition

Trails of the Feather River Region: A Treasure Trove of Northeastern California Trails.

All rights reserved. This book may not be reproduced in full or in part in any form, by any electronic, mechanical, or other means, without the written permission of the publisher, except for use by a reviewer in the context of a review. Inquiries and excerpt requests should be addressed to:

Valderi Valdera Publishing
10 Sugar Pine Drive
Blairsden, CA 96103
530-836-4112

All photographs by the author except as noted and all historic photos courtesy Plumas County Museum, Quincy, California.

Front cover: South side of Mt. Washington above Johnsville. Cover by Kevin Mallory

No liability is assumed with respect to the information or content of this book. No one should participate in any of the activities in this book unless they recognize and personally assume the associated risks.

Cataloging-in-Publication Data

Lawson, Scott J.
    Trails of the Feather River Region: A Treasure Trove of Northeastern California Trails / Scott J. Lawson.
p. cm.
Includes bibliographical references, index.
ISBN 1-59109-739-8
1. Hiking—California, Northeastern—Guidebooks. 2. History—California, Northeastern. 3. Sierra Nevada and Cascade Range—California—Description and travel--Guidebooks. I. Title
GV

Printed in the United States of America.

TRAILS OF THE FEATHER RIVER REGION

A TREASURE TROVE OF NORTHEASTERN CALIFORNIA TRAILS.

Over 200 Trails Anyone Can Hike.

SCOTT J. LAWSON

Valderi Valdera
Publishing
Blairsden, California

TABLE OF CONTENTS

Locator Map for Plumas County	11
Dedication and Acknowledgements	12
Introduction and Disclaimer	13
Historical Overview	14
How To Use This Book	17
Essentials	17
Rating System	18
Mileage and Elevation	19
Pacific Crest Trail	19
Maps	19
Switchbacks	20
Other Rules of the Trail	20
Things To Be Aware Of...	21
Getting Lost (or Unlost)	21
Fire Danger	21
Private Property	21
Water	22
Dogs and Domestic Animals	22
Snakes	22
Bees	23
Ticks and Lyme Disease	23
Bubonic Plague and Hanta Virus	24
Bears and Lions	24
Poison Oak	24
Heat Stroke	25
Heat Exhaustion	25
Hypothermia	25
Injuries	26
Communities and Cultural Attractions	27
American Valley	27
Chester-Lake Almanor	28
Eastern Plumas and Sierra Valley	29
Feather River Canyon	31
Indian Valley	32
Mohawk Valley	33
Southern Plumas and the Lost Sierra	35
North Yuba Canyon	36
Sierra Valley (Sierra County)	37
Susanville-Westwood	40
List of Trails	
Northern Sierra County and Eastern Yuba County	41
Locator Map for Sierra County	42
Badenaugh Canyon Trail 17E01	43

Bellevue Mine Flume Trail	44
Bellevue Mine-Howland Flat Wagon Road Trail	45
Bellevue Mine-Wallace Creek Trail	46
Brandy City Trail	46
Brandy City Pond Trail	48
Bullard's Bar-Dark Day Trail	48
Bullard's Bar Trail 8E07 (Sunset Vista to Schoolhouse)	48
Bullard's Bar Trail 8E10 (Schoolhouse Trail)	50
Butcher Ranch Trail	50
Canyon Creek Trail	51
Castle Rock Trail	52
Chapman Creek Trail	52
Chimney Rock Trail	53
Craig's Flat Trail	54
Cut-Eye Foster's Bar Trail	55
Downie River Trail	55
East Branch Canyon Creek Trail	56
Empire Creek Trail	57
Eureka Diggings-Little Canyon Creek Trail	58
Fiddle Creek Ridge Trail	60
Hall's Ranch Trail	61
Haskell Peak Trail	61
Illinois Creek Trail	62
Lavezolla Creek Trail	63
Little Grizzly Creek Trail	64
Morristown-Canyon Creek Trail	65
Mountain Boy-Pat's Gulch Trail	65
Mt. Fillmore Trail	66
Mt. Lola Trail	66
Old Poker Flat Trail	67
Pacific Mine-Canyon Creek Trail	68
Pauley Creek Trail	68
Port Wine Trail	69
Port Wine Ridge Trail	70
Ramshorn Trail	70
Rattlesnake Creek Trail	72
Second Divide Trail	73
Spencer Lakes Trail (via Spencer Creek)	74
Spencer Lakes Trail (via the PCT)	74
St. Charles Hill Trail (Brown Bear Mine Trail)	75
Stafford Mountain-West Branch Canyon Creek Trail	76
Third Divide Trail	76
West Branch Canyon Creek Trail	77
West Coast Mine-Canyon Creek Trail	78
Lakes Basin Recreation Area (Plumas and Sierra Counties)	**79**
Bear Lakes Trail	81

Berger Creek-Saxonia Lake Trail	82
Deer Lake Trail	83
Fern Falls Overlook Trail	83
Frazier Falls Overlook Trail	83
Grassy Lake Trail	84
Gray Eagle Creek Trail	84
Lily Lake Trail	85
Little Jamison Creek Trail	85
Long Lake Dam Trail	87
Long Lake Trail	87
Long Lake Trail (from Gray Eagle Lodge)	88
Mount Elwell Trail	88
Mount Elwell Trail (Smith Lake Trailhead)	88
Mt. Washington Trail	90
Mud Lake Trail	90
Pacific Crest Tie Trail (Upper Salmon Lake)	91
Red Fir Nature Trail	92
Round Lake Trail	92
Sand Pond Interpretive Trail	94
Sardine Lakes Overlook Trail	94
Sierra Buttes Trail	95
Silver Lake Trail	95
Smith Creek Trail	96
Smith Lake Trail (from Gray Eagle Lodge)	97
Smith Lake Trail (via Little Jamison Creek Trail)	97
Summit Trail	98
Tamarack Connection Trail	99
Upper Salmon Lake-Deer Lake Trail	100
Wades Lake Trail	101
Southern Plumas County and Northeastern Butte County	102
Abandoned Feather Falls Trail	103
Belfrin Mine Extension Trail (Seymour Trail)	104
Butte Bar Trail	105
Buzzard's Roost Ridge Trail	105
Dixon Creek-Union Creek Trail	106
Eureka Peak Trail	107
Feather Falls National Recreation Trail	108
Fingerboard Trail (Minerva Bar Trail)	110
Fish Creek-McRae Meadows Trail	110
Grass Valley Bald Mountain Trail and PCT Tie Trail	112
Graves Cabin-Kennedy Cabin Trail	113
Hanson's Bar Trail	114
Hartman Bar National Recreation Trail (South)	115
Hewitt Mine-Hopkins Creek Trail	116
Hottentot Bar Trail	116
Illinois Ridge-China Bar Trail	117

Joe Taylor Trail	117
Kennedy Butte Trail 7E27	118
Little Grass Valley Lakeshore Trail	119
Madora Lake Nature Trail	119
Minerva Bar Trail (Wilson Gomez Route)	120
Nelson Creek Bridge-Union Creek Trail	121
Nelson Point-La Porte Road Trail	121
Nelson Point-Turntable Trail	122
Onion Valley Creek Mine Trail	122
Onion Valley Creek Trail	123
Overmeyer Trail	124
Poormans Creek Road-Hopkins Creek Trail	125
Richmond Hill-Berg Creek Trail	125
Sawmill Tom Trail	126
Sawpit Flat Trail	127
Sawpit Flat Wagon Road Trail	128
Seven Falls Trail	128
Shake Cabin Trail	129
Upper Nelson Creek Trail	130
Watson Cabin-Abandoned Feather Falls Trail	130
Watson Ridge Trail	131
West Branch Nelson Creek Trail	132
Zumwalt Flat-Nelson Creek Trail	133
Central Plumas County (Including Bucks Lake Wilderness)	134
Big Bald Rock Trail	134
Buckhorn Mine Trail	135
Bucks Creek Trail	135
Camp Rodgers Saddle Trail	136
Cascades Trail	137
Deadman Springs Trail	138
Dome Trail	139
Five Bear Mine-Bach Creek Trail 10E16	140
Grizzly Forebay Gauging Station Trail	141
Grizzly Forebay Trail	141
Hartman Bar Trail (North)	142
Heinz Creek Trail	143
Hunter's Ravine Trail	144
Jackson Creek-Middle Fork Feather River Trail	144
Little California Mine Trail	145
Little North Fork Trail	145
Long Valley Trail	146
Lost Cabin Springs-Sugar Pine Mine Trail	148
Marble Creek Trail	148
McCarthy Bar Trail	150
Middle Branch Mill Creek Trail	150
Mill Creek Ditch Trail	151

Mountain House Creek Trail	151
No Ear Bar Trail	152
Oddie Bar Trail	153
Silver Star Mine-Baker Creek Trail	153
Summit Trail	154
Tobin Trail	154
West Branch Mill Creek Trail	156
Wildcat Creek Trail	156
Bucks Lake Wilderness Trails	**159**
Granite Gap Trail 7E12	160
Mill Creek Trail	160
Right Hand Branch Mill Creek Trail	161
Silver Lake-Gold Lake Trail 8E04	162
Spanish Ranch-Rich Bar Trail	163
Three Lakes-PCT Tie Trail	164
Three Lakes-Rich Bar Trail (via Kellogg Lake)	164
Three Lakes Trail	166
Northern Plumas County and Southern Lassen County (Including Caribou Wilderness and Lassen National Park)	**167**
Antelope Lake Nature Trail	167
Antelope Lake-Taylor Lake Trail	168
Belden-Soda Creek Trail	171
Ben Lomond Trail	173
Bizz Johnson Trail	173
Blue Lake-Ridge Lake Trail	174
Blue Lake-Spencer Meadows Tie Trail	175
Chambers Creek Trail	175
Cold Stream Trail	177
Dixie Mountain Trail	178
Homer Lake-Deerheart Lake Trail	178
Hosselkus Creek Trail	179
Hungry Creek Trail	181
Indian Falls Trail	181
Indian Springs Trail	181
Lake Almanor Recreation Trail	182
Middle Creek Trail	183
North Arm Rice Creek Trail	184
Peter's Creek Trail	185
Providence Hill-Schneider Ravine Trail	186
Round Valley Lake Nature Trail	187
Spencer Meadows National Recreation Trail	187
Star Lake Trail	189
Sunflower Flat-Saucer Lake Trail	190
Sunflower Flat-Soda Creek Trail (to Peacock Point)	190
Trail Lake Trail (Echo Lake to Silver Lake Trail)	192
Yellow Creek Trail	193

Caribou Wilderness Trails 194
    Caribou Lake-Black Lake Trail 195
    Caribou Lake-North Divide Lake Trail 196
    Cypress Lake Trail 196
    Hay Meadow-Cone Lake Trail 197
    Hay Meadow-Long Lake Trail (via Beauty Lake) 199
    Hay Meadow-Long Lake Trail (via Hidden Lakes) 199
    Indian Meadows-Hidden Lakes Trail 200
    Triangle Lake Loop Trail 200
Lassen National Park Trails 201
    Boiling Springs Lake Trail 201
    Bumpass Hell Trail 201
    Cinder Cone Trail 201
    Forest Lake & Brokeoff Mountain Trail 201
    Kings Creek Falls Trail 201
    Lassen Peak Trail 201
    Lily Pond Nature Trail 202
    Manzanita Lake Trail 202
    Mill Creek Falls Trail 202
    Mt. Harkness Trail 202
    Summit Lake to Echo Lake & Twin Lakes Trail 202
    Terrace Shadow & Cliff Lakes Trail 202
Unexplored Trails 203
Eastern Yuba County
    Cherokee Creek Trail 203
    Council Hill-Brandy City Trail 9E132 (via Canyon Creek) 203
    Gophner Ravine-Wambo Bar Trail 203
    Kelly Bar Trail 204
    Oak Flat-Race Track Point Trail 204
    Slate Range Bar Trail 204
Sierra County 206
    Bee Ranch Trail 206
    Craycroft Ridge Trail 206
    Smith Lake Trail (Smith Lake to Lavezolla Creek Trail) 206
Butte County 207
    China Gulch Trail 207
    Fall River Trail 207
    French Creek Trail 207
    Jackson Ranch Trail 207
    Skyhigh-Little North Fork Feather River Trail 208
Plumas County 209
    Barker's Cabin-Onion Valley Creek Trail 209
    Hartman Bar Ridge-South Branch MFFR Trail 209
    High Ridge Trail 209
    Hopkins Creek-West Nelson Creek Trail 209
    Hottentot Creek-Winters Creek Trail 210

Montgomery Creek Trail	210
Weber Bar Trail	211
Dead Trails	212
Bach Creek Ridge Trail	212
Cable Crossing Trail	212
Clippership Mine-Gardiner's Point Reservoir Trail	212
Cold Springs-Claremont Trail	212
Fiddle Creek Trail	212
H&G Mine Trail	212
Hartman Bar Ridge-Hunter's Ravine Trail 7E26	213
Hog Gulch Trail	213
Hopkins Creek-Peak 6908'	213
Little Grizzly Valley-Peacock Point Trail	213
Mountain House-12 Mile Bar Trail	213
Mt. Alma Trail	214
Mt. Etna via Hopkins Creek Trail	214
Nelson Creek Trail	214
Onion Valley-Richmond Hill Trail	214
Rock Creek to Rock Creek Crossing Trail	214
Yellow Creek Trail (Parallel to County Road 307)	215
Glossary	216
Information Centers	219
Hiking Information & Clubs	220
Map Sources	220
Suggested Reading	221
List of Sources	221
Index of Trails	223
About the Author	229

PLUMAS COUNTY & THE FEATHER RIVER REGION LOCATOR MAP

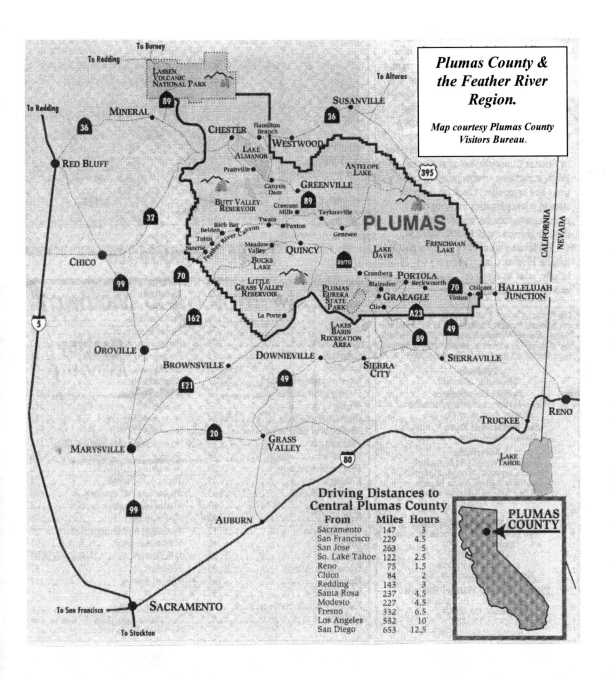

DEDICATION

I dedicate this book to my daughter, Sarah J. Lawson, who has hiked with me since she was just a little tyke, and in memory of Sally, our faithful 16-year old Golden Retriever, who made almost every one of these hikes (at least three times!).

ACKNOWLEDGEMENTS

My sincere thanks go to the following people who have helped in many ways over the years: Judy Buck, editing and encouragement; Tim Dembosz, U.S. Forest Service, trails information; Michael Ellwood, hiking buddy; Andrew Harris, encouragement and information; Becky Herrin, proof-reading; Dean & Diane Lawson, my parents-they let me go out and about hiking at a young age; Melanie Lawson, encouragement, car shuttling; the late Ronald Marsh, shuttling cars, encouragement, and his experiences; and Heidi Wightman, proof-reading.

INTRODUCTION

I love history, especially California and local history. My original idea was to list and describe only the historic trails of the Feather River watershed, but I soon found that even the newer ones were fun and interesting and so the idea for this reference-guide was born. I thought perhaps it would be a benefit not only to hikers and backpackers, but fishermen, hunters, equestrians, mountain bikers, foresters, and search and rescue personnel. Many of the trails presented here are done so in the hope that someone will adopt them. Many are listed for their historic value rather than hiking value due to their extremely deteriorated condition. Some great trails are not even on maps, and some that are indicated on maps are in such a state of decline that they are almost unusable. I have listed these with what I hope are appropriate notes. Others no longer even exist and so I have listed them as dead trails in a separate section. On some of the trails described, special care must be taken to look for blaze marks (many of which are overgrown but evident), cuttings on the ends of brush, ducks or cairns (small stacks of rocks along the trail) and other features that indicate the trail route. These particular trails are generally extremely rough and should only be attempted by persons in extremely good physical and mental condition.

It is strongly advised that you attempt only trails that you are physically and mentally conditioned for.

Sometimes the roads used to access these trails are also narrow, steep, rough, or require four-wheel drive (4WD) vehicles. Whenever possible, I have tried to note when 4WD is required; however, man's activities, the weather, or other events could change conditions without notice. Please be careful not to over-extend yourself or underestimate the power of Mother Nature. Always let a responsible person knows where you are and when you plan to return, and stick to your plan.

As with all maps, atlases, or guides, the user of these tools must assume risk and responsibility for themselves. The compilation of these trails into a guide does not infer that I assume a responsibility for them or those who use them. No guidebook can be expected to diminish hazards or be a guarantee of safety. Events beyond anyone's control can turn a simple hike into a dangerous situation. This guide is meant only as an aid in hiking some of the many trails in Plumas, Lassen, Butte, Yuba, and Sierra counties. I have tried, by walking the trails myself, to verify everything in this guide as much as possible, but assume no responsibility for errors in writing, description, or direction, or for any accidents, or incidents, that may occur directly, or indirectly, as a result of using this guide. The years 1997-2001 are an excellent example of how conditions change. This region endured extreme floods and fires both. But we must remember that this also gives us the opportunity to observe nature recover.

HISTORICAL OVERVIEW

The following is a brief historical and geographical narrative of the area this book covers. Further along are sections on how to use this book, a glossary of terms related to hiking in general, cultural attractions. The remainder consists of detailed descriptions of over 200 trails available for hiking throughout this area.

Plumas, Lassen, Butte, Yuba, and Sierra counties, located in northeastern California, were born of the California Gold Rush. Prior to that event, the Mountain Maidu Indians inhabited the area. Living in small groups, they gathered roots, berries, grasses, seeds, and acorns, supplementing these staples with large and small game, fowl, and fish. During the summers they inhabited the mountains, gathering acorns and seeds, hunting and fishing, and in the fall and winter returned to the mountain valleys and foothills. Their placid existence was rudely disturbed in the spring of 1850 when a flood of gold-seeking miners poured into the mountains and canyons of the region in search of a fabled lake of gold.

During the fall of 1849, gold seeking emigrant Thomas Stoddard staggered into a mining camp telling a tale of a lake whose shores were lined with gold. Crazy Stoddard, as he became known, led a large party of miners into the mountains in search of this elusive treasure the next spring. The lake of gold proved to be a farce, and Stoddard, after receiving an ultimatum and an invitation to a necktie party, disappeared. The disappointed treasure seekers broke off into small groups to prospect, the result of which was the discovery of many rich gold deposits all over Plumas County and northern Sierra County. Overnight, mining camps exploded to life, rivers were turned from their ancestral beds, ditches were carved along the hillsides to bring water from distant sources to the diggings, and the earth was turned upside down. Chinese miners, mostly male, took up residence in the area, remaining until the early 1900s when, with a decline in mining, most left for metropolitan areas such as San Francisco and Sacramento.

The Feather River, originally named Rio de las Plumas by Spanish explorers, has three main branches. The North, Middle, and South forks were the primary sites of early mining activity with many smaller camps located on their tributaries. For the entire second half of the 19th century, gold mining remained the main industry of Plumas County.

In 1850, African-American mountain man James P. Beckwourth discovered the lowest pass across the Sierra Nevada (5,212 feet). The following year he navigated a wagon train for California-bound emigrants from what is now Reno, Nevada, through present day Plumas County, to the Sacramento Valley.

Several years later, in March of 1854, Plumas County was formed from the eastern and largest portion of Butte County. The town of Quincy was chosen as the county seat after a heated election between rival towns. In 1864, a part of northern Plumas County was carved off to form present-day Lassen County. Following this, Plumas County annexed a small portion of northern Sierra County, which included the mining town of La Porte. In the late 1850s, Greenville came into existence as a mining and farming community at the head of Indian Valley; Chester, on the shores of Lake Almanor, prospered as a result of damming Big Meadows for hydro-electric power in 1914. Since that time, along with tourism, the lumber potential from the timber stands blanketing the area have provided their economic basis. Soon after the turn of the century, and with the completion of the Western Pacific Railroad in 1910, Portola became the hub of activity in eastern-central Plumas County. With the railroad for transportation, and a general decline in mining, the timber industry began to emerge as the primary economic force in the county. Until that time lumber was milled strictly for local use. Finished lumber could now be shipped nationwide from Plumas County's forests. The timber industry contributed enormously to the growth and prosperity of Plumas County and continues to do so to this day.

Riding upon the new railroad, sportsmen and leisure-seekers poured into the county. Resorts and lodges popped up all along the Feather River Route to accommodate fishermen, hikers, and sightseers. In 1937, the Feather River Highway, touted as the Sierra's only all weather route, was opened. It ran through the Feather River canyon from Oroville to Quincy, linking Plumas County year round to the Sacramento Valley. After the construction of the highway and World War II, passenger-train travel dropped and the last Zephyr passenger train ran in March 1970. The line, now owned by Union Pacific Railroad, is devoted exclusively to freight traffic.

Since the Gold Rush, the region has continued to grow in population, although very slowly. Part of what brought our pioneers, and kept them, has also succeeded in keeping present-day residents. The attractions of the Feather River and Yuba River drainages are many; old growth forests and cascading streams, lush mountain valleys, crystal blue lakes, and sage-covered high deserts. Quiet towns, golf courses, a state park, museums, several airports, water and winter sports, a national park, and a relaxed lifestyle are a part of this, one of California's best-kept secrets. The population of Plumas County in 2000 was 20,824 with a land base of 1,675,780 acres, of which 71% is public land. National forest covers most of Plumas County's 2,613 square miles, with the Plumas National Forest occupying 1.2 million acres. Known for its high alpine lakes and thousands of miles of clear-running streams, Plumas County sits at the top of a watershed that supplies water to many millions of California's citizens.

The largest town, centered in the geographic area described in this guide, is Quincy, Plumas County, with a population of about 5,500 people. There is one stoplight, recently installed, but no freeways or smog. The major highways crossing this region are east-west State Route 70, and north-south state routes 49 and 89, all of which now enjoy National Scenic Byway status. Plumas County is accessible from the Sacramento Valley within a couple of hours, and Reno, Nevada, is about one hour to the east. The drive through this region alone is worth the trip; the trails only make it better.

Many of the trails in the Feather and Yuba watersheds were first used by wildlife and the Maidu Indians, expanded on by the Argonauts of the California Gold Rush, and further developed through the turn of the century for mining, hunting, recreation, and fire suppression. A number of the trails were mule packers' routes, a few became narrow wagon roads, but most, simply footpaths. Some are so ancient they seem hardly to exist any more. Plumas County, where the majority of the trails in this guide are located, also has the most inadequately maintained trails. The Plumas National Forest has for years neglected trail building and maintenance, though lately their efforts have been renewed in that area. On the other hand, Tahoe National Forest in Sierra County seems to have a generally more aggressive trail program. The trails tend to be in overall better condition. The Plumas, Lassen, and Tahoe national forests also administer an Adopt-A-Trail program. If you are interested in maintaining or refitting one or more of these trails, contact the District Ranger Office nearest the trail you are interested in. Contacting the Forest Service and expressing your interest in seeing them maintain the trails as a regular program may also be beneficial.

Throughout the region are reminders of Native Americans, miners, lumbermen, and ranchers. Grinding rocks, old ditches, cabin sites, mining camps, sawmills, ranches, and homesteads are mute testimony to their existence. As interesting and tempting as they are, these pieces of our heritage are protected under federal and state laws. Bottle digging, relic collecting, or disturbing of these sites is prohibited and, when apprehended, violators are vigorously prosecuted. Severe fines are a reality if you are caught in these activities. Please respect and enjoy our heritage, don't degrade or destroy it. Leave it for others to enjoy.

I hope you enjoy your visit to the Feather-Yuba river country. If you live here, you know what I mean. Unparalleled scenery, towering pines, deep craggy canyons with wild rushing streams, windswept ridges, placid lakes, and gentle valleys offer something for everyone. The beauty of the man-made and natural wonders to be found here are a reward well worth the effort of a hike. I hope this guide will serve to make your experience a very enjoyable one.

"Homeward Bound" September 11, 1921

HOW TO USE THIS BOOK

This reference-guide is arranged geographically into five sections. Within each section the trails are listed alphabetically. Although this separates some related trails, it makes it easier to locate them in the guide. The five sections are comprised of the Lakes Basin area, Northern Sierra & Eastern Yuba counties, Southern Plumas & Northeastern Butte counties, Central Plumas County, and Northern Plumas & Southern Lassen counties. Included in the appropriate sections are subsections on Bucks Lake Wilderness, Caribou Wilderness, and Lassen Park.

The following information is by no means all-inclusive and if you are not familiar with any of these topics it is recommended that you consult more in-depth sources. The intent here is to assist you with some of the more basic subjects related to hiking. Further sources of information that you may wish to contact, and a glossary of terms relative to hiking and the outdoors are also provided at the end of this section. It is strongly recommended that you take a Red Cross course in first aid and CPR. That knowledge could save your life or the life of another.

ESSENTIALS

Wear clothing appropriate for the occasion. If necessary, carry extra clothing, food, etc. In spring and autumn, weather can change rapidly and drastically, so be prepared! Some recommended items to carry on a hike are: a daypack, this guide, lunch, first aid kit, candy, emergency food, whistle, small mirror, small flashlight, can opener, pocket knife, maps, compass, emergency tarp, toilet paper, matches and candle in waterproof container, small plastic garbage bag, bug repellent, sunscreen, sunglasses, water, and anything else you feel will benefit you on your hike. This may seem excessive, but if you end up in a negative situation, these common items may mean all the difference. I have several emergency kits and first aid kits that I keep in each pack all the time.

RATING SYSTEM

Keep in mind that any rating system is inherently flawed. Individual perceptions differ, trails change, conditions change, but for lack of a better way of concisely describing the effort required to hike a trail, some kind of system is required. There are so many variables that affect effort: weather, personal attitude, individual physical condition, time of day, time of year, etc. There is one variable that I have used to help determine effort, and that is trail condition. Conditions may change on a particular trail for better or worse at any time, but it is such an integral part of hiking that I feel justified in using it. Therefore, I have opted to use the following system. A trail may contain any one or more of the following features to warrant a particular rating:

Very Easy: Level, smooth, well maintained.
Easy: Fairly level, good tread, little or no brush overhanging the trail, no scrambling. Well maintained.
Moderate: Some up and down. Some brush, rugged tread, or obstructions in the trail. Adequate maintenance.
Difficult: Steep, many ups and downs, rugged tread, brush or obstacles in trail. Adequate to little maintenance.
Very Difficult: Overgrown, brushy, obstacles in trail, little or no route indications. Steep, loose, rugged tread. Little or no maintenance.
Extremely Difficult: Don't do it! Either the trail is almost nonexistent, the brush is so thick you have to be a bear to walk through it, or there is some other non-redeeming feature to the trail. Some of these border on dead trail status.

ICONS

The various icons you will see to the right of the trail information heading are a quick way to determine some features of the trail. Of course the icons cannot possibly describe everything about the trail, so if you are seeking certain features you should read the entire description.

Summit climb or good views

Forested (limited views)

Historic (mining, ranching, packing, wagon road)

Waterfall

ADA accessible

No OHVs or motorized vehicles or equipment

Fishing

MILEAGE AND ELEVATION

Mileage is something that seems to be a preoccupation with many hikers. Since everyone, including the sign makers, seem to have their own idea about how far it is from one place to another, I have given mileages as approximate. Because there generally are never more than 1/4 to 1/3 mile variances, this should allow you an idea of how you would like to budget your time. Remember, you are in mountain country and must expect there could be lots of up and down on the trail, so plan accordingly.

In this book the first elevation given is the starting point and the second the destination. There may be higher or lower points between the start and end, but elevations are given only for each end. Conversely, you may want to start at the other end. The second elevation is then your starting point. This is also the case as far as hike time. If a trail is fairly level or easy, the time to hike it would be about the same regardless of which end it is started. However, as a rule of thumb, it is wise to allow yourself at least double the time to return on a trail, especially if it is a steep one, For example, the trails that drop into the Middle Fork of the Feather River. The times I have given are for steady hiking with no extended stops along the way. You may take much longer or not as long as the guide describes.

PACIFIC CREST TRAIL (County-wide)

Other than tie trails or where a trail connects with the Pacific Crest Trail, I have elected not to describe this trail. Though many short segments of it make great day hikes, there are enough well executed guides on this trail that I feel it would be redundant for me to cover it here.

MAPS

U.S. Geological Survey (U.S.G.S.) topographical maps are well detailed, and indicate the elevations above sea level of a given spot by use of contour lines. Towns, mines, trails, roads, and other features are indicated on them. Generally, the Forest Service designates their roads with a lettering and numbering system such as 24N32 or 24N32Y. The 24N refers to the township the road originates in, the 32 is the road, and the Y (or other letter) denotes a spur of the road. As with anything, the maps are not

Rustic signs made by William Shuster, Fire Control Officer.

infallible and you may come across mistakes in the placement of sites, trails, and sometimes a whole stream! For the most part though, these are the best maps available and can be obtained from most sporting goods stores, some stationary and office supply houses, Plumas County Museum, and the U.S.G.S. itself. The maps included in this guide are very basic, and are intended only as locator maps. It would probably be best to obtain full quadrangles to show more detail, as well as the surrounding countryside.

SWITCHBACKS

Now about the one feature of a trail most hikers seem to hate: Switchbacks. Switchbacks are repetitious and therefore can become monotonous. One thing inconsiderate and impatient hikers do is cut switchbacks. **Please do not do this**! Switchbacks may represent a bit of extra walking, but they are necessary. They maintain trail integrity and make a walk uphill much easier. If you cut a switchback, then the next person will, and the next, and so on, and soon the trail is beset with erosion problems.

OTHER RULES OF THE TRAIL

Hike with a partner whenever possible and be sure to let a responsible party know your intended route, and stick to that route. When hiking with others, keep out of alignment with each other while hiking up or down in steep terrain to make sure loose rocks or debris dislodged from above won't hit the hiker below you. Always carry out your own trash, and any other trash you find. It really will make you feel better knowing you did more than your part to keep our wild lands clean. As for Off-Highway Vehicle (OHV) travel, I have noted the trails or areas where these machines are specifically prohibited. These areas include Lakes Basin, Bucks Lake Wilderness, Caribou Wilderness, the Middle Fork of the Feather River Wild Area, and certain individual trails. Riding OHVs can be fun, but please respect these restrictions. I have treated mountain bikes as I have horses. I am not a biker or equestrian so I don't presume to know which trails are suitable for those modes of travel. I can only plead with mountain bikers to please repair the trails they use so that others might enjoy them.

THINGS TO BE AWARE OF...

GETTING LOST (Or Unlost)

Although getting truly lost is a fairly difficult thing to do, it still happens. Sometimes becoming disoriented is just as bad. In any case, **do not panic!** Stop, try to relax, calm down, and determine just where you are, where you have been, and where you can go. In most cases a road or large stream is not too far off. If you hit a road, stay on it. Following large streams downward will **almost** always bring you to a road, but not always. The best way to avoid ever getting into a situation like this is to have the proper maps for your hike, a compass, and the knowledge to use them. If lost, hug a tree or other large landmark until someone can find you. It is always easier to hit a stationary target than a moving one. Blow on a whistle rather than shout, or your voice will soon be lost also.

FIRE DANGER

This is without a doubt the greatest danger to everyone, especially the forest. I cannot stress enough the responsible use of fire in the forest. Always have water or a suitable fire extinguisher handy when using campfires. Never build bonfires and always clear the surrounding area down to soil at least 10 feet away from the fire pit. In fact, not even using open campfires is strongly advocated. Besides being messy, they take too much time out of a day to make, maintain, and put out. A fire permit is required also. You may obtain one from any U.S. Forest Service office.

PRIVATE PROPERTY

Some of these trails start on, end on, or cross private property. Please respect the owner's rights. Do not disturb, destroy, or remove anything on their property. Many trails have no legal easements, so in essence you may be trespassing even though the public has used the trail for years. I am not condoning the use of trails on

Old outhouse for the Pilot Peak Lookout in 1974.
Photo by Michael Ellwood.

private property, they are only listed because they are on maps or are commonly known.

WATER

An ample supply of drinking water should be carried since water from springs, streams, lakes, and ponds may be contaminated. It is said giardia and other microscopic bacteria may be present now in just about every water source, including snow. If you can't carry water, one recommended method for purification is to bring clear water to a rolling boil for not less than 1 minute. Commercially available tablets and filters can also be found at most outdoor sports stores. Giardia can be transmitted between humans and animals. Feces can contain the organism. Waste should be buried 8 inches deep and at least 200 feet away from water sources. Dogs, like people, are susceptible to infection with giardia. Unless they are carefully controlled, dogs can contaminate the water and continue the chain of infection from animals to humans. Keep this in mind when taking dogs with you on hiking trips, which leads us into...

DOGS AND DOMESTIC ANIMALS

I love dogs, but must stress here that responsible dog owners should have a leash or other type of restraining device available to them while hiking. That way, if a trail requires a leash, the restriction can be exercised. Rather than indicate every trail that requires a leash, to be on the safe side, at least carry a short length of rope to use as a leash. I have tried to indicate trails that specifically prohibit dogs, but, as a precaution, a phone call ahead to the proper administrative authority is the best bet. Generally, dog restrictions apply in state, local, and national parks. Horses, mules, and llamas are a popular mode of travel in certain areas, but due to ever-changing trail conditions, and the fact that I am not an equestrian, I have not indicated if a trail is suitable to horses. I am not anti-horse by any means, but I have seen the Forest Service recommend trails for horses that I could barely walk, and I don't want to get people or animals injured. I hope the trail descriptions are clear enough that an experienced rider will be able to ascertain whether the trail is suitable for horse or other animal travel.

SNAKES

Say snake and most people envision a repulsive, slithery reptile that lurks in wait to bite the unwary. Contrary to this notion, most snakes, including rattlesnakes, prefer to remain away from the company of humans and strike only in self-defense. Do not kill rattlers unless absolutely necessary, and most certainly do not kill harmless snakes such as gopher snakes, water snakes, and king snakes. Incidentally, more people die of bee stings every year than snakebites. In fact, in 1993, of the 604 rattlesnake bites reported nationwide to the U.S. Poison Control centers, none were fatal. When in snake area use common sense and keep a sharp lookout. Don't reach under brush, rocks, or into places where you can't see. Step on logs or obstructions rather than stepping over them. It is also wise to use a hiking stick to beat brush, and poke in and around rocks, logs, etc. on the hiking trail. Most snakes will try to get out of your way given half a chance. Fortunately, the rattlesnake is the only venomous snake we need to be concerned with in this country, and since they normally will try to warn you with the buzzing of their tail, you have the advantage. Stand still and determine the location of the snake, then move away from the snake as quickly as possible.

In case of snakebite, the first thing is to determine if the bite injected venom. As many as 20 percent of rattlesnake bites are venomless. Venom causes the following symptoms: burning pain near the wound, rapid swelling of the infected area, tingling and a metallic taste in the mouth, muscle twitching, and general weakness. Try to remain calm and warm, but not over-heated. Cool the bite, but don't use ice. Treat for shock, and give fluids as desired. If possible, get to a doctor as quickly as possible but do not run or move briskly. The affected part should be immobilized. It is very important to keep the spread of venom in your system to a minimum. If it is not possible to get to a doctor quickly (within 2 hours), or have one brought in, the use of a snakebite kit is justified, but know how to use it and read the instructions carefully. Never cut or suck on snakebite wound. Venom from the bite can enter even the smallest wound in your mouth with serious consequences. Do not give aspirin or any medication containing aspirin. Do not give stimulants, alcohol, or use tourniquets. The Sawyer Extractor Pump, available at sporting goods stores, is considered the safest in snakebite first aid. Again, read the instructions and know how to use it.

As an interesting aside, the old snake bite medicine myth was dispelled years ago when in 1897 it was reported that: A Philadelphia scientist declares the idea that whisky is a cure for snake bite has been completely exploded. It is a wonder these men of science cannot let laymen enjoy at least this one of the old and comforting traditions.

BEES

Hornets and wasps are about our only real concern when it comes to venomous flying insects. Hornets (commonly called meat bees or yellow jackets) are particularly vicious and will attack with little or no provocation. Pay attention when you hear their distinct hum and try to quickly get out of their way. These angry fellows can be found in nests in the ground, in rotten logs and snags, and in paper-like nests hanging from branches. The bald face hornet, a dark, larger, more potent relative is another ornery one to watch out for. If stung, cool the wound and don't exert yourself. There are commercially available first aid kits with suction devices that work well on bee stings. If you are allergic to stings you should carry a bee sting kit, available by prescription.

TICKS & LYME DISEASE

Ticks are generally picked up when hiking in brushy areas. Most forest animals also carry ticks so stay away from dead or dying creatures. Frequently check your clothes and skin for these small, oval shaped bloodsuckers. The smaller black and brown ticks are deer ticks and are the ones that may be carrying Lyme disease. If you find one has bitten you or burrowed in, remove it, put it in a sealed bag or container, and take it to your doctor to be checked for the disease.

BUBONIC PLAGUE & HANTA VIRUS

Although relatively rare, the bubonic plague and the hanta virus have been found throughout the Sierra. Both chipmunks and ground squirrels carry the fleas that transmit plague, while deer mice carry the hanta virus in their blood and transmit it through that medium and in their droppings. To reduce risk, do not set up a tent or your sleeping area near rodent holes or nests. Do not leave food out, and clean your dishes thoroughly after each meal. Check regularly for ticks and fleas. If you come down with flu-like symptoms within 45 days of camping, you should check with your family doctor or health department.

BEARS AND LIONS

The area in this guide is bear and mountain lion country. Although bears will try to go out of their way to avoid you, they also understand that people have food. Never leave food unattended in a picnic area or campsite. Store your food in your vehicle and never leave a pack unattended. The latter may seem unrealistic, especially if while backpacking you want to make a side trip and need to leave your pack for a time. Hanging it out of reach in some manner, usually by suspension from a stout limb, is a good choice. If spending the night, hang food well out of reach.

Mountain lion attacks on people are extremely rare. Nevertheless, never leave children, pets, or pet food unattended. If you meet a cat on a trail, give the animal an escape route. Generally, mountain lions will try to avoid a confrontation. Don't run. Hold your ground or back away very slowly, always facing the cat. Never crouch or turn your back, and do all you can to appear larger than you are. If you are with children, pick them up without stooping over. If a cat behaves aggressively, wave your arms, shout, and throw objects at it. You must convince the animal that you are not prey, and are dangerous yourself.

THE POISON OAK.

POISON OAK

Poison oak is a very hardy plant that is common all over California. It can grow to altitudes of 5,000 feet, but is generally found below 3,000 feet. It is poisonous all year, whether in leaf or not. The oil from the plant is what causes an allergic reaction. The plant is also peculiar in that it takes the form of a vine, a bush, or a spindly plant. In some regions the leaves remain green during the entire time they are on the stem. In other areas they change to various colors such as red and purple with the changing seasons. It is most recognizable by its triple leaf and shiny surface. Remember, Leaves of three, let them be. Not all people are susceptible, but why push your luck? I get it, and I can tell you it is no fun. Be sure to wash whatever comes in contact with the plant, and never touch your eyes, mouth or other sensitive areas if you think you have been infected.

HEAT STROKE

Over-exertion and dehydration can result in heat stroke. Some symptoms of heat stroke include: Dry skin that is red and hot, very high body temperature of 104 degrees or more, headache, coughing, nausea or vomiting, no appetite, stumbling or lurching, confusion, a strong, rapid pulse, and unconsciousness. If someone exhibits any of these symptoms, it is imperative that they are cooled down as quickly as possible. *Heat stroke can kill quickly!* Red Cross advice is to disrobe the individual and apply cold packs. At the least, get the victim out of the sun and bathe them with the coldest water you have, paying special attention to the head. Shock is a very real part of heat stroke and needs to be treated. Keep the patient cool and elevate the feet. Monitor the temperature and do not leave for help until the patient is conscious and at least a temperature of 102 degrees.

Grave of Nancy Ann Bailey, a miner's wife and mother of three children. Mrs. Bailey died at Rich Bar in 1852 while Dame Shirley was there.

HEAT EXHAUSTION

This condition can lead to heat stroke so do not take it lightly. The symptoms for heat exhaustion are somewhat the same as for heat stroke and also include: Clammy, pale skin, heavy perspiration, body temperature under 100 degrees, fainting or dizziness, stumbling, vomiting or nausea, and cramps. Again, shock is a major concern here. Remember, *shock can kill!* Administer aid in the same manner as described for heat stroke.

HYPOTHERMIA

Hypothermia, the result of over-exposure to cold, is a real killer. Symptoms include: Slowed, slurred speech, lack of reasoning ability, a drunken-like appearance, uncontrollable shivering, loss of memory, inability to perform simple tasks with hands, stumbling, and drowsiness. The latter is the one that ultimately conquers. Drinking plenty of fluids (no alcohol), covering your head, and layering your clothing can go a long way toward preventing hypothermia. Numerous books and pamphlets on this subject have been written, and it is strongly advised that you make yourself very familiar with the information in them.

INJURIES

Remember that when you are in the backcountry you are usually far from medical aid, so always try to minimize your risk for injury. If you become injured for whatever reason, don't *panic!* Calm yourself and try to think of how to get yourself back to help. If a hiking partner is injured, determine the extent of the injury and apply suitable first aid. Never leave an unconscious person unless *absolutely* necessary! Get help or have someone summon help and get back to the injured person as quickly as possible. Again, a Red Cross certified course in first aid and CPR is strongly recommended.

Longboard racers are "Ready to Start" at the annual Alturas Snowshoe Races held at La Porte from 1867 until 1911. These skis, or longboards, are up to twelve feet in length and speeds of 88.8 miles per hour were achieved.

PLUMAS COUNTY
COMMUNITIES & CULTURAL ATTRACTIONS

American Valley

Quincy: Nestled against the southern edge of the lush American Valley, Quincy, the seat of Plumas County, is situated on the western slope of the Sierra Nevada Range. The town was named in honor of community founder H.J. Bradley's hometown of Quincy, Illinois. Quincy is known for its attractive downtown historic buildings that have been the focus of preservation and restoration. The four-story courthouse on Main Street is the county's most dominant and impressive structure. Built in 1921, it features huge columns, a brass chandelier and marble flooring and staircases. The self-guided Heritage Walk, a tour of thirty-three of Quincy's historic homes and businesses is available at the Plumas County

Museum. There are numerous accommodations in the town itself, as well as in outlying regions such as Bucks Lake, Cromberg, and the Feather River Canyon. Besides a very strong commitment to the arts, it is home to the Feather River College, a two-year community college, the Plumas-Sierra Counties Fairgrounds, and numerous community functions throughout the year.

Museums:

The 1878 Variel Home: *137 Coburn Street, Quincy (530) 283-6320:* A painstakingly restored Victorian, it is operated by the non-profit Plumas County Museum Association, Inc. The home is furnished with Plumas County pioneer artifacts, including material from Joshua Variel, the original builder and owner. Guided tours can be arranged by contacting the staff at Plumas County Museum. Donations are appreciated.

Plumas County Museum: *500 Jackson St., Quincy. Behind the courthouse. (530) 283-6320. www.countyofplumas.com. Open year round.* This is one of the most comprehensive, well-presented, and complete museums in rural California. A dynamic living museum, it features dozens of events, exhibits, meetings, and functions year-round.

Quincy's Main Street in 1877 after the completion of the I.O.O.F. Hall. These three brick buildings still stand today.

Period rooms, historic photographs, mining, logging and natural history displays are presented in the main gallery, along with a permanent exhibit that focuses on an outstanding collection of baskets created by the area's original Mountain Maidu Indians. Along with its devotion to the county's historical fabric, the museum remains contemporary, with periodic cultural displays and artwork by local artisans in the second floor Mezzanine Gallery. Also featured is steam railroad memorabilia, a large doll collection, natural history specimens and many other permanent and rotating exhibits such as country stores, saloon, kitchens, etc. A working blacksmith shop and restored miner's cabin and stamp mill is located in the exhibit yard along with many implements used by ranchers, farmers, miners and lumbermen. Area literature, histories, artwork, and other items are on sale at the museum bookstore.

Chester-Lake Almanor Region
Canyon Dam: This small community serves as the gateway to Lake Almanor from the east. Located on Highway 89, it has cabins, RV camp facilities, and a store.

Chester: The youngest of Plumas County's towns, Chester sits at the northwestern end of beautiful Lake Almanor. The town was the site of early day cattle ranching and was near the Humboldt Road to the Idaho mines, as well as the Lassen Emigrant Trail. Hydroelectric power and lumber have played a vital part in the area's economic growth. Lake Almanor was created in 1914, with the damming of the North Fork of the Feather River, at Big Meadows. Chester offers a full range of amenities. There is a wide range of motels, bed and breakfast inns, vacation rentals, resorts, and campgrounds. Besides being a mecca for water-sports, annual art shows, Fourth of July fireworks, and other special events help make this a popular vacation spot. Nearby is Lassen Peak in the Lassen

National Park, the Caribou Wilderness, the Ishi Wilderness, and the historic sites of Humbug Valley, Seneca, and Butt Valley, the latter now under the waters of Butt Lake.

Lake Almanor with Lassen Peak in back.

Museums:

Chester-Lake Almanor Museum: *200 First Avenue, Chester. (530) 258-3777.* Housed in a log structure, the all-volunteer facility features a photographic history of the Lake Almanor basin, including dairy farming, logging, and tourism. Also included is Maidu Indian basketry and artifacts.

Eastern Plumas and Sierra Valley
Beckwourth and Sierra Valley: The vast expanses of the Sierra Valley occupy a major portion of Eastern Plumas and play a major role in the county's cattle-producing industry. Situated in the valley are the towns of Beckwourth, Loyalton, and Vinton, at the end of State Highway 49. Chilcoot, the gateway to Frenchman Lake, a popular fishing, and water-sports area, is also nearby. Fossils, quartz, and astounding natural sculptures of volcanic rock found in places like Frenchman Canyon on Little Last Chance Creek are evidence of the valley's unique geological formation. Accommodations range from secluded cabins, family style resorts, golf course condos, or quaint bed and breakfast inns.

Portola: Plumas County's only incorporated city, Portola, population 2,300, sits on State Highway 70, the Union Pacific Railroad, and the Middle Fork of the Feather River. First named Headquarters in 1905, then Mormon in 1907, this was changed to Imola and Reposa in 1908, with the final change to Portola in 1909. Portola's existence has been due to railroads since its very beginning. Now spanning both sides of the river, Portola's older section is on the south side. Commercial Street, its main and oldest business street retains its early 20th century charm. At the end of this street and along the railroad is the world-renowned Portola Railroad Museum, definitely worth a visit.

Museums:

Jim Beckwourth Museum: *Rocky Point Road, 2 miles east of Portola off State Route 70. (530) 832-4888.* Plumas County pioneer Jim Beckwourth's refurbished hotel and trading post, circa 1853, has been restored. It is operated by volunteers on a limited basis. Beckwourth, who for a time lived among the Indians, was one of the few pioneer leaders of African-American descent. In 1850 Beckwourth discovered one of the lowest passes over the Sierra Nevada, just east of this cabin. It became a well-used trail that in sections has evolved into present day highways and secondary roads.

The Beckwourth Cabin, contrary to the caption on the photo, was built in the 1850s. It is near the city of Portola and has been restored. It is now open seasonally as the Jim Beckwourth Cabin Museum and is maintained and staffed by volunteers.

Portola Railroad Museum: *Off Commercial Street in downtown Portola. (530) 832-4131. Open year round.* The Portola Railroad Museum is world-renowned. Established in 1983 by the Feather River Rail Society, it preserves equipment, photos, artifacts, historical information, and data. Housed in a former Western Pacific diesel shop, the museum has approximately 12,000 feet of track. Visitors can climb about an extensive collection of train cars and locomotives, and can even operate a locomotive themselves. Train rides in cabooses and vista flats are available around a one-mile track during the summer.

Feather River Canyon

Belden, Caribou, Paxton, and Twain: These small communities are located in the Feather River Canyon along State Route 70 west of Quincy. They resulted because of the gold rush and later, railroad construction. Though quite small, they offer opportunities for sightseeing, gold panning and other activities. About 29 miles west of Quincy is the Eby Stamp Mill historic site and rest area. Across the river via a 1911 bridge, Belden is home to a large store-tavern complex with rental cabins. Caribou sits at the junction of the North Fork and the East Branch and has a small restaurant and store. Camping and great fishing are available nearby, and for the adventurous, a mountain road winds its way up the canyon through Seneca to Lake Almanor. Twain, about 14 miles from Quincy, hosts a store and post office and camping. Every fall the residents of the Twain community put on an outdoor

The Feather River canyon at Belden.

mining and western event as a fund raiser to help local projects. Paxton, 12 miles from Quincy, was once a railroad destination site and the junction of the Western Pacific and Indian Valley railroads, but is now a collection of rental cabins and the rambling three-story historic Paxton Hotel.

Indian Valley

Crescent Mills: This tiny community is nestled against the western edge of Indian Valley on State Highway 89. A mining boomtown between 1862 and 1882, it now features a nine-hole golf course, a general store, a bed and breakfast inn and restaurant, a service station and several gift shops. The town's main business section burned in 1926 and was rebuilt, but there are still structures from the early days such as the school, residences, and the picturesque cemetery atop the hill north of town.

Greenville: The largest community in the Indian Valley, Greenville offers a full range of business and service establishments. Located mid-way between Quincy and Chester and at the western edge of Indian Valley, Greenville's historic Main Street still retains the charm of its early days. Community events such as the annual Gold Diggers Celebration recall the mining and ranching history of the area. Greenville was born as a town in the late 1850s as a result of the Round Valley gold strikes nearby. Since then, farming, ranching and logging have been the main industries of the area. Nearby is Round Valley Reservoir, a warm-water fishery containing bass and bluegill.

An old cabin at the Lucky "S" Mine above Indian Valley.

Taylorsville: Located on Plumas County road A-22, this gem of Indian Valley was settled in 1853 and has changed little since. A number of period buildings and ranches remain, and along with the Indian Valley Museum, offer visitors a rare glimpse of yesteryear. Flour from Jobe Taylor's mill was produced here and hauled by pack mules to the Idaho mines in the 1860s. The town becomes a mecca for cowboys over the Fourth of July, when the Silver Buckle Rodeo comes to town. A parade and pancake breakfast accompanies this event. There is a county campground east of town and a Grange Hall renowned for its unique spring-loaded floor. A post office, Young's Store (dating from the 1860s), a tavern, and a cafe make up the business section of town. About twenty-two miles further east by paved road is the popular Antelope Lake recreation area. Be sure to stop at the historic Genesee Store for an ice-cold beverage on the way.

Museums:

Greenville Cy Hall Memorial Museum: *Located at 208 Main Street, Greenville. (530) 284-6633.* This all-volunteer museum, still under development, features displays depicting the mining and logging history of the area dating back to the mid-1800s, as well as local theater memorabilia from the mid 1900s. A collection of pictures and books gives an overview of early life in the area.

Jamison Mine in foreground, the town of Johnsville in back, about 1908. The Jamison Mine produced over $2 million in gold until it closed about 1919.

Indian Valley Museum: *Located at the Mt. Jura Gem & Mineral Society Building, on the corner of Cemetery and Portsmouth streets in Taylorsville. (530) 284-6511.* The Indian Valley Museum features displays and data relating to the rich traditions of mining, ranching, and logging in the area, as well as Native American materials. The museum has a collection of artifacts from the 1850s to the present, representing the settling of the Indian and Genesee valleys. Mining equipment is on display outside the museum.

Mohawk Valley
Blairsden, Clio, Graeagle, and Johnsville: These small communities are situated in and around the beautiful and historic Mohawk Valley. They have gained prominence as

planned residential centers for vacation and retirement residents. The area's five pristine golf courses have made it a renowned golf vacation destination. Blairsden, named for a Western Pacific Railroad official, came into being early in the 20th century because of that railroad. It was also the jumping-off point for the Lakes Basin Recreation area. Today it hosts several restaurants, a store, bakery, and other businesses. Clio, at the east end of Mohawk Valley, was also a lumber and railroad town. Originally known as Wash, its present name was bestowed in 1903 from a brand name for a popular heating stove. A post office and delicatessen-store are the businesses in this town. Nearby is the 1853 White Sulphur Springs Ranch, in ownership by the same family since 1867. The village

The once prosperous mining town of La Porte about 1911. The long white building left of center is the Union Hotel, still standing. The town is framed by hydraulic mining scars, while uniquely shaped Table Rock is in the background.

of Graeagle, a former lumber mill town, features a quaint array of identical red buildings that house gift shops and services. The World Famous Graeagle grocery, a cafe, tavern, and service station are near the Mill Pond, a favorite swimming hole and site of the Fourth of July fireworks. Graeagle is the northern Gateway to the Lakes Basin. Nearby is the historic town of Johnsville, located in the heart of Plumas Eureka State Park. An 1870s mining town, it features picturesque private homes and one restaurant that is open seasonally. The old Plumas Eureka Ski Bowl, now known as Ski Gold Mountain, above Johnsville attracts history buffs as well as Nordic and alpine skiers. The annual Lost Sierra Longboard Ski Revival Series, an historic reenactment of the famous 19th century downhill ski races, is held here in January, February, and March. Slightly deranged participants hurtle down the slopes on ten-foot to sixteen-foot handmade wood skis as in years past. The March race culminates the series as the World's Championship Race.

Museums:

Plumas Eureka State Park Museum: *Located just outside the town of Johnsville, six miles from Graeagle on Johnsville Road (A-14 west of Highway 89). (530) 836-2380.* This indoor-outdoor museum at the Plumas Eureka State Park preserves the rich heritage of the Feather River Country's gold mining legacy. Housed in a restored miners' boarding house, the museum displays mining tools, photographs, pioneer household items, working models of antique mining machinery and antique longboard skis as well as animals native to the park. The rustic, five-story Mohawk Stamp Mill, which processed raw gold-bearing quartz is among the restored buildings nearby, which also include a blacksmith shop, a bunkhouse, and a miner's home. Once a month during summer, costumed docents recreate the lives of pioneer residents on Living History Day. Blacksmith demonstrations, mining lore, and samples of homemade ice cream and other foods take visitors back to the 1890s.

Southern Plumas and the Lost Sierra

La Porte: Originally known as Rabbit Creek, La Porte was a bustling gold mining town until the prohibition of hydraulic mining. Its gold now lies in the recreational opportunities available in the surrounding Plumas and Tahoe national forests and at the Little Grass Valley Reservoir, about two miles north by paved highway. La Porte is also known for its winter recreation, and in 1867 was the site of the world's first organized downhill ski racing when miners strapped on twelve-foot longboards and reached speeds of eighty-eight miles per hour. This tradition, though not the speeds, is kept alive today at Johnsville, another old mining town about twenty-five miles east. La Porte hosts miles of snowmobiling and cross-country skiing terrain, as well as a number of warming huts. The town features the historic three-story Union Hotel, a restaurant, and Reilly's Cafe, the local watering hole. Connected to Quincy by a winding mountain road built in 1867, during winter La Porte is accessible by road only from the lower elevation Marysville side.

Museums:

Frank C. Reilly Museum: *P.O. Box 189, Main Street, La Porte: (530) 675-1922 or 675-2841.* This small, but very attractive and informative museum is volunteer-organized and maintained by residents and the fraternal organization of E Clampus Vitus. It features a host of local artifacts, as well as the restored Hewitt Bros. stamp mill from the Oro Fino Mine on Hopkins Creek, moved to this site in 1980.

SIERRA COUNTY
COMMUNITIES & CULTURAL ATTRACTIONS

North Yuba Canyon

Bassets Station: Originally located on the south side of Highway 49 and west of its present site, Bassett's Station has served travelers in this region for over 100 years. Today there is a restaurant, gas station, fire hall, and snowmobile staging area. Information on the Lakes Basin area is available here also.

Downieville, "away back when." Note the absence of trees on the hillsides.

Downieville: The county seat of Sierra County, population 300 or so, is located on Highway 49 at the forks of the North Yuba and Downie rivers. Major William Downie discovered gold here in the summer of 1849. By May of 1850, the town had fifteen hotels and gambling houses, four bakeries, and four butcher shops. As the population of the area grew, Downieville became the trading center for the Northern Mines, and by the mid-1850s, was California's fifth-largest town. Now it relies on summer tourists and gold mining and logging. Main Street in Downieville is narrow and full of character. Lined with tree-shaded walks and historic buildings, it is considered the least changed of all the gold rush towns in California. The Gallows in Downieville was only used once, but it remains today as a reminder of justice in the gold rush era. Downieville offers self-guided walking tour brochures that detail the history and sites of the community. A ninety-minute, self-guided audio tour combines entertainment with the town's colorful history.

Goodyears Bar: Once a bustling mining camp, Goodyears Bar still sports one of the oldest hotels in the gold country and a schoolhouse built about 1872. Located on the south side of the North Yuba, the post office and a number of residences are located along Goodyears Creek on the north side of the river and Highway 49.

Sierra City: At an elevation of 4,200 feet, this picturesque little town was established in 1850 because of gold mining. By 1852, miners were retrieving gold from several tunnels in the nearby Sierra Buttes. At that time Sierra City had two large buildings, a bakery shop, and several gambling houses and saloons. The buildings were crushed under an avalanche of snow in the winter of 1853, forcing the inhabitants to rebuild at the present, lower elevation. Main Street in Sierra City is charmingly narrow and lined with many turn of the century structures, complete with wooden walks. The Masonic Hall, built in 1864, is the oldest building in town. As the southern Gateway to the Lakes Basin, Sierra City also provides dramatic views of the Sierra Buttes. The Busch and Herringlake Building typifies 19th century Federalist-style architecture. The brick two-story structure was used as a mercantile store and Wells Fargo Express & Company stagecoach stop in the 1870s.

Museums:

The Downieville Museum: *Main Street across from the Community Hall. P.O. Box 484, Downieville, CA 95936.* This stacked-rock building dates back to 1852 when Chinese emigrants built it as a store. Today it contains a number of informative collections that depict life in this area from Gold Rush days to the present.

The Foundry Building: *Pearl Street, on the south side of the Yuba River. (530) 289-3261.* Built in 1855, it was the site of mining machinery manufacturing, and has now been restored for museum use. Tours are offered by reservation only. It features a detailed model of turn-of-the-century Downieville as well as logging and mining exhibits.

The Kentucky Mine, Stamp mill, and Museum: *Located just east of Sierra City on Highway 49. (530) 862-1310.* The museum offers guided tours into the underground mine and also into California's only remaining historic tourable and operable gold ore stamp mill. The museum depicts the gold rush era of Sierra County, life in a mining camp, and the local American Indian culture. For tour information and operating hours, call the Sierra County Historical Society.

Sierra Valley
Sierra Valley is the largest alpine valley in North America. It is part of the continental crust that was dropped by the same faulting that raised the Sierra Nevada. The overlooks on Highway 49 east of Yuba Pass (6,700') and Highway 70's Beckwourth Pass (5,000') provide spectacular panoramic views of this beautiful valley and surrounding mountains. The scenery in Sierra Valley varies from sage, conifer, and aspen forests, to crops, pastures and, in spring, wildflowers. Adjacent smaller valleys and meadows are laced with meandering streams. The Sierra Valley ranches were settled in the 1850s and provided dairy products, hay, and cattle for Sierra and Plumas counties and the Comstock mines of Nevada. By the 1880s it was one of the finest agricultural regions of California. Numerous historic barns and ranches dating back to the mid-1800s dot the valley. The

lumber industry was also part of this healthy agricultural economy. Sierra Valley timber supplied the Comstock Lode, Central Pacific Railroad, Western Pacific Railroad, and the California Fruit Exchange from the 1860s to the 1900s.

Loyalton on the 4th of July, 1910. Loyalton's past includes ranching, sawmilling, and railroading.

Calpine, Loyalton, Sattley, and Sierraville: These towns all share California's largest inter-montane valley with Plumas County. Calpine, named for the California White Pine Lumber Company, began about 1916 as a lumber mill and logging town. Today, the Calpine Lodge is a favorite vacation spot in this pine-shaded town on Highway 89. Loyalton, originally known as Smith's Neck, was renamed due to the sentiment of loyalty to the Union Cause during the Civil War. Today it is the largest and only city in Sierra County, topping out at about 2,800 people. There are a number of historic homes and business buildings to see in this quiet, little town tucked into the southeastern edge of the Sierra Valley. The museum at the city park is well worth the visit. Sattley sports the historic Sattley Cash Store and several homes and ranches at the intersection of Highway 89 and County Road A-23. Sierraville, at the intersection of highways 49 and 89, boasts the restored Globe Hotel, a bar, several stores and restaurants, and a large number of beautiful Victorian ranch houses.

Museums:

The Loyalton Museum: *City Park off A-24. (530) 993-6754.* This historic building features displays on logging, agriculture, the Washoe Indians, domestic life, and early Sierra Valley. Outdoor exhibits include logging wagons, a donkey engine, and farm equipment, which includes the oak hay press hand-built by the Penmans of Mohawk Valley in Plumas County.

Roop's Fort, now part of the Lassen County Historical Society holdings in Susanville. This was the site of the short-lived "Sage Brush War" between Honey Lakers and Plumas County in 1863 that ultimately resulted in the creation of Lassen County in 1864.

LASSEN COUNTY
COMMUNITIES & CULTURAL ATTRACTIONS

Susanville: Although not within the geographic scope of this guide, Susanville is the county seat of Lassen County, where some of these trails are situated. Originally settled by disgruntled residents of Plumas County, after a protracted bureaucratic war and the short but violent Sage Brush War, in 1864 Lassen County was formed from a portion of Plumas and Shasta counties. Susanville has since grown to become a very good sized community. Just to the west is the Lake Almanor recreation area, the Caribou Wilderness, and Lassen National Park.

Westwood: Westwood was brought into existence in 1913 through the Red River Lumber Company. With the town came the legend of Paul Bunyan and his blue ox, Babe. The first printed stories and pictures of Paul were generated from Westwood, turning him into a nationally known legend. Logging railroads soon stretched in every direction into the thick, virgin forests of the region. With its unique, rustic architecture, Westwood was a model company town until the Red River Company shut down business and the mill. It is now the northeastern gateway to the Lake Almanor basin and features a number of gift shops, restaurants, and lodging.

Museums:

Lassen Historical Museum: *75 N. Weatherlow St., Susanville, CA 96103. (530) 257-3292.* This is a regional history museum connected with the Lassen County Historical Society. The facilities include a stamp mill. In the 1940s, local Explorer Scouts constructed a log building to house artifacts. The two-room museum displays farming, mining, and logging equipment, photos, journals, bottles, Native American items, and a host of other Lassen County artifacts. Next door is Roop's Fort, Susanville's original trading post and site of the regionally famous 1863 Sagebrush War between Plumas County and Honey Lake Valley residents. Local history books are available for sale here.

Westwood Museum: *311 Ash Street, Westwood, CA 96137. (530) 256-2233, www.museum@psln.com.* This small, one room museum offers a nice look into the colorful past of Westwood and its surroundings. This volunteer operation is open during the summer only.

NORTHERN SIERRA COUNTY & EASTERN YUBA COUNTY

Sierra County is located in the Yuba River drainage in the northern section of the Sierra Nevada. Accessible by State highways 49 & 89, it remains today much as it has for over 100 years, when gold-seeking miners toiled in the rivers and mountains in search of a fortune. Sierra County is rich with beauty, natural resources, and friendly people. The Washoe and Maidu Indians, early gold miners, loggers and ranchers have left it as a priceless possession - a window to the past. Historic buildings and landscapes provide a rare and unique look into American history as they span over time and into the present. Rugged peaks, craggy ridges, and steep canyons typify this beautiful portion of California's '49er country. It is easy to imagine yourself back in time while traveling some of the ancient pack trails. Sierra County has year-round recreation for every visitor. For all its wilderness and pristine beauty, Sierra County is easily accessible year round. Fishing, hiking, and camping are available for all levels of interest and ability. Much of Sierra County is located within the Tahoe National Forest. Further west along the North Yuba and lower in elevation is eastern Yuba County. This country is characterized by steep canyons, brushy slopes with stands of large timber, large oaks, poison oak, and hot summers. Water to drink is scarce but the North Yuba River provides pleasant swimming in mid to late summer. The Bullard's Bar Recreation Area in particular is a very popular summer playground. There are three trails at Bullard's Bar listed in this section.

The Port Wine trails, Craig's Flat Trail, Eureka Diggings-Little Canyon Creek Trail, and West Coast Mine-Canyon Creek-Morristown Trail were all part of an interconnected transportation network between Downieville, Eureka, La Porte, and the towns on the Port Wine Ridge. Historically, the area has been referred to by Sierra County residents as Over North. Used as pack mule routes, these trails soon added the luxury of mule saddle trains to carry passengers. In the 1860s, one could ride this saddle train from Downieville to La Porte for $5, and early accounts tell of travelers skiing between points along the route. Later, some of the trails were improved into very narrow wagon roads for hauling mining freight. In 1854, Seth Chandler of St. Louis, Sierra County, wrote of women of a low character: It is not an uncommon occurrence to see them dressed in men's clothes astride a mule cantering over our mountain trails. He went on to complain that there were these sorts of women all over the mining region, and that they complemented the drinking and gambling. Another interesting account regarding these trails is contained in the Fall/Winter 1998 issue of The Sierran, a publication of the Sierra County Historical Society. Belle Alexander, Superintendent of Sierra County Schools from 1908 to 1940, recounts how she traveled by horseback to the various schools Over North using these old trails.

As you follow these trails, be sure to exercise due caution as many are unmaintained, and also to respect the historic features and archaeological sites you may encounter.

SIERRA COUNTY & THE YUBA-FEATHER RIVER REGION LOCATOR MAP

Sierra County and the Yuba-Feather River Region.

Map courtesy Design Works.

BADENAUGH CANYON TRAIL 17E01

Elevation: 6600' to 8760'
Length: +/- 2 1/2 miles
Effort: Difficult
Hike Time: About 3 hours
Location: T20N R17E, sections 7,8
Quadrangle Map: Loyalton

This trail is demanding but gives a good example of the destructive power of fire. The trail is now becoming overgrown with brush, while no trees have been replanted, but overall it is a worthwhile hike. To reach this trailhead from Loyalton, proceed about 1/2 mile east on **Highway 49** to the **Lewis Canyon Road (Sierra County 860).** This road is paved the first 4 1/2 miles as it passes through the Sierra Brooks subdivision and the starkness of the 1994 Cottonwood Fire. Take this road south about 8 1/2 miles to an unsigned left turn. This three-mile road leads to the trailhead. Its first 1/2 mile or so is gravel, which then turns to rough dirt for about 1 1/2 miles, and then back to gravel the last mile. The trail itself begins as a gated road with an information sign board on the left. The first section is wet and grassy and passes along the edge of a recovering burn. The easy ascent passes ruins of a 1930s era logging camp, and within a short distance, crosses the small creek and arrives at a trail sign pointing left. The trail here is somewhat faint with heavy ground cover. After a second crossing of the creek, note the volcanic rock formations to the right. The trail begins a moderately light ascent away from the creek and is easy to follow as it skirts a grassy area and enters the East Smith burn. The first of very old blazes are noted as the trail makes a moderate ascent and winds upward to a sign proclaiming Babbit Research Natural Area and a K-tag for sections 5,6,7,8. The ascent is now steeper with a dry gully on the right. The faint trail has had no maintenance and the blazes are badly burned. The steep ascent bears left, away from the gully, while on the left is a large rock formation. Keep an eye on the boulders lining the route of the path, especially as the trail veers right and levels for a short distance. Make a light ascent between a gully and the ridge, then cross the dry gully under a mass of boulders. Occasional ducks show the steep route as it winds through

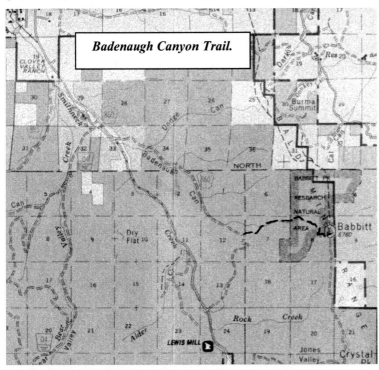

Badenaugh Canyon Trail.

burned big timber. Soon it cuts right, into unburned trees, makes a switchback, ascends along the edge of the burn, switchbacks again, and steeply ascends back to the burn. A small field of mullen is on the left of the winding ascent, and soon a rock knob spotted with orange and lime-colored lichen is also passed. The trail works back into a stunted white fir forest, levels with limited views of the burn and the Sierra Valley, and then makes a moderate ascent into western white pine cover. A switchback and a light ascent are a welcome change on this well-blazed and defined trail, but the ascent soon goes from moderate to very steep. There is a great view to the left of the Dodge Canyon area, Sierra Valley, Mt. Lassen, and Loyalton. In a short distance the trail intersects a firebreak and a sign on a tree reading **Badenaugh Canyon Trail 17E01.** You can either pick your way through the sagebrush to the Babbit Peak Lookout or follow the firebreak right to the lookout road. From Babbit Peak (elevation 8760') there are outstanding views of eastern California and western Nevada as well as Stampede Reservoir.

BELLEVUE MINE FLUME TRAIL

Elevation: 4600' to 4650'
Length: +/- 1 mile
Effort: Easy
Hike Time: About 1 hour
Location: T21N R9E, section 1
Quadrangle Map: La Porte

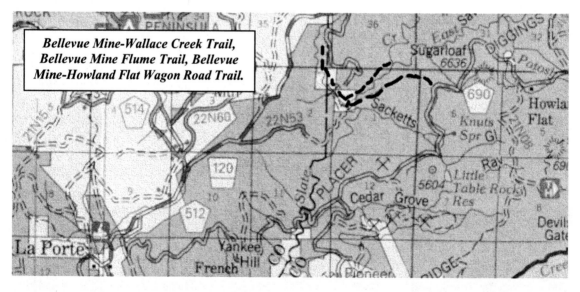

Bellevue Mine-Wallace Creek Trail, Bellevue Mine Flume Trail, Bellevue Mine-Howland Flat Wagon Road Trail.

To reach the trail from the town of La Porte, take the **Quincy-La Porte Road** north from La Porte about 3 miles to the signed turnoff to Slate Creek and the Bellevue Mine. This two-mile road is in good condition but is very narrow. It was built in the late 1800s as a wagon road, with the last mile remaining pretty much intact. If drop-offs and heights bother you, these may not be the roads or trails for you. It is best to take the right hand fork of the road as you approach the mine, as it has an area to turn around. After parking, follow the road to the mouth of Wallace Creek. Carefully cross that stream and make a winding ascent up the narrow ridge to the old flume. This watercourse was blasted out of solid rock, and then a wood flume was constructed upon it. The water was used at the Bellevue Mine for power and gold recovery. Look along the banks 20 to 30 feet above the present creek and you will see white gravel patches. These are remnants of the tailings that once filled the Slate Creek basin from the hydraulic mining on the Gibsonville and Port Wine ridges. At one time, horse-drawn stages were able to run up and down the streambed because of the leveling nature of the gravel. Most of the gravel has since been reworked and washed away. A good view of the old wagon road ascending the hillside across the canyon, and the rugged bed of Slate Creek, are seen from this almost level walk. Cross a seasonal draw on planks laid on a beautiful rock wall abutment, then make a steep drop (about 8') and resume the level walk. As the trail progresses along the Big Bend, it makes small ins and outs, and occasionally some ups and downs, where the rock walls have failed. Just down from the confluence of the East Branch and Slate Creek the trail drops off the flume grade to the streambed. By walking upstream 50 yards you will come to the confluence.

BELLEVUE MINE-HOWLAND FLAT WAGON ROAD TRAIL
Elevation: 4600' to 5321'
Length: +/- 1 mile
Effort: Moderate
Hike Time: About 1 hour
Location: T21N R9E, section 1 and T21N R10E, section 6
Quadrangle Map: La Porte **(For map see page 44)**

Use the *Bellevue Mine-Flume Trail* description above to reach this trail. After parking, follow the road to the mouth of Wallace Creek, cross both creeks, and make a light scramble to the very wide trail. This is actually an old stagecoach road that was a continuation of the one just driven in on. It ran from La Porte to Howland Flat during the late 1800s. When the tailings became quite deep in Slate Creek, the stage was able to run upon them up and down Slate Creek. This trail makes an almost unchanging mild ascent the entire distance. There is some sloughing and the rock walls are starting to give out so stay a good distance from the edge. The trail enters the shade of trees, then goes back into the open several times. Great views of Slate Creek far below, the *Bellevue Mine Flume Trail*, and a shot of Pilot Peak are had here. In one area about two-thirds the way up, brush has crowded the trail enough that you have to pass along the outside edge. The knob visible at left is the divide between the East Branch and Slate Creek, the gray ridge to the north is Sawmill Ridge, and the mountain ahead is Mt. Fillmore. The placer diggings of the Pine Grove area are now visible ahead also. As the trail hits the top it levels and enters trees. Blazes mark the route as it bears east and enters overgrown placer diggings. Ascend onto a ditch and follow it left a short time. Bear right and cross 150 feet of diggings to a primitive spur road that will wind about 1/4 mile up to an obscure spot on the *Howland Flat Road (USFS 21N17)* about 2 1/2 miles northeast of St. Louis, and 3 1/2 miles southwest of Howland Flat.

BELLEVUE MINE-WALLACE CREEK TRAIL
Elevation: 4800' to 5200'
Length: +/- 1/2 mile
Effort: Very Difficult
Hike Time: About 1/2 hour
Location: T21N R9E, sections 1,2
Quadrangle Map: La Porte **(For map see page 44)**

Though still historically important, this poor old trail has seen better days. Unfortunately, the trail has been recently logged over, destroying much of its upper half. To reach the trail from the town of La Porte, take the ***Quincy-La Porte Road*** north from La Porte about 3 miles to the signed turnoff to Slate Creek and the Bellevue Mine. This two-mile road is in good condition but it is very narrow. It was built in the late 1800s as a wagon road, with the last mile remaining pretty much intact. If drop-offs and heights bother you, these may not be the roads or trails for you. Park at the intersection where one road drops to the right, as there is very limited parking

Cherokee Creek Bridge in 1995.

and turn-around space further on. After parking, follow the level road to its end at Wallace Creek at the entrance to the now-closed mine. Cross the creek and ascend a very rough, dry draw about 50 feet to just above the old flume (ditch) line. The trail begins at left, though it is quite sloughed at first. The trail becomes defined, though brushy, as it makes a medium ascent along rock walls. A nice view of the old ditch systems and tortured Wallace Creek canyon is had. Make a steep switchback at a medium-size ponderosa pine, another switchback, and ascend along decaying rockwalls. Fallen trees occasionally require you to go around them on this open, hot hillside. Contour along the hillside about 100 feet above the creek, then begin a mild ascent (note the double-decker rock wall in a seasonal gully) as the trail reaches the ridgeback. As it ascends to the brush you might as well stop here. Another 75 feet and you will lose the trail completely in recently logged ground. Just above here is a big ditch out of Slate Creek that apparently served some placer diggings nearby.

BRANDY CITY TRAIL
Elevation: 2200' to 3500'
Length: +/- 1 1/2 miles (4 miles including access)
Effort: Very Difficult
Hike Time: About 3 hours
Location: T19N R8E, sections 12,13
Quadrangle Map: Strawberry Valley **(For map see page 47)**

Poison oak is neck-high, and madrone, oak, and other brush have overgrown this historic trail quite heavily. Several sections are very faint and there is considerable fallen timber. To reach the trail, park at the trailhead on the north side of the North Yuba River Bridge on **State Highway 49** about 12 miles southwest of Downieville. There is a locked gate here so park clear of it. Follow the mostly-level road through Shenanigan Flat to the end of the road at Cherokee Creek where a new bridge was installed in the fall of 1995. Cross the creek and ascend to a switchback. The old trail going straight ahead leads to Cut Eye Foster's Bar. Take this switchback to another switchback. Here, another old trail continues up Cherokee Creek but is so overgrown it is almost impenetrable. That trail was the original route to Brandy City from the south side of the Yuba River. Make this switchback and round the ridge out of the Cherokee Creek drainage onto the hillside above the North Yuba River. On the right is the old, very overgrown *Brandy City Trail.* A sign reads: Canyon Creek 1 1/2 (straight), *Brandy City Road* 1 1/2, Cherokee Creek 1/4. Climb the bank, make six short switchbacks, and ascend the ridgeback a short distance to a large Douglas fir with an overgrown undercut. The trail now runs north along the ridge side. Make two more faint switchbacks onto the ridgeback and ascend along a kind of hogsback. Level out, then ascend two switchbacks along the east side, do another six switchbacks, ascend sidehill, switchback seven times onto the south side, then make three switchbacks to the east side for a short distance. Make four more switchbacks to a view up-river of *Highway 49* as it ascends Depot Hill. The trail then mellows out along the south side of the mountain, making a

Brandy City Trail, Canyon Creek Trail, Cut Eye Foster's Bar Trail.

gentle ascent for a long distance before rounding the ridge at a blazed ponderosa pine and a large rock. Continue the ascent on the west side of the ridge now with a view down river. The trail is much more open now also. After quite a distance, make a switchback at a dry ravine and ascend to a blazed oak near the ridgeback where the trail makes another short switchback to the top. Follow this almost level walk along a hogback, then make a light ascent on rocky ground with a great view up river. This pleasant ascent is through live oak. The trail continues in this fashion, making light ascents and descents along the ridgeback, to evidence of past logging. The trail now hits an old spur road. Follow it along the west side of the ridge to an intersection with another overgrown spur running east and west. Cross this spur and continue north about 1/2 mile through thick forest to the *Brandy City Road* (which makes a large U) and a ponderosa pine plantation.

BRANDY CITY POND TRAIL
Elevation: 3700' to 3700'
Length: +/- 1/2 mile
Hike Time: About 1/2 hour
Effort: Easy
Location: T19N R8E, section 1
Quadrangle Map: Strawberry Valley

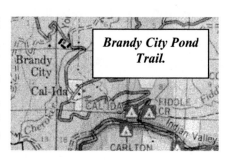

Reach this trail by taking the **Brandy City Road** about 5 miles to the site of the old Cal-Ida sawmill. Take a left at the Y and follow signed **Road 491** about 2 miles to the site of the historic Brandy City Mine. Although not an historic trail in its own right, it gives a great view of the devastation of hydraulic mining and the historic Brandy City hydraulic mine pit.

BULLARD'S BAR-DARK DAY TRAIL (Yuba County)
Elevation: 2243' to 2250'
Length: +/- 3 miles
Effort: Easy
Hike Time: About 2 hours
Location: T18N R8E, sections 17,18,19
Quadrangle Map: Camptonville, Challenge **(For map see page 49)**

This trail is a segment of the seven-mile long **Bullard's Bar Trail** from Sunset Vista to Dark Day picnic area. To access the trailhead take **State Route 49** either from Nevada City about 20 miles, or from Downieville about 25 miles to the **Marysville Road (County Road 117)** and turn left. Follow this road for 2 3/4 miles to the Dark Day Picnic Area/Boat Ramp access. Take a right here and travel 1/2 mile to an intersection, go straight to the picnic area, tent camping area and trailhead. This is an easy walk along the lake with good fishing and swimming. Huge Douglas fir and ponderosa pine form a canopy over large groups of wildflowers.

BULLARD'S BAR TRAIL 8E07 (Sunset Vista to Schoolhouse Trail) (Yuba County)
Elevation: 2243' to 2250'
Length: +/- 1/2 mile
Effort: Easy
Hike Time: About 1/2 hour
Location: T18N R8E, section 13,18,31
Quadrangle Map: Camptonville, Challenge **(For map see page 49)**

This is a segment of the seven-mile long **Bullard's Bar Trail** from Sunset Vista to Dark

Day. To access the trailhead take *State Route 49* north from Nevada City about 20 miles, or south from Downieville about 25 miles to *Marysville Road (County Road 117)* and turn left. Follow this road for about 5 miles to the Sunset Vista turnoff. Pull in here and park in the large lot. The trail leaves to the left. A sign reads: Schoolhouse Campground 3 1/4, Dark Day Picnic Area 5 1/2. Almost immediately the trail is transformed to an old paved road. Follow this down almost to the lake where the trail cuts away to the right. The trail is well-maintained, although there is nothing remarkable about it. It is almost level the entire way, with a few minor ups and downs. Occasional portions of it utilize old roads, there are a number of piped stream crossings and one small section of moss-covered rock walls, an old bench, and lots of huge ferns. The canopy is so thick that a heavy cloudburst did not even wet me while there. There are a few good views of the lake here and there. No motorcycles or OHVs are allowed. It is a great jogging trail.

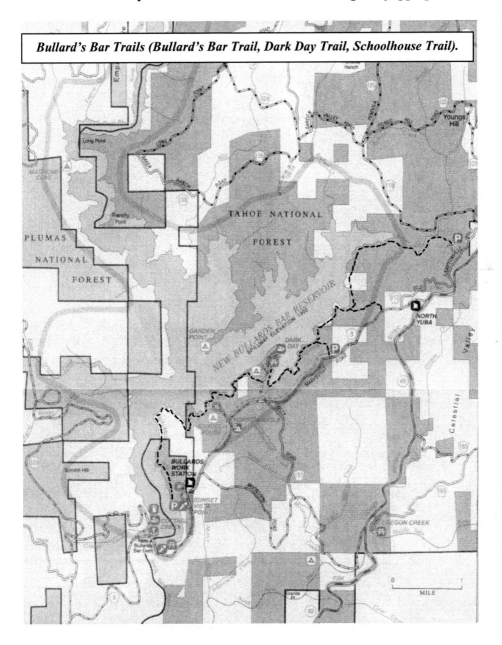

Bullard's Bar Trails (Bullard's Bar Trail, Dark Day Trail, Schoolhouse Trail).

BULLARD'S BAR TRAIL 8E10 (Schoolhouse Trail) (Yuba County)

Elevation: 2243' to 2250'
Length: +/- 1/2 mile
Effort: Easy
Hike Time: About 1/2 hour
Location: T18N R8E, section 19
Quadrangle Map: Camptonville, Challenge **(For map see page 49)**

To access the trailhead take **State Route 49** south from Camptonville 2 miles to **Marysville Road (County Road 117)** and turn left. Follow this road about 4 miles to the Schoolhouse Campground turnoff. Turn right into the campground and take the one-way road to the first left. Take the left and follow it around to the trailhead and sign: Bullard's Bar Reservoir 1/2, Dark Day Picnic Area 3, Sunset Vista Point 3. This is a tie trail to the **Bullard's Bar Trail**. It is actually an old road used in the construction of the reservoir. It makes a light-to-moderate descent to a small sign pointing right. Follow this onto an actual trail that leads to two signs: **Bullard's Bar Trail 8E01, Schoolhouse Trail** 1/2 mile, Vista Point 2 1/2 miles, and **Bullard's Bar Trail 8E07, Schoolhouse Trail** 1/2 mile, Dark Day 2 1/2 miles. This is the center point of the **Bullard's Bar Trail**.

BUTCHER RANCH TRAIL

Elevation: 6200' to 4320'
Length: +/- 2 miles
Hike Time: About 1 hour
Effort: Difficult
Location: T20N R11E, sections 1,2,3,9,10
Quadrangle Map: Sierra City

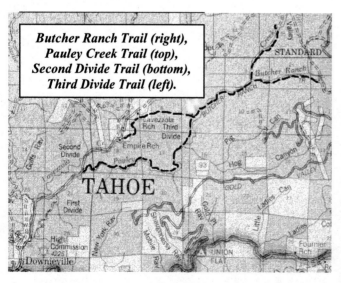

Butcher Ranch Trail (right), Pauley Creek Trail (top), Second Divide Trail (bottom), Third Divide Trail (left).

To access the trailhead from Downieville use the **Pauley Creek Trail** description. Otherwise, to reach the trailhead travel 5 miles east of Sierra City on **State Route 49** to the **Gold Lake Road** at Bassett's Station. Turn left (north) on that road and travel 1 1/2 miles to the Salmon Creek bridge. Cross and follow the road for about 1/4 mile to the **Packer Lake Road.** Turn right on this road and follow 2 1/2 miles to Packer Lake. **Packer Saddle Road (USFS Road 93)** goes left here. Follow it 2 miles to Packer Saddle and turn left. Another 1/2 mile and **USFS Road 93** makes a 90-degree turn to the right. Follow it another 1/2 mile to a sign reading Gold Valley 5 1/2, **Highway 49**

11, Butcher Ranch 1, Pauley Creek 4. Take the right fork, traveling 3/4 mile to a sign pointing out the trailhead. Up to 1/2 mile from this point the road is paved. Though 4WD vehicles may continue a little further, it is recommended to park here and walk the last mile to the trailhead. At a fork in the **Gold Valley 4WD Road** and the **Butcher Ranch Trail** access are several signs. One is rather misleading as it points out the **Butcher Ranch Trail** as heading north. Another points to the OHV trail, and a third sign reads Pauley Creek 1 1/2, Gold Valley 4, Third Divide 4, Empire Ranch 6. From here proceed west 100 yards to parking at an abrupt gully. Cross and begin a gentle descent with several loose spots, crossing springs, and water on the trail. After this the trail becomes steep and in poor shape. There is heavy use by mountain bikes, so exercise caution. The trail follows the course of Butcher Ranch Creek for 1 1/2 miles to the confluence of Butcher Ranch and Pauley Creek. From here you can head up Pauley Creek to Gold Valley, or continue down Pauley Creek on the **Pauley Creek Trail** to either **Third Divide Trail** or **Second Divide Trail.** Pauley Creek abounds with beautiful, deep pools. Good fishing and numerous campsites are found.

CANYON CREEK TRAIL

Elevation: 2200' to 2100'
Length: +/- 1 mile (3 1/2 miles including access)
Effort: Moderate
Hike Time: About 2 hours
Location: T19N R8E, sections 11,13,14
Quadrangle Map: Strawberry Valley **(For map see page 47)**

A very good, enjoyable description of the history of this trail and the surrounding area can be found in the guidebook <u>Yuba Trails</u>. The actual single tread section of this trail is only about 1 mile in length, but in order to hike it you need to walk 2 1/2 miles of historic dirt road. Park at the trailhead on the north side of the North Yuba River Bridge on **State Highway 49**, about 12 miles southwest of Downieville. There is a locked gate here so park clear of it. Follow the mostly-level road through Shenanigan Flat to the end of the road at Cherokee Creek where a new bridge was installed in the fall of 1995. Cross the creek and ascend to a switchback. The old trail going straight ahead leads to Cut Eye Foster's Bar. Make the switchback to another switchback. Here another old trail continues up Cherokee Creek, but is so overgrown it is almost impenetrable. This old trail was the original route to Brandy City from the south side of the Yuba River. Make this switchback and round the ridge out of the Cherokee Creek drainage onto the hillside above the North Yuba River. On the right is the old, very grown-over **Brandy City Trail.** A sign reads: Canyon Creek 1 1/2 (straight), **Brandy City Road** 1 1/2, Cherokee Creek 1/4. The trail from here is mostly level with light ascents and descents. Cross a seep spring, dry gulch, and a K-tag for sections 13 and 14. The trail crosses into Brummel Ravine, which is dark and lush, then rounds the ridge, and makes a moderate descent with views of the river below. The trail in this section is quite rocky and the fallen leaves make it very slick. Carefully descend to the confluence of Canyon Creek and the North Yuba River.

CASTLE ROCK TRAIL
Elevation: 5550' to 6860'
Length: +/- 1 1/2 miles
Effort: Moderate
Hike Time: About 2 hours
Location: T20N R12E, section 1 and T21N R12E, section 36
Quadrangle Map: Clio

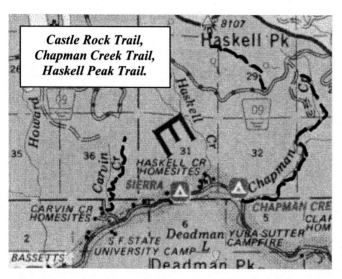

Castle Rock Trail, Chapman Creek Trail, Haskell Peak Trail.

This trail is maintained by the summer-home owners at Carvin Creek Forest Service Homesites. To reach the trail take **State Route 49** about 1 1/2 miles east of Bassett's Station. It is best to park on the south side of the highway and walk the 1/2 mile to the trailhead to avoid disturbing the residents or raising dust. Follow the dirt road across Carvin Creek, past a left fork, and continue up along the creek to a switchback in the road. A large cedar has a homemade sign attached to it pointing out the trail. The trail drops across Carvin Creek and soon begins a series of switchbacks up the mountain. This may have been an old miners trail originally. Nice views of the Yuba Canyon are seen from here.

CHAPMAN CREEK TRAIL
Elevation: 5600' to 6546'
Length: +/- 2 miles
Effort: Easy
Hike Time: About 1 1/2 hours
Location: T21N R13E, sections 28,32,33
Quadrangle Map: Clio

To reach the trailhead travel east on **State Route 49** 8 1/2 miles from Sierra City to Chapman Creek Campground, where the trail begins. It gently runs up the east side of Chapman Creek about 1 mile where it crosses a small creek out of Beartrap Meadows. A light ascent in an open area is somewhat rutted. Contour along and cross another tributary above this confluence and work along the creek. Large red and white fir shade this pleasant walk as it begins a light ascent into old logging, contours, ascends, and then crosses Chapman Creek. Make a light ascent and cross a small stream and wet grassy area to another old logging skid trail. Follow this as it winds up lightly and passes a large cairn and a rock bluff on the left. A light descent on the well-defined trail comes to another crossing of Chapman Creek and the trailhead at an old log landing on *USFS 09-13*. A sign here reads *Chapman Creek Trail 13E03*, No Motorized Vehicles. This very pleasant, well-maintained trail is just right for picnicking, or relaxing and enjoying the scenery.

CHIMNEY ROCK TRAIL
Elevation: 6400' to 6800'
Length: +/- 4 miles
Effort: Moderate
Hike Time: About 3 hours
Location: T21N R10E, sections 13,14,23 and T21N R11E, section 18.
Quadrangle Map: Mt. Fillmore

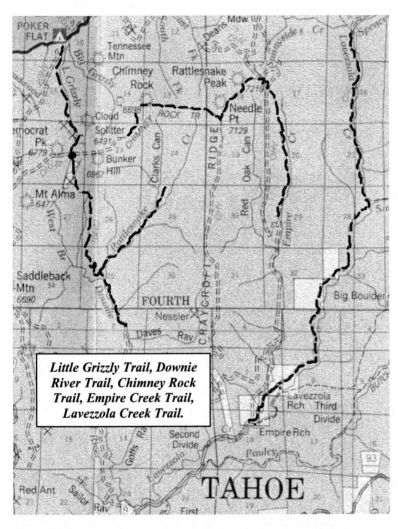

Little Grizzly Trail, Downie River Trail, Chimney Rock Trail, Empire Creek Trail, Lavezzola Creek Trail.

To reach the trailhead take the **Saddleback Road** 1/4 mile west of Downieville. Travel about 8 miles to a five-way intersection. Go straight ahead onto **USFS 25-23-1** for about 1/4 mile past the now dead-and-gone Bee Tree (still on the maps). Keep straight ahead another mile and bear right onto **USFS 25-23-1-2.** A sign notes the road is a dead-end and not maintained. Proceed straight through another mile to a Y intersection. Go right and continue for another 1/2 mile to the **Poker Flat OHV Trail** (going left). As you pass Democrat Peak on your left, the **Downie River Trail** drops right and the **Little Grizzly Creek Trail** drops left. From the base of Bunker Hill the road is 4WD only the last 1/2-mile to the trailhead. The entire access distance from Downieville is about 13 miles. At the trailhead is room for only one or two vehicles. The road makes a very sharp right and is closed here by a metal post and cable in its center. The trail starts out level with great views of the area to the north. Soon it makes a light descent into a thickly forested saddle where it then begins to make a moderate climb along the south side of the hill. It then makes seven switchbacks before breaking out into the open on the west again. Wind along to Chimney Rock, an interesting volcanic plug twelve-feet in diameter at the base and about twenty-five-feet tall. Beautiful views of Saddleback, Fir Cap, Table Rock, Mt. Fillmore, Pilot Peak and even far away Spanish Peak are a few of the rewards of this hike. The trail continues east, winding along the ridgeback separating the Yuba River and Canyon Creek drainages. As you work around the north side of the ridge, the trail descends through a light forest cover with some very rocky sections. The trail now becomes five switchbacks up Needle Point. A fantastic view of the area is had from the top switchback. As you round the point and leave this vista, an old pack trail down Craycroft Ridge bears away to the right. This trail, though blazed, is not maintained and in about 400 yards hits the **Craycroft Ridge 4WD Road**. Continue an easy descent along the south side of the ridge to the **Empire Creek Trail**. A sign indicating the **Rattlesnake Peak Trail** is near the end of this trail. From here you can take either the **Empire Creek Trail** down to its trailhead or use the **Red Oak OHV Road**, eventually reaching Downieville.

CRAIG'S FLAT TRAIL
Elevation: 5000' to 2800'
Length: +/- 2 miles
Effort: Difficult
Hike Time: About 1 hour
Location: T21N R9E, sections 25,36
Quadrangle Map: La Porte
(For map see page 49)

Old cabin along the Downie River Trail.

This trail is one of the old mule pack and passenger trails from the North Yuba River over to the Port Wine Ridge. A large portion has been destroyed by the now closed **USFS 21N71Y**, but enough exists at the lower end to be able to follow it. Since a road now drops into Canyon Creek about where this trail hits Canyon Creek, the trail has no real function anymore, except as a walk. Additionally, the route out the south side is now a 4WD road. To reach the trailhead take the **Howland Flat Road (USFS 21N17)** to **USFS 21N69** about 1 mile north of Port Wine and Queen City. Proceed about 1 1/2 miles, passing the **Pacific Mine Road** and the **West Coast Mine Road**. Cross a small rise and log landing and descend through a sweeping turn past the shared **Port Wine Trail** and **Port Wine Ridge Trail** trailheads. Continue straight a short distance to **USFS 21N71Y**, which makes a sharp left. The road is blocked here so you will have to walk the 1/2-mile of road to the end at a log landing and clearcut. At the landing there is a small pile of rocks on the left. Drop off the edge here staying left of the clearcut. Make a steep descent with several ducks but no real trail to a very much overgrown skid road. This is the trail.

Follow it left for a bit before the trail drops to a switchback at a large sugar pine log. You might note an old wood chisel poking out of the log. Make a moderate descent to another skid trail and the edge of the clearcut. Go left and follow the skid trail along the ridgeback and the edge of the clearcut. Bear left and drop down the ridgeback to the rotted remains of an old footbridge across the stupendous and enormous Scales Ditch from Poker Flat to Scales. Cross here, (note the stacked rock abutment) and drop straight down the ridge through evidence of logging from the 1960s, then through a small, but obvious basin. As the skid trail begins to drop straight down, there is a small pile of rocks on the left. Make a left here and the trail will descend easily for a long way to a switchback and Canyon Creek. From here you can walk downstream on a miner/fisherman trail to the end of a spur off *USFS 21N77*. Another route out of the canyon is to cross Canyon Creek, then take the 4WD road out to Craig's Flat.

CUT EYE FOSTER'S BAR TRAIL

Elevation: 2200' to 2200'
Length: +/- 1/2 mile (3 miles including access)
Effort: Easy
Hike Time: About 1 1/2 hours
Location: T19N R8E, sections 13,14
Quadrangle Map: Strawberry Valley **(For map see page 47)**

A very good description of historic Cut Eye Foster's Bar can be found in <u>Yuba Trails</u>, Fariss & Smith's <u>1882 History of Plumas, Lassen & Sierra Counties</u>, and Major Downie's <u>Hunting For Gold</u>. Reach this trail by using the directions for the ***Canyon Creek Trail*** and ***Brandy City Trail*** hikes. After crossing Cherokee Creek ascend to a switchback, but instead of making the switchback, continue straight and descend along Cherokee Creek to a small plot fenced with wire. Skirt the fencing and bear right around a point. The trail picks its way along the bedrock and foot of the hill to a gravel bar. It then meanders past a substantial picnic table and continues up through brush, before dropping again to the river. Locust trees and blackberries abound here. The trail seems to be maintained mostly by miners and fishermen.

DOWNIE RIVER TRAIL

Elevation: 6400' to 3000'
Length: +/- 6 1/2 miles
Effort: Moderate
Hike Time: About 5 hours
Location: T21N R10E, sections 22,27,34,35 and T20N R10E, sections 2,11,14
Quadrangle Map: Downieville and Mt. Fillmore **(For map see page 53)**

Though not maintained, this trail is very prominent from its past use as a packing trail. There are two trailheads available, with the upper one being the way I will describe this trail. The alternate trailhead from Downieville is described below. The upper trailhead is reached by traveling north from Downieville on the ***Downieville-Poker Flat Road*** about

10 miles, turn right (east) on the **Bunker Hill-Clark's Canyon Road**, and travel 2 miles to the saddle at the head of Little Grizzly Creek and the West Branch of the Downie River. Start at the saddle where the unsigned **Little Grizzly Creek Trail** tops out. The **Downie River Trail** begins a moderate descent past the Herkimer Mine (private property) all the way to the Downie River. Extensive views of the Yuba River canyon make this an enjoyable hike. Approximately two miles from the top, the **Rattlesnake Creek Trail** connects with this trail. Near the confluence of Rattlesnake Creek and the Downie River is a new hiking and pack bridge. Continue down to another bridge and in 1/4 mile reach the parking area at the end of the five-mile road from Downieville.

Alternate trailhead: To reach the lower trailhead, take Upper Main Street through Downieville. About 1/2 mile east of the Post Office take the unpaved **Downie River Road,** do not cross the Downie River bridge. A sign notes that the **Downie River Trail** is 5 miles. Stay left, passing the **Gold Bluff Mine Road**. Park at the end of the road and take the **Downie River Trail** about 1/4 mile to the Downie River bridge. Cross to the east side and continue along the nicely rebuilt trail. The creek is quite pretty through this section. Cross a small stream via a new timber bridge, pass a maintained cabin, and ascend around the ridge through old growth timber to a moderate descent to Rattlesnake Creek. Until October of 1995 the trail forded the creek, but now there is a 65-foot-long twin beam steel bridge with wood decking. It was delivered via helicopter. Cross here and ascend through an active mining claim with a maintained cabin. The **Downie River Trail** faintly veers left and uphill.

EAST BRANCH CANYON CREEK TRAIL
Elevation: 4800' to 5800'
Length: +/- 5 miles
Effort: Moderate
Hike Time: About 4 hours
Location: T21N R10E sections 1,2,12 and T21N R11E, section 7
Quadrangle Map: Mt. Fillmore **(For map see page 63)**

To hike this trail upstream one must first get to Poker Flat, a now all but abandoned mining camp that originated in 1850. Thought by some to be the setting of Bret Harte's famous Outcasts of Poker Flat, a 4WD vehicle is required to reach this historic spot. The road in from the north is considerably rougher than the access from the south, but either one is rough at best.

Once on the trail it is a pleasant hike, running from the junction of the West Branch and East Branch of Canyon Creek up the East Fork to the Gibraltar Mine. From this point the trail has been converted to a 4WD road. A locked cable gate is maintained by mine owners at the saddle between Rattlesnake Peak and an unnamed peak to its north. On the east side of the saddle, with a sharp eye one may find the abandoned wagon road that was once used to get to and from Sunnyside Meadows. The present road contours south off the saddle to connect with **USFS 514B.** Begin at the junction of the **Tennessee Mine Road** and the combined West and East Branch Canyon Creek trails approximately 1 1/2 miles east of Poker Flat via the **Tennessee Mine Road.** The trail is well-defined and maintained by mine owners and crosses to the east side of the East Branch of Canyon Creek at the creek junction. About 1/2 mile up the trail is a standing historic shake cabin. Continue in a southerly direction another 1/2 mile to the mouth of the North Fork of Canyon Creek. Cross this creek about 75 yards upstream from its confluence with the East Branch. About 100 yards south from the crossing, and on the left (east) is the **North Fork Trail.** This is a dead end-trail about 3/4 mile long. 300 feet above this trail junction, another trail also branches off the **North Fork Trail** to the right (southeast) and runs directly up a ridge. The **East Branch Trail** continues through heavy forest with occasional views of the opposite side of the creek. Near the mouth of Deans Ravine is an old growth incense cedar grove and the ruins of miners' cabins. Cross Deans Ravine and connect with the 4WD road through Gibraltar Mine and on to Sunnyside Meadows. This 4WD road is moderately steep with many switchbacks and lots of loose cobble. Portions of the original pack trail/wagon road are evident here and there between present switchbacks all the way to the top.

EMPIRE CREEK TRAIL

Elevation: 4820' to 6760'
Length: +/- 2 1/2 miles
Effort: Moderate
Hike Time: About 2 1/2 hours
Location: T21N R11E, sections 29,20,17,18
Quadrangle Map: Downieville, Mt. Fillmore **(For map see page 53)**

To reach the trailhead take Upper Main Street in Downieville about 1/2 mile past the post office. Cross the Downie River bridge and proceed 4 1/4 miles up Lavezolla Creek to a well-defined fork in the road. Take the left fork signed Craycroft Ridge and **Red Oak O.H.V. Trail** 4. Follow this road another 2 miles to a 90-degree turn. Here you will find a sign reading **Red Oak Road** and pointing to a narrow road straight ahead. Take this road 1 1/2 miles to a ford across Red Oak Canyon Creek. Continue another 3/4 mile to the signed trailhead, which is at a sharp switchback in the road. As the trail makes a moderate ascent it will soon come to a spring dominated by a huge incense cedar. Continue the ascent for a considerable distance with the trail finally making a nice contouring walk through a beautiful old growth forest. Occasionally you may see remnants of an old telephone line. Soon you will again begin to ascend with several refreshing springs and a small creek along the way. The trail continues to get steeper for a time, then mellows out for a nice vista down the Empire Creek canyon. As you near the top of the trail and its intersection with **Red Oak Road** it runs along several semi-dry meadows. After crossing the road the trail begins a series of five switchbacks constructed in the summer of 1993 to replace the loose, highly eroded original route. At the top of the switchbacks you will hit the virtually non-existent **Rattlesnake Peak Trail** and the newly reconstructed, wonderful **Chimney Rock Trail.** One sign points out the **Chimney Rock Trail,** the other tells us that the **Rattlesnake Peak Trail** is not maintained. The **Rattlesnake Peak Trail** is a short, unmaintained climb to the top of 7219' Rattlesnake Peak. There are outstanding views from this point, so it is worth the effort of making the side trip. The **Chimney Rock Trail** is definitely a worthwhile hike. At the top of the **Empire Creek Trail** is a nice, but dry campsite also accessible by the **Red Oak Road**.

EUREKA DIGGINGS-LITTLE CANYON CREEK TRAIL
Elevation: 5000' to 4000'
Length: +/- 1 1/2 miles
Hike Time: About 1 hour
Effort: Very Difficult
Location: T20N R10E, sections 6,7 and T20N R9E, section 1
Quadrangle Map: Goodyears Bar, La Porte **(For map see page 59)**

Take the **Eureka Diggings Road (USFS 25)** about 15 miles off of **Highway 49** at Fiddle Creek, about 12 miles west of Downieville. Look for a sign on the right (south) side of **USFS 25** reading Snow Creek. At this intersection turn left (north) onto a small road that leads to a fallen cabin and the trailhead. This is one of many old mule packers' trails in Northern Sierra County. During the early 1860s Vaughn and Bryant used it as a route for their saddle passenger train taking passengers and express from Downieville to Port Wine. From Downieville the mule train would pass through Eureka and Morristown into Canyon Creek and up the other side to Port Wine. Though the blazes are well grown over, brush is crowding it, and small fallen trees are numerous, it is still a very interesting hike. Head almost north from the fallen cabin where you parked, looking for old blaze marks. They are plentiful. The trail makes a slight ascent across a ditch and up and over a low ridge. It is a very wide, well-defined route that skirts the west side of the historic Eureka hydraulic diggings. As the trail drops down to Little Canyon Creek there are several slip-outs on the way to watch for. Care must be taken using this trail, as it has had no maintenance in at least 40 years. After about 1 1/2 miles you will reach **USFS 35-50**.

Old hydraulic mine diggings at Eureka North.

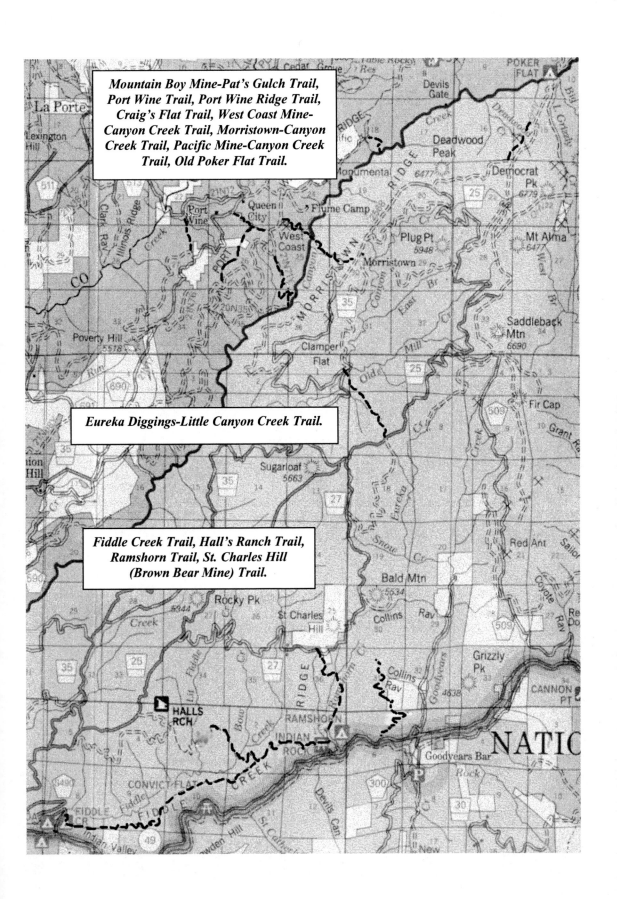

FIDDLE CREEK RIDGE TRAIL
Elevation: 2291' to 4100'
Length: +/- 4 miles
Hike Time: About 3 1/2 hours
Effort: Difficult
Location: T19N R9E, sections 8,9,10,16,17
Quadrangle Map: Goodyears Bar **(For map see page 59)**

This is another old trail that was rebuilt in 1994-95. Although some locals say it is a new trail, old blazes along the route are evidence that it's not. Most of the grade is moderate, and for a great distance is in decomposed granite. To reach the trailhead, take **State Highway 49** about 12 miles west from Downieville to Indian Valley. Turn right on the paved **Eureka Diggings Road (USFS 25)** just before the Indian Valley Outpost and the bridge over Fiddle Creek. Follow the road less than 1/4 mile to the signed trailhead on the right. Just past the sign is milepost .25. There is a small parking area opposite the trailhead. This trail is restricted to pedestrians and equestrians only. The trail makes two quick switchbacks up to a running water ditch. This is a domestic water supply so please keep yourself and any animals with you out of it. Pass a large, gnarly live oak as you follow the ditch a short distance, then cross and ascend the hill, crossing an old dry ditch. A switchback and winding ascent brings the trail to the ridgeback and another switchback. Ascend the ridgeback, then back along the west side of the ridge. Another switchback and ascent takes the trail back to and around the ridgeback and onto the south side of the mountain. The trail ascends this side with short glimpses of the old Indian Hill hydraulic mine across the Yuba River to the west. Make another switchback and return to the west side. There is a long arc around another ridge into mostly young Douglas fir, then a switchback and winding ascent onto the ridgeback and the north side of the ridge. Make a light descent along the north side of the ridge, swing around to the east, and descend through a small saddle back to the ridge top and an old CAT trail. The trail now makes a number of light ascents and descents along the top and side of the ridge to a survey monument and private property at section corners 8,9,16,17. The trail makes a light ascent on the north side of the ridge among evidence of past logging. Contour under heavy fir and tan oak to a saddle. The trail again ascends and descends along the ridge through several open areas showing evidence of the Indian Fire of 1987. Ahead can be seen the heavily timbered ridge the trail is about to ascend. Make light ups and downs along the south side winding through live oak, black oak, poison oak, and firs, pass around a draw and head south along the west side through a rocky section. There is a nice view down river and back over the trail route. The trail now rounds onto the south side of the ridge as it continues east and makes four switchbacks into the Indian Fire. From here there is a view up river of **Highway 49** and of the Sierra Buttes (after all this walking the highway doesn't seem that far below!) Bearing east, make two switchbacks and ascend along the ridgeback, meandering up through brush and dead oaks in a partial burn. There is a good view of the Indian Fire on the north side of Fiddle Creek from here. The trail passes in and out of the burn along the ridge top before making a quick, steep descent to another saddle. Continue along the ridge top to the intersection with **Hall's Ranch Trail**, which climbs up from **Highway 49**.

HALL'S RANCH TRAIL

Elevation: 2600' to 4400'
Length: +/- 5 miles
Hike Time: About 2 hours
Effort: Moderate
Location: T19N R9E, sections 1,2,3
Quadrangle Map: Goodyears Bar **(For map see page 59)**

The trailhead is at Ramshorn Campground, 6 miles west of Downieville on **State Route 49**. There is no sign when coming from Downieville so look for a USFS sign pointing out Indian Rock Picnic Area. The trailhead is opposite it. Park here, cross the highway and walk up the **Ramshorn Summer Home Tract Road** about 75 feet to the trail sign on the left. It says that Fiddle Creek is 2 miles and Hall's Ranch is 5 miles. Make a gradual ascent to a switchback, pass under the phone line and make two more gradual switchbacks. The trail levels out on a nice flat in heavy forest, then makes four more switchbacks. From here you may see the heavily forested south side of the Yuba River (and incidentally, the Ramshorn Campground dumpster on the east side of Ramshorn Creek). Make three more switchbacks before breaking out along the south side of the ridge. There is a sweeping view down the Yuba River. The trail makes a gentle ascent through fairly open, though rocky, country. The trail is a little loose and narrow here. Make three more switchbacks, a long ascent, another switchback, and you are on top of Fiddle Creek Ridge. The **Fiddle Creek Ridge Trail**, finished about 1995, intersects here. Small signs point out the trail since there are trail-like firebreaks from the 1987 Indian Fire that burned 8,600 acres of forest around Hall's Ranch and Fiddle Creek. Bear left along the ridge top then descend, bearing right. Two more little signs point out the trail. The trail is faint through here due to the resurgence of manzanita. What *looks* like the trail dropping to the left isn't. Stay to the right and begin dropping to a switchback. Make a moderate descent, cross two dry gulches in a nice forest that suffered minor fire damage, and make three more switchbacks. Fiddle Creek is a beautiful little stream with exposed bedrock. To continue, cross here where the trail runs upstream, makes a switchback, and ascends quickly to another faint switchback at the edge of a gully. It then makes another switchback and winds straight up the hill to make two more switchbacks and then a long, sweeping switchback. It then works up the ridge to a skid trail and a sign reading **Hall's Ranch Trail**, pointing toward Fiddle Creek.

HASKELL PEAK TRAIL

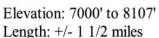

Elevation: 7000' to 8107'
Length: +/- 1 1/2 miles
Effort: Moderate
Hike Time: About 1 1/2 hours
Location: T21N R13E, sections 29,30
Quadrangle Map: Clio **(For map see page 52)**

From Bassett's Station travel east on **Highway 49** about 5 miles to a left-hand turn onto

Haskell Peak Road (USFS 21N09). Proceed on this road 4 1/2 miles to the four-way intersection at Chapman Saddle and turn left, still on ***21N09***. Another 1 1/4 mile will bring you to a log landing on the left and the signed trailhead on the right. The sign notes that Haskell Peak is 2 miles and that no motorized vehicles are allowed. The trail begins by crossing a meadow shared with lodgepole pine and mule ear, and soon makes an easy, winding ascent into small white fir. Rock ducks as well as occasional signs indicate the trail route. As the trail winds up through ferns and signs of logging, you may notice old blazes. A short contour leads to a light ascent in lodgepole pine and several dry gully crossings. Skirt the left side of a tree-studded meadow, then veer right to cross the meadow into trees. A steeper ascent under mostly red fir also becomes somewhat rocky as it leads to two switchbacks and a glimpse of Sierra Valley. The trail mellows amid trees then tops the saddle. An old segment of the trail continues west (see end of description), but to reach the peak veer right sharply and make a slightly rocky, moderately steep ascent to the summit. From here are outstanding views of the Sierra Valley, Sierra Buttes, Lakes Basin, Mt. Lassen, and most days, Mt. Shasta. There are also three impressive rock cairns constructed over the years by hikers. The westerly-running segment from the saddle was by appearances, originally a wagon road. It contours along under timber with occasional trail signs to indicate the route. A big clearcut on the left gives a view of the Sierra Buttes and a light ascent along its right side takes the trail to a saddle and view to the north of Mohawk Valley, Portola, and Sierra Valley. The trail (signed as no longer maintained) once ran up the steep west flank of Haskell Peak. Although maps show a trail running through to the Kelly-Locke Mine area, it appears that the area has been heavily logged and I could find no more traces of a single-track trail.

ILLINOIS CREEK TRAIL

Elevation: 6400' to 4800'
Length: +/- 2 miles
Effort: Very Difficult
Hike Time: About 2 hours
Location: T21N R10E, section 2 and T22N R10E, sections 34,35
Quadrangle Map: Mt. Fillmore **(For map see page 63)**

This is a tough trail to follow and a sharp eye for route indicators is a must, as this trail makes some unexpected zigs and zags. Besides, it doesn't even remotely follow the route officially indicated on the quad map. A portion of it almost borders on an Extremely Difficult rating. Reach the trailhead by taking the ***Johnsville-La Porte Road*** east about 5 1/2 miles from Gibsonville to ***USFS 22N43***. The unsigned turn off is on the north shoulder of Mt. Fillmore. Turn right and follow the road about 1 1/2 miles to an iron gate. Just past the gate you will see the private property line. The trail begins just below the road at this point and angles moderately down about 1/4 mile to a saddle. After crossing through the saddle the trail is distinct to where it hits a USFS survey monument on the government-private line. From here on you must watch very carefully for overgrown blazes. From the monument the trail angles down to the left toward a large open area resembling a meadow. As you descend, cross a large miner's ditch, then hit the top of the open area, and head right (south) through the trees to another open area on the other side of the ridge. Skirt the top of the meadow to a large white fir in a thicket. From here you can again follow overgrown blazes in a meandering fashion down the ridgeback. The trail itself is almost nonexistent except for the blazes. Pass through another small saddle and begin descending along a shale outcropping. From here the trail drops quickly and steeply west and down hill to cross several very steep, dry ravines. Extreme care should be used on this trail. After working through the dry ravines the trail becomes much more apparent as it parallels Illinois Creek about 100 feet below. It makes a moderate ascent to a small and very steep stream. Cross the stream and make a moderate-to-heavy ascent, then a light-to-moderate descent crossing two dry ravines. After crossing a wet ravine and a very open sidehill where the trail is again faint, descend across a spring in a ravine and make some minor ups and downs. Below are an old ditch and diggings. Pass along the top of a very high, steep bank and make a light descent with two short switchbacks to cross an old ditch. In a short distance the trail hits another old ditch coming down the ridgeback. Cross the ditch and parallel it down the ridge through brush and red and white fir. There is a switchback in some old diggings, then the trail goes across and down to the left. Just below is Illinois Creek and some maintained mining cabins. The trail runs along a bedrock shelf as it passes an old tin shed into a mining draw and old diggings. Veer right and switchback down past an outhouse to the end of a 1/4 mile spur road off the **Tennessee Mine-Poker Flat Road.** Poker Flat is west about 1 mile via rough road that may now be closed due to storm damage.

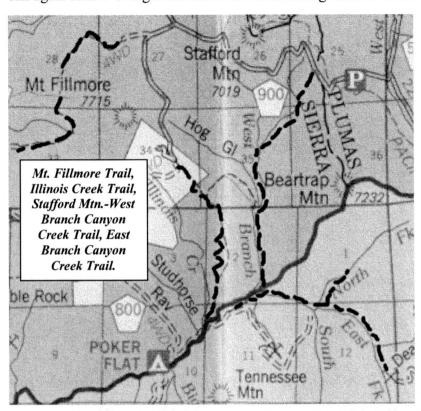

Mt. Fillmore Trail, Illinois Creek Trail, Stafford Mtn.-West Branch Canyon Creek Trail, East Branch Canyon Creek Trail.

LAVEZOLLA CREEK TRAIL
Elevation: 4200' to 5200'
Length: +/- 3 1/2 miles
Effort: Moderate
Hike Time: About 4 hours
Location: T21N R11E, sections 9,16,21,28,33
Quadrangle Map: Downieville, Mt. Fillmore, Gold Lake **(For map see page 53)**

This trail, though a pretty hike, is difficult to access. There are two trailheads, one near Johnsville in Plumas County and the other above Downieville. For simplicity we will use the Downieville end for a starting point. To reach the trailhead, take Upper Main Street in Downieville about 1/2 mile past the post office. Cross the Downie River bridge and proceed about 5 miles up Lavezolla Creek. You will pass a well-defined left fork in the road and continue through the Empire Ranch to a gate at the Lavezolla Ranch where you must park. After passing by the house, beautiful rock walls and other ranch buildings, you must still walk about 2 miles of road to the trailhead. The trail begins on the left near the end of the road in a logged area. It has been repaired here and is easy to follow, though it is not signed. As you leave the logged area there is one last view of Lavezolla canyon from a rocky point. There are two small creeks to cross via footbridges and for the most part the trail makes very gradual ups and downs for the approximately 1 mile to the old bridge crossing. At one time a large, high bridge spanned the canyon here. On the other side the **Old Lavezolla Creek Trail** continues up the right side of the creek for several miles, but is very brushy and overgrown. Just past Smith Creek (on the old trail) is the **Smith Creek Trail** to Smith Lake, also overgrown. To stay on the **New Lavezolla Creek Trail**, backtrack to where the trail made a distinct ascent (a jeep sign adorns a tree here) and follow up the left side of the creek. About 2 miles up, the trail suddenly becomes a 4WD road, though a very primitive one. Although the miscreants who made the road degraded a very good hiking trail, you can still make a pleasant walk of it. The route meanders through huge incense cedars and firs with views of the opposite hillside. The road gets progressively better as you ascend but has three fords to make before climbing steeply the last 1 1/2 miles to the A Tree, **Four Hills Mine Road**, and the **Pacific Crest Trail.** From here the main road runs down to the **Johnsville-La Porte Road** and Johnsville. Gus Poggi, an old-time packer, described the trail to Hank Meals in 1993: Those trails were all county trails when I was a kid. The...Lavezolla Trail, that was a county trail. It was maintained all the way from Downieville to the A-Tree. It goes right up the Lavezolla; in those days it was called the Middle Fork, clear up to the Ten Mile Bridge, up to the old Four Hills Power House, and right on up to the A-Tree. That was the county line. From there on, Plumas County maintained the trail, down Florentine Canyon to the Plumas-Eureka I believe.

LITTLE GRIZZLY CREEK TRAIL
Elevation: 4800' to 6400'
Length: +/- 2 miles
Effort: Difficult
Hike Time: About 2 hours
Location: T21N R10E, sections 10,15,22
Quadrangle Map: Mt. Fillmore **(For map see page 53)**

This trail is also known as the **Old Downieville Trail.** Start at a point on the west side of Little Grizzly Creek about 1/8 mile south of the Poker Flat Cemetery on the **Downieville-Poker Flat 4WD Road (USFS 25N58)**, or use the directions for the **Downie River Trail** and **Rattlesnake Creek Trail** trailhead. There is heavy usage for the first 1/4 mile from miners camped along the trail. Crossing an abandoned mining ditch and skirting their camp, the trail begins a moderate ascent up the canyon. This trail is no longer maintained but for the most part is in very good condition until the tailings from the long dormant Golden Scepter Mine are encountered. Here the trail becomes vague, though several small switchbacks are very evident. From the trail you can see a natural hole through the bedrock in the creek, which makes an interesting side trip. Continue along roughly the same course, passing through recent miner's workings. The trail becomes markedly steeper now as it approaches the saddle between Democrat Peak and Bunker Hill. There is a long sweeping switchback under Democrat Peak that will take you to the top. Here you connect with the **Downie River Trail** and the **Bunker Hill-Clark's Canyon Road.**

MORRISTOWN-CANYON CREEK TRAIL
Elevation: 5200' to 4200'
Length: +/- 1 mile
Effort: Very Difficult
Hike Time: About 1 hour
Location: T21N R10E, section 30 and T21N R9E, section 24
Quadrangle Map: La Porte **(For map see page 59)**

Reach the trailhead by taking the **Downieville-Poker Flat Road** north about 11 miles to a left on the **Deadwood Peak-Morristown Road**. Proceed approximately 4 miles, pass the Morristown Cemetery, and make a sweeping turn 1 1/2 miles down into the Morristown Diggings. Starting at the west edge of the Morristown Diggings follow the overgrown, brushy, but distinct mule trail down across an intermittent stream. The trail makes a descent into Canyon Creek where in summer the shade is welcome. You can hike up the **West Coast Mine Trail** described later, and continue to the site of Port Wine via the **Port Wine Trail.**

MOUNTAIN BOY MINE-PAT'S GULCH TRAIL
Elevation: 4800' to 4400'
Length: +/- 1 mile
Effort: Very Difficult
Hike Time: About 1 hour
Location: T21N R9E, sections 27,22
Quadrangle Map: La Porte **(For map see page 59)**

In the winter of 1938, a group of men transported a miner with a spinal injury by sled from the Mountain Boy Mine to Strawberry Valley by way of La Porte. The arduous journey over snow took them two days, but at that time they had no choice. Reach the trailhead from La Porte by taking the **La Porte-Port Wine Road (USFS 21N47)** about 3 1/2 miles to the **Scales-Howland Flat Road (USFS 21N17)**. Turn right on that road and proceed west 1 1/2 miles past the old mining camp of Port Wine. Just before leaving private property, unsigned **USFS spur 21N48Y** turns right (northwest). A Sierra County road marker reading 690 SIE 76 sits opposite the turnoff. Follow this about 1/10 mile to a definite right angle turn at the base of a steep grade. The overgrown, unsigned trail drops steeply down the ridge spine to Pat's Gulch and its junction with Port Wine Ravine.

MT. FILLMORE TRAIL
Elevation: 6490' to 5800'
Length: +/- 3 1/2 miles
Effort: Very Difficult
Hike Time: About 3 hours
Location: T22N R10E, sections 27,28,33
Quadrangle Map: Mt. Fillmore and La Porte **(For map see page 63)**

In 1974 I walked this old trail and was taken with the views it afforded. Sadly, sometime between then and now a large portion of it was logged and turned into a 4WD road. At the end of the 4WD section the old foot trail continues on, but is very vague. To reach the trailhead, take the **Johnsville-La Porte Road (USFS Road 900)** about 16 miles west of Johnsville or 5 1/2 miles northeast of La Porte. Turn south onto **USFS 22N43** and almost immediately make a right. This is the trail. It contours around the north and west slopes of Mt. Fillmore at an elevation of about 6,000 feet with nice views of Howland Flat and Sawmill Ridge, but blazes are occasional and difficult to spot. As the trail skirts the head of Pearson Ravine, dense manzanita brush becomes prevalent. Take care to stay on the trail as it descends to a dead-end road 1/2 mile long that connects with the old **Howland Flat Road** one mile north of Howland Flat.

MT. LOLA TRAIL
Elevation: 6640' to 9143'
Length: +/- 4 1/2 miles
Effort: Moderate
Hike Time: About 3 hours
Location: T19N R15E, sections 20,29,32 and T19N R14E, sections 1,25 and T18N R14E, sections 11,12
Quadrangle Map: Weber Lake, Independence Lake

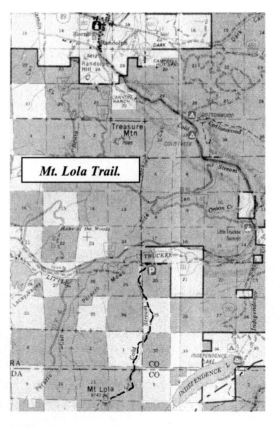
Mt. Lola Trail.

Reach the trailhead by taking the **Jackson Meadows Reservoir Road (USFS-07)** at Little Truckee Summit on **State Highway 89** about 12 miles south of Sierraville and 20 miles north of Truckee. Proceed west 1 1/4 miles to a left turn. Cross a small bridge and travel a short distance to an unsigned four-way intersection. Turn right onto **Sierra County Road S301** and follow about 4 1/2 miles to the signed trailhead on the left. Along the way are remnants of the original **Henness Pass Road** to Nevada. A message board and trail signs are at the large parking area. The trail meanders up at an easy grade following old logging skid trails. It makes several short, steep pitches and two switchbacks then meanders along an open ridgeback. As it climbs it swings into the side of a small canyon with Cold Stream flowing north about 50 yards below. The trail now becomes a definite single track at an easy ascent. As you pass from private land into national forest and then back onto private land (Santa Fe Pacific), there is ample evidence of the logging in 1997. Contour along under a haul road and log landing. After a bit the trail leaves the predominantly red fir forest and enters lodgepole pine. It skirts above a meadow area with riparian brush, crosses a seasonal ravine, and continues an easy ascent along the east side of the live stream. At the crossing of Cold Stream you again enter private land. Continue upstream, entering Nevada County and crossing the head of the creek. Begin a steep winding ascent to the summit of 9,143' Mt. Lola. Trails continue from here to White Rock Lake, the *PCT,* and the Basin Peak area.

OLD POKER FLAT TRAIL
Elevation: 5200' to 5900'
Length: +/- 1/2 mile
Effort: Difficult
Hike Time: 1/2 hour
Location: T21N R10E, section 15
Quadrangle Map: Mt. Fillmore **(For map see page 59)**

The only real reason to walk this trail is if you happen to be hiking in or out on the *Poker Flat-Downieville Road* and you want to take the historic route or avoid dust from OHVs (and it may be just a bit quicker than the road to walk). It is a nice old trail but rather short. The trail can be picked up just above the road about 3/4 to 1 mile out of Poker Flat. It parallels the road for a distance at a heavy grade before crossing it on a switchback. Continue to ascend along the west side of the hill as the road heads east. The trail winds in around the top of Cleghorn Ravine and another unnamed ravine, crosses a small ravine with some water seepage, and then tops a black-colored serpentine ridge where it intersects an OHV trail off the *Poker Flat-Downieville Road*. Cross the OHV trail and contour along the west slope in short cedars and pine to the head of Deadwood Creek and a reuniting with the *Poker Flat-Downieville Road*. As you walk along you might notice

The 1886 Scott Home at Poker Flat, though heavily vandalized, is now under restoration by volunteers.

the large number of old cedar stumps, the trees of which were used for the extensive mining in the area. In his journal <u>Up and Down California In 1860-1864</u>, Professor William H. Brewer described his trip from Eureka to Poker Flat in September of 1863: From the town of Eureka it was ...a vile trail, nine miles, <u>very</u> rough, across canyons and ridges...We at last sank into a very deep canyon, perhaps two thousand feet deep, to Poker Flat, a miserable hole - but what we lacked in accommodations was made up in prices. Ten white men and two Chinamen slept in the little garret of the hotel. Our horses fared but little better, and our bill was the modest little sum of fifteen dollars.

PACIFIC MINE-CANYON CREEK TRAIL

Elevation: 5000' to 4300'
Length: +/- 1/2 mile
Effort: Difficult
Hike Time: About 1 hour
Location: T21N R10E, section 18
Quadrangle Map: La Porte **(For map see page 59)**

From La Porte, take the **Howland Flat Road (USFS 21N17)** to **USFS 21N69** about 1 mile north of Port Wine and Queen City. Proceed about 1 mile to a left-hand turn. Just before the turn the road doubles back as you cross the ridge. The left-hand road is the **Pacific Mine Road**. Continue along the mostly level road about 2 1/2 miles. At the now non-existent Pacific Mine the road makes a sharp left up the hill. This is 4WD only. Park here and walk 25 feet northeast to the overgrown Scales Ditch. This is our trail. It is not maintained and can be somewhat dangerous in spots, but the views into Canyon Creek are well worth the effort. About 1/4 mile out the trail to Canyon Creek leaves the ditch and drops quickly and steeply down the side of the canyon. Although the view is pleasant, the hike out is not. If you would rather not go into the canyon you can continue along the ditch to its abrupt end. Do not try to go further as it is very loose, steep, and hard to negotiate. I stood on the end of it early one autumn morning with the wind blowing at what seemed 100-miles-an-hour. What a great feeling, leaning into the view of upper Canyon Creek! The ditch itself is a stupendous work. Carved out of solid rock, it demonstrates the sheer will of the early miners.

PAULEY CREEK TRAIL

Length: +/- 3 miles
Effort: Difficult
Hike Time: About 3 hours
Location: T21N R11E, section 35, T20N R11E, section 3
Quadrangle Map: Downieville, Sierra City, Gold Lake **(For map see page 50)**

The Pauley Creek Trailhead is reached by following the **Third Divide Trail** or the **Second Divide Trail** to their junction with the **Pauley Creek Trail.** To reach the first two trails use the trailhead access descriptions given for the respective trails. At the trailhead, signs on posts and attached to a huge ponderosa pine tell you that Gold Valley is 5 miles and

Butcher Ranch 4 miles. Follow the trail at an easy descent to Pauley Creek, which you cross via a long iron bridge built in 1952. There are many nice campsites here and all along the creek, which in this section is known as the Devil's Den. The trail climbs moderately with three switchbacks after crossing the creek. Continue climbing steadily with views of beautiful pools and old growth timber along the creek. Remnants of an old telephone line can be seen occasionally, also. The trail through here is rather loose due to heavy use by mountain bikers. Great views of the rugged canyon sides are frequent and several miner's cabins sit just below the trail. As you pass these maintained claims (and a unique privy built against a huge cedar), the trail works through a very nice flat area with large trees. Fish can be seen jumping in the pools and, if you are lucky, a mother bear and her cubs. Just before you cross Butcher Ranch Creek on a new footbridge is the intersection with the **Butcher Ranch Creek Trail**. One sign says Lavezolla Creek 4 miles, Butcher Ranch 2 miles; the other **Pauley Creek Trail**, Gold Valley 2 1/2 miles. Both signs are well shot up. Cross Butcher Ranch Creek and continue along a pleasant grade to an open area with quaking aspen. Here the trail ascends some winding switchbacks paved with interlocking cement blocks to reduce trail erosion. Continue past a nice campsite on the creek. Across the creek is a 4WD road. Pass several springs and one small creek to the footbridge crossing Pauley Creek. From here the trail makes a steep ascent for over 1/4 mile to the end of a 4WD road from Gold Valley. Gold Valley is an alternate trailhead. Use the directions for access to the **Butcher Ranch Trail** from Sierra City, but continue on past that trailhead following the signs to Gold Valley if you decide to start at the top end.

PORT WINE TRAIL
Elevation: 5200' to 5000'
Length: +/- 1 mile
Effort: Moderate
Hike Time: About 1 hour
Location: T21N R10E, sections 23, 25, 26
Quadrangle Map: La Porte **(For map see page 59)**

To reach the trailhead from La Porte, take the **La Porte-Port Wine Road (Plumas County 513, Sierra County 791)** to the site of Queen City. Turn left on the **Port Wine-Howland Flat Road (USFS 21N17)** and proceed to **USFS 21N69**, about 1 mile north of Port Wine and Queen City. Maps show this road as making a loop back to Queen City, but it doesn't. After about 1/2 mile **USFS 21N69** becomes **USFS 21N77**. Turn right and travel about 1 1/2 miles, passing the **Pacific Mine Road** and the **West Coast Mine Road.** Cross a small rise and log landing, and just as you begin descending into a sweeping turn, the shared **Port Wine Trail** and **Port Wine Ridge Trail** trailhead is on the right. It is best to park in the log landing. Head west through a recently logged area to the foot of the slope at your right. A skid trail covers the trail for 200 yards or so, but the route has been recently re-blazed. The trail is quite wide, though not maintained and climbs moderately to the ridge top. Here the **Port Wine Ridge Trail** bears left. We drop down to the right into dense timber and soon hit a now-closed logging spur **(USFS 21N03X)**. Follow this approximately 1/4 mile to **USFS 21N17**.

PORT WINE RIDGE TRAIL

Elevation: 5200' to 4800'
Length: +/- 2 miles
Effort: Moderate
Hike Time: About 2 hours
Location: T21N R9E, sections 23,26,35
Quadrangle Map: La Porte **(For map see page 59)**

To reach the trailhead from La Porte, take the **La Porte-Port Wine Road (Plumas County 513, Sierra County 791)** to the site of Queen City. Turn left on the **Port Wine-Howland Flat Road (USFS 21N17)** and proceed to **USFS 21N69**, about 1 mile north of Port Wine and Queen City. Maps show this road as making a loop back to Queen City, but it doesn't. After about 1/2 mile **USFS 21N69** becomes **USFS 21N77**. Turn right and travel about 1 1/2 miles, passing the **Pacific Mine Road** and the **West Coast Mine Road.** Cross a small rise and log landing, and just as you begin descending into a sweeping turn, the shared **Port Wine Trail** and **Port Wine Ridge Trail** trailhead is to the right. It is best to park in the log landing. Head west through a recently logged area to the foot of the slope at your right. A skid trail covers the trail for 200 yards or so, but has been recently re-blazed. The trail is quite wide, though not maintained and climbs moderately to the ridge top. The trail to the townsite of Port Wine drops quickly to the right. Our trail bears left and ascends gradually up the ridgeback. Note the overgrown blaze marks on many of the trees. As you make a slight descent, there are nice views of the La Porte area to the west and Saddleback Peak and Craig's Flat to the east. As you pass onto private property, note the Quartz Hill survey monument. Make a slight ascent as you leave the private property and soon cross an old skid trail, ascending along the very edge of the ridge and an old natural wash. More nice views of the La Porte area are seen from here. On a clear day, the Coast Range, High Sierra, and unfortunately, many clearcuts can be seen. An old skid trail covers the trail again for about 1/2 mile, though it has healed very well. It then descends into heavy timber on the east side of the ridge, still on the skid trail. The trail proper resumes and breaks out into the open for a short distance before again hitting an old logging area. From here the trail has been destroyed, but by staying right on the ridgeback you can drop down to an abandoned logging road, cross it and follow a large skid road to **USFS 21N77**, about 1/4 mile or so. Unless you have transportation back to the trailhead, returning via the trail is easier, as the road is a long walk. Though this trail has been logged over in spots, it is still a pleasant hike.

RAMSHORN TRAIL
Elevation: 5000' to 2640'
Length: +/- 2 3/4 miles
Effort: Very Difficult
Hike Time: About 4 hours
Location: T20N R9E, section 36 and T19N R9E, section 1
Quadrangle Map: Goodyears Bar **(For map see page 59)**

The topographic maps show this trail as heading out at the lower end from **Highway 49** and making a gradual ascent for quite a distance. Looks can be *very* deceiving! There is absolutely no reason I can think of to utilize this trailhead if you don't have to. If you want to hike up the trail, it is preferable to start from Ramshorn Campground (originally known as St. Joe Bar) about 5 miles west of Downieville. I have used both trailheads and the Ramshorn Campground one is much easier. However, the best way to hike this trail is to start at the upper trailhead. I will describe all three trailheads as a part of the trail description just for drill. To reach the upper trailhead take the **Eureka Diggings Road (USFS 25)** about 6 miles from Fiddle Creek Campground (about 12 miles west of Downieville) to a sign reading **Ramshorn Trail.** Take the white-graveled road *(USFS 27)* 5 miles to the signed trailhead. There are two signs: **Ramshorn Trail 9E08** and Ramshorn Campground 2 3/4, **Highway 49** 2 3/4. The trail almost immediately crosses a seasonal creek and an old ditch. Descend at a moderate grade and round the ridgeback. The grade becomes steeper, crosses an old mining wash, brushes along the edge of private property, and makes two switchbacks. Note the porcelain insulators from an old phone line. There are a number of old prospects above and below the trail through here. As you pass three caved adits, watch the mine rail across the trail, it's at shin's height. The trail makes five switchbacks with a steep grade down to a refreshing creek. Cross the creek and a small spring at a 1950s cabin site (no digging!) and continue down a nice grade through oaks, maples, and firs to a small rock field. There are a number of large logs across the trail in this area. Make a sharp left and two switchbacks with a moderate grade, then drop through a forested swale, making about five switchbacks. A large oak along the trail has an X blazed in its bark. Continue down through the swale, noting the small rock walls. The trail works out onto the ridge spine and makes three switchbacks down to a switchback and K-tag for the quarter corner of section 1, T19N R9E. Make three short, steep switchbacks and descend a short distance to where the trail switches back and makes a long, easy descent, rounds the ridge, crosses a dry gully, and hits the top of a steep woodcutter's road. Follow the woodcutter's road down to the Ramshorn Campground, approximately 1/2 mile or so. At the pavement there is a wire gate and two metal white diamonds nailed to two trees. The road is steep and rocky and much more pleasant to walk down than up. Now, if you insist on taking the route given on some topographical maps, pass the last switchback described and descend to what appears to be an old ditch with some nice rock walls on it. Follow this into a drainage with a large blazed cedar. There is a short, miserable descent

Chimney Rock Trail above Downieville.

of several switchbacks. The blazes are quite overgrown here. Cross a small stream in heavy brush onto the east side and contour along the hill. The trail is brushy now, but blazed and obvious. It makes a moderate descent toward a large brushy flat area. The trail is very faint, but keep contouring to the next wet drainage where the trail now becomes an old, overgrown logging skid road. Strangely, there is a huge rose bush in the road just after crossing the creek! The road descends steeply to another flat. Stay on the uphill side of it. On the left end of the flat pick up the trail again and contour along the hillside. Cross a small spring and a small washout and break out onto another flat area. Cross a dry drainage, pass under the phone line, contour through a thicket, gently round the ridge, and make a moderate descent in Douglas fir cover to another dry drainage. The trail is now definitely an old ditch. Contour along the hillside, pass a galvanized iron post, pass under the phone line again, and make a light ascent to the intersection with the **Old St. Charles Hill Trail**. From here, switchback down, cross a small gully, and descend to the concrete drainage and parking area on **Highway 49**. Again, I heartily discourage use of this route until it has been worked on.

RATTLESNAKE CREEK TRAIL
Elevation: 4000' to 5000'
Length: +/- 2 1/2 miles
Effort: Difficult
Hike Time: 2 hours
Location: T21N R10E, sections 25,26,35
Quadrangle Map: Mt. Fillmore **(For map see page 53)**

The U.S. Forest Service has begun revitalizing a number of old trails in this region, and the **Rattlesnake Trail** is one of them. I recently ran across an article that was written in 1892 regarding the origin of the name of Rattlesnake Creek. In early 1850, miners prospected their way up the North Fork to the junction of Clark's Canyon. It was said that several parties ...discovered more rattlesnakes than any one before had probably seen at one spot in the United States. Supposedly, two enterprising Downievillians went up to the spot on a Sunday and shot and killed at least 300 reptiles, ...until the air was so loaded with that peculiar sickening odor that comes from them, that [the two] were attacked with vomiting and had to leave in a hurry.... At any rate, in time the site was mined away and no snakes, at least in those numbers, remain. To reach the trailhead, take Upper Main Street through Downieville. About 1/2 mile east of the Post Office take the unpaved **Downie River Road,** do not cross the Downie River bridge. A sign notes that the **Downie River Trail** is 5 miles. Stay left, passing the **Gold Bluff Mine Road**. Park at the end of the road and take the **Downie River Trail** about 1/4 mile to the **Downie River Trail** bridge. Cross to the east side and continue along the nicely rebuilt trail. The creek is quite pretty through this section. Cross a small stream via a new timber bridge, pass a maintained cabin, and ascend around the ridge through old growth timber to a moderate descent to Rattlesnake Creek. Until October of 1995 the trail forded the creek, but now there is a 65-foot long twin beam steel bridge with wood decking. It was delivered via helicopter. Cross here and ascend through an active claim with a maintained cabin. The **Downie River Trail** faintly veers left and uphill. Continue along a moderate ascent through old diggings and fir cover, into live oak, then make a descent back into heavy cover. The trail soon crosses a small creek with waterfalls below. Round the ridge and enter a rocky area with predominantly live oak. Cross two dry ravines and a spring with a lean-to just below. The trail now ascends steeply, crosses an old ditch, ascends easily across another seep spring under very heavy cover, contours to another spring, crosses a small stream with four-foot banks via a log bridge, then moderately ascends around the ridge. A heavy descent through large Douglas fir and live oak mellows into a contour along the hill above the creek, then works through old diggings to a short but steep drop to the creek. Cross here, just above the cliffs along the creek. Make a steep but short climb into old diggings, two switchbacks, and a short, heavy ascent into a section of old growth. Gently ascend to a set of bluffs where the trail rounds the ridge and makes a moderate descent along the bluffs to a crossing of Rattlesnake Creek on fairly permanent looking boulders. The trail ascends steeply past a campsite to skirt the bluffs on this side, then drops down to cross Clark's Canyon just upstream of its confluence with Rattlesnake Creek. The trail then continues at a moderate to steep ascent up the ridgeback to a very overgrown section of closed 4WD road from Bunker Hill. For all practical purposes at this time there is no reason to continue past Clark's Canyon. The 4WD road is one of the most miserable, loose, steep, wretched roads I have ever walked. If you do hike it, take care not to drop off on the Clark's Canyon side of the trail, for it is aptly named.

SECOND DIVIDE TRAIL

Elevation: 3480' to 4440'
Length: +/- 5 miles
Effort: Difficult
Hike Time: About 3 hours
Location: T20N R11E, sections 9,16,17,18
Quadrangle Map: Downieville, Sierra City **(For map see page 50)**

Take Upper Main Street through Downieville. About 1/2 mile east of the Post Office, cross the Downie River bridge. Take the dirt road 2 3/4 miles to the ***Second Divide Trailhead,*** on your right. This trail is characterized by numerous ups and downs, with most of the trail out of sight of the creek. Within 1 mile you will reach a trail cutting off to the creek to your right. A sign here tells you it is 2 miles back to Second Divide, and 3 miles to Third Divide. It isn't. It is more like 4 miles to Third Divide. Ascend the two switchbacks just past this sign. The trail continues along the creek, which through here is very pretty. After a distance you will see signs requesting gun-toters not to shoot as there is a cabin along the trail. It is a maintained mining claim and should be respected. Begin ascending again, at one point right alongside a huge, fallen pine tree. Reaching an old mining ditch-turned trail is a welcome relief. Follow this not quite a mile to a maintained log cabin. After leaving this quaint scene the trail makes some minor switchbacks up the hill with occasional glimpses of the creek. From here the trail is narrower and has many more short up and down spots. A homemade sign indicates the trail in a level section of the forest. From here you again ascend moderately to the intersection with the ***Third Divide Trail*** and the ***Pauley Creek Trail.*** Signs on posts and attached to a huge ponderosa pine direct you either back to Second Divide 5 miles; Butcher Ranch 4 miles, and Gold Valley 5 miles ahead; or to Lavezolla Creek 3 miles. If you elect to return via Third Divide you will have another 1 1/4 miles of road to walk also to get back to the Second Divide trailhead.

SPENCER LAKES TRAIL (via Spencer Creek)

Elevation: 6400' to 5200'
Length: +/- 1 mile
Effort: Extremely Difficult
Hike Time: About 1 hour
Location: T21N R11E, sections 9,10
Quadrangle Map: Gold Lake

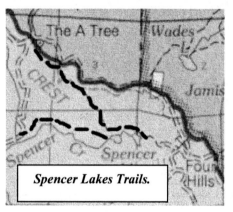

Spencer Lakes Trails.

Don't do it! It was once a fairly good pack trail, but until it is refitted I highly discourage this hike. This trail is not only hard to find at either end, it is only discernible for a short distance at each end before it becomes so heavily overgrown with brush that it is almost impossible to stay on it. Steep switchbacks, tall, dense brush, sudden drops off of boulders, and an eroded trail base all combine to make this trail a real nightmare.

SPENCER LAKES TRAIL (via the PCT)

Elevation: 6600' to 6400'
Length: +/- 2 miles
Effort: Easy
Hike Time: About 1 hour
Location: T21N R11E, sections 3,4,10
Quadrangle Map: Gold Lake

Reach the trailhead by taking the rough **Johnsville-La Porte Road** about 4 miles southwest of Johnsville to the **Four Hills Mine Road**. This road is well graveled and makes a distinct left off the main road. It crosses Jamison Creek via a bridge and continues about 2 miles to a saddle and the A Tree. The A Tree is about 31 miles from Quincy by this route. There are actually about three A Trees at this spot. All are marked with an A blazed into the bark, one has a sign on it. Park here and take the **Pacific Crest Trail** east (the left side). The trail runs along smoothly for about 1 1/4 miles, makes a switchback, enters an open area, and then as you re-enter the trees, the unsigned **Spencer Lake Trail** drops to the right. Make several switchbacks down the hill and as the trail leaves the trees there is a nice view of the huge monolith above Lower Spencer Lake. There is a spring on the trail just before it enters a brushfield. From here it makes eight more very gradual switchbacks down to the lake.

ST. CHARLES HILL TRAIL (BROWN BEAR MINE TRAIL)

Elevation: 2640' to 5000'
Length: +/- 2 miles
Effort: Difficult
Hike Time: About 2 hours
Location: T19N R10E, sections 5,6 and T20N R10E, section 31
Quadrangle Map: Goodyears Bar **(For map see page 59)**

James J. Sinnott, in his book Sierra City and Goodyears Bar, gives the following information regarding this trail. A[n]...early trail, which is believed was laid out in 1866, ascended the mountain northwest of Goodyears Bar. This trail had its origin about a half mile west of Goodyears Bar, goes by St. Charles Hill, the Brown Bear Mine and on to Eureka. Gus Poggi also called it the ***Brown Bear Trail.*** It shares the same trailhead as the original ***Ramshorn Trail*** and for the most part is a moderate hike. However, at this writing only half of the trail had been refitted leaving enough rough sections to warrant a difficult rating. Reach the trailhead about half a mile west of ***Mountain House Road*** at Goodyears Bar, about 4 miles west of Downieville on ***Highway 49***. There is no sign, but look for a large dirt turnout with a cemented drainage ditch and culvert. Park by the ditch, the trail starts on the other side of it. Once on the trail immediately cross a dry gulch, switchback, recross the gulch, and pass the very unmaintained ***Ramshorn Trail***, which takes off to the west (left). Keep heading east with a phone line above paralleling the trail. Just above the trail note the impressive live oak with a huge butt. Pass a K-tag (section 5), go under the phone line and into the Goodyears Creek drainage. Pass another K-tag just under the section 5 corner. Make four more switchbacks, then a long, easy ascent, all under heavy forest. Another four switchbacks, a long easy ascent and two more switchbacks brings the trail onto a small flat. As of 1994 trail maintenance stopped here. Cross the flat and keep on an easy ascent. Soon you will note old stumps from logging, you are now just inside private property. Make a switchback and ascend around the ridgeback to where you can see down the Yuba River. The trail is very faint through here. Switchback at a gray pine stump about twenty-feet tall and again switchback almost immediately at a large oak. Head west, looking for clippings on the end of branches and small blazes on oak and fir trees. Stay slightly sidehill, then ascend onto the spine of the ridge, pass through a small opening and continue ascending. Switchback at a blazed oak (the trail seems to keep going straight, but doesn't) and go up the ridgeback and onto the east side again. Make another switchback in very heavy cover, ascend to the ridge again, switchback, ascend the east side again past a blazed ponderosa pine and flat area directly below the trail. There is a nice stand of old growth Douglas fir and pine here. Just past a 4 1/2 foot diameter ponderosa with blaze marks is another switchback. Make three more switchbacks after this, cross the ridgeback and contour along the southern exposure. Here are your first real views of the south side of the Yuba River drainage. Make two more switchbacks and ascend the very ridgeback to a logging skid trail. Follow this a short distance to ***USFS 27N16 spur*** off the ***St. Charles Hill Road.***

STAFFORD MTN.-WEST BR. CANYON CREEK TRAIL
Elevation: 6200' to 5000'
Length: +/- 1 1/4 miles
Effort: Very Difficult
Hike Time: About 2 hours
Location: T22N R10E, sections 26,35 and T21N R10E, section 2.
Quadrangle Map: Mt. Fillmore **(For map see page 63)**

The trailhead is on the **Johnsville-La Porte Road (Plumas Co. 507, Sierra Co. 900)** about 13 1/2 miles west of Johnsville, or about 7 1/2 miles northeast of La Porte off the **La Porte-Quincy Road**. The trail is very vague at first. A blazed, flat-topped old Jeffrey pine more or less marks the start of this trail. Straight downhill about 50 yards and to the left (east) are the remains of an old mine. Bearing right, or southwesterly, begin a gradual descent that will take you to the unnamed eastern fork of the West Branch of Canyon Creek. From the beginning of this trail to about 1/4 mile from its intersection with the **West Branch Trail** it is very brushy, though the trail is generally discernible. It also makes several crossings of the creek that can be vague. As noted in the preface of this guidebook, it is advisable to keep a sharp eye out for old trimmings, blazes, rock piles, or other indications of previous traffic. As the West Branch is neared the trail becomes much more defined. Overgrown blazes on trees mark this route pretty well, and it also rarely gets more than 100 feet from the creek itself. Connect with the **West Branch Canyon Creek Trail** at the confluence of the West Branch and the unnamed fork.

Pauley Creek Bridge built in 1952 on the Pauley Creek Trail.

THIRD DIVIDE TRAIL
Elevation: 3500' to 4440'
Length: +/- 3 1/2 miles
Effort: Moderate
Hike Time: About 1 1/2 hours
Location: T20N R11E, sections 9,16,17,18
Quadrangle Map: Downieville, Sierra City **(For map see page 50)**

Take Upper Main Street through Downieville. About 1/2 mile east of the Post Office, cross the Downie River bridge. Take the dirt road 4 1/4 miles up Lavezolla Creek, passing the ***Second Divide Trail*** about 2 3/4 miles up. Just past here you will cross Lavezolla Creek via a bridge. A sign 1/4 mile south of the trailhead reads: Attention Hikers, Park Here for the ***Third Divide Trail***. Walk the road, taking the right fork into the Empire Ranch (private land) and continue 1/4 mile to the trailhead sign on the right. Cross Lavezolla Creek on an iron bridge and begin the moderate ascent along the creek. On the opposite side you may see a miner's cabin. Soon you will leave the creek, walking under predominately Douglas fir cover. Several Forest Service K tags along the trail help to indicate your position if you are interested. Several times there is a nice view of the old Lavezolla Ranch and meadow across the creek. Passing through an old logged over area you will cross a spring then another with a tub and pipe. Ascend to a bench-like area with mostly white fir cover. Very soon you will climb to the top of Third Divide. From here begin the descent through Douglas fir and black oak to an intersection with the ***Second Divide Trail*** and the ***Pauley Creek Trail.*** Signs on posts and attached to a huge ponderosa pine direct you either to Second Divide, 5 miles; Butcher Ranch 4 miles, and Gold Valley 5 miles; or back to Lavezolla Creek 3 miles. From here you can take the longer, rougher ***Second Divide Trail*** back to the road and walk to the parking area, about 1 1/4 miles or back track the ***Third Divide Trail.***

WEST BRANCH CANYON CREEK TRAIL
Elevation: 5000' to 6300'
Length: +/- 2 1/2 miles
Effort: Difficult
Hike Time: About 2 hours
Location: T22N R10E, sections 26,35
Quadrangle Map: Mt. Fillmore **(For map see page 63)**

The West Branch is a fairly wide stream bed with steep canyon sides. Much mining was conducted along its lower half during the late 1800s. The upper reaches become steeper and much brushier. This trail is moderate for the first 1 1/2 miles but becomes much rougher after that point. It is well marked with grown over blazes, but a keen eye should still be kept for sections where the trail becomes vague. Begin at the junction of the ***Sunnyside Trail*** and ***Tennessee Mine Road,*** approximately 1 1/2 miles east of Poker Flat via the ***Tennessee Mine Road***. The ***Tennessee Mine Road*** climbs to the southeast while our trail continues east on the level. Take the trail 1/4 mile to the junction of the East and West branches of Canyon Creek. The trail crosses the East Branch and goes through a present-day miner's camp along the right or south side of the West Branch. 1 mile up at the junction of Hog Gulch are noteworthy rock piles and stacked rock sluiceways from the miners of the 19th century. The trail is adequately maintained by a mining claim owner for about 1 1/2 miles to the junction of the ***West Branch-Stafford Mountain Trail***, at an unnamed eastern fork of the creek. There are about five creek crossings in this 1 1/2 miles, most of which are fairly obvious.

WEST COAST MINE–CANYON CREEK TRAIL
Elevation: 5200' to 4200'
Length: +/- 1 mile
Effort: Difficult
Hike Time: About 1 hour
Location: T21N R9E, sections 24,25
Quadrangle Map: La Porte **(For map see page 59)**

To reach the trailhead see the instructions given for the **Port Wine Ridge Trail**. Just before reaching the trailhead to that trail is the obscure, unsigned **West Coast Mine Road** on the left. Parking is available at the remains of a fallen cabin. The trail starts about 50 feet south of this spot, and descends along the side of a shallow ravine before descending rather steeply down the ridge. The original large switchbacks have been shortened by hikers. Descend past the interesting, rusting machinery of the West Coast Mine where you will cross a small stream. Continue your descent to beautiful, cool Canyon Creek. From here it is possible to cross the creek and continue up the unmaintained pack trail to Morristown (see *Morristown-Canyon Creek Trail.*)

View of the rugged ridge south of Mt. Fillmore from a meadow on the Illinois Creek Trail.

LAKES BASIN RECREATION AREA TRAILS
(Plumas & Sierra Counties)

Most of the trails in this area provide wonderful loop hikes. By using different trailheads and transportation you can make longer through hikes. *No motor bikes or other motorized vehicles are allowed on the trails in this region.*

This popular area is a beautiful place to spend a day, a week, or longer. Cool in the summer and brimming with alpine lakes, it is easily reached by traveling south on the Gold Lake Highway from Graeagle on State Route 89, or north from Bassett's Station on State Route 49. From Sacramento travel east on I-80 to State Route 49 or State Route 89, and head north. From Reno take US 395 to State Route 70 and continue to State Route 89 at Graeagle.

Overnight camping is <u>allowed</u> in the area of Tamarack Lake, Grass Lake, Wades Lake, Rock Lake and Jamison Lake. Most campsites are taken during summer weekends.

Overnight camping is <u>prohibited</u> at Hidden Lake, Lily Lake, Grassy Lake, Long Lake, Hellgrammite Lake, Mud Lake, Silver Lake, Cub Lake, Little Bear Lake, Big Bear Lake, and Round Lake due to the heavy day-visitor usage.

The Lakes Basin Recreation Area features some of the most pristine lakes in North America. Small resorts tucked among trees and lakes offer comfort and amenities for those wishing to forego the sleeping bag. Also provided are different levels of services such as prepared meals and housecleaning.

Pauley's Stage from Blairsden to Lakes Basin, 1909.

Development of communities and recreation in Sierra County was the direct result of the discovery and search for gold in California. As the roads were improved, travelers began to stop and enjoy the beauty and the wildlife. The late 1800s brought a surge of interest among Californians in primitive environments for the purposes of recreation and relaxation. Wilderness camping and mountain climbing were important aspects of this movement, and had a special appeal to city people as a temporary relief from the frantic pace of urban life. A form of medical treatment known as the wilderness cure enjoyed considerable popularity in California during the late nineteenth century and brought many recreationists to the area. By 1926, the Lakes Basin area boasted a number of popular resorts with fishing, swimming, boating, and lodging available. The lodge at Sardine Lake was first constructed in 1941, and six guest cabins were added in 1945-46. Packer Lake was on the course of an early pack trail, and in 1926 a lodge was built, along with platform tents and log cabins. Shortly after the mid-1850s, a recreation lodge was also built at Gold Lake. Gold Lake Road was constructed in 1913, providing easier access to the resorts. Bassett's Station, at the intersection of State Route

49 and Gold Lake Road, began as a way station over 125 years ago and continues to provide a rest stop and supply point for travelers.

Graeagle and Blairsden are early-day lumber towns that now are the gateway to the Lakes Basin Recreation Area. Quaint shops line the main streets of these small communities. At Graeagle is the mill pond, a favorite summer swimming hole, as well as languid stretches of the Middle Fork of the Feather River where fishing and swimming and other water sports are enjoyed. Additionally, there are six golf courses nearby.

The whole Lakes Basin system of trails underwent heavy maintenance during 2001 with upgrading of many of the trail treads.

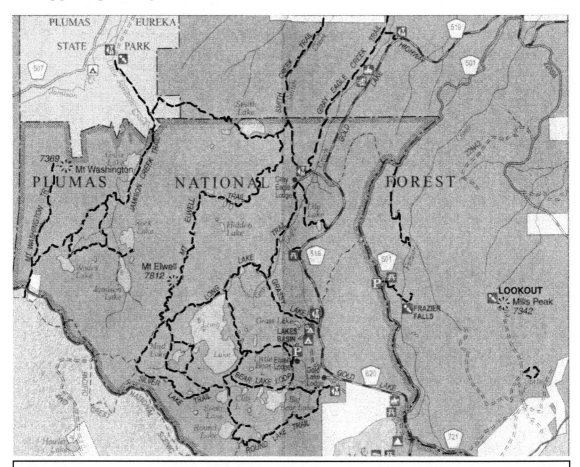

Bear Lakes Trail, Fern Falls Overlook Trail, Frazier Falls Overlook Trail, Grassy Lake Trail, Gray Eagle Creek Trail, Lily Lake Trail, Little Jamison Creek Trail, Long Lake and Long Lake Dam Trails, Mt. Elwell Trails, Mt. Washington Trail, Mud Lake Trail, Red Fir Nature Trail, Round Lake Trail, Silver Lake Trail, Smith Creek Trail, Smith Lake Trail, Summit Trail, Wades Lake Trail.

LAKES BASIN CAMPGROUND TRAILHEADS

To reach the trailheads for Grassy Lake Trail, Silver Lake Trail, Summit Trail, Mud Lake Trail, Long Lake Trail, Bear Lakes Trail, Mt. Elwell Trail, and the Pacific Crest Trail, take the Gold Lake Road (USFS 24) south from State Route 89 about a mile or so east of Graeagle. Proceed about 6 1/2 miles to a signed turnoff on the right to Lakes Basin Campground. The road is now paved the 3/4 mile to the trailheads. There is a group camp and a regular campground on the way to the trails, along with an interpretive site for prehistoric petroglyphs. Ample parking and restrooms can be found at the trailhead. To reach this area from the south, take State Highway 49 to Bassett's Station, then take the Gold Lake Road about 10 miles south to the above intersection.

Another trailhead to consider is the Round Lake trailhead at the historic Gold Lake Lodge. The lodge, established in 1912, has been listed in the National Register of Historic Places. From the north take the Gold Lake Road about 1 mile past the Lakes Basin Campground turnoff to the summit. A sign on the left side of the road points to the turnoff on the right. Turn in here and park in the large dirt parking area. Gold Lake Lodge is just to the right and downhill.

BEAR LAKES TRAIL

Elevation: 6300' to 6485'
Length: +/- 1 1/2 miles
Effort: Moderate
Hike Time: About 1 hour
Location: T21N R12E, sections 7,8,18
Quadrangle Map: Gold Lake **(For map see page 80)**

There are actually 3 trailheads to the ***Bear Lake Trail***. One is at Lakes Basin Campground, one at Elwell Lodge, and the other at Gold Lake Lodge. From Lakes Basin Campground head south on a wide, level trail that soon makes a light ascent, crosses the water line to Elwell Lodge (just visible), then contours along the side of the mountain. It then touches on the large stream running out of Bear Lake, leaves the stream, and makes a meandering ascent to the intersection with the trail from Gold Lake Lodge.

Alternate Trailhead: From Elwell Lodge go about 1/4 mile up a steep and rutted trail to a blocked intersection with the trail just described.

Alternate Trailhead: For the third trailhead, park in the lot for the ***Round Lake Trail***. Follow that trail about 1/4 mile to a signed intersection: Round Lake 1 3/4 (straight), Bear Lake 3/4 (right). Drop down this trail and make several easy ups and downs, passing a pond on the right and a K-tag for sections 7 and 8. Make a moderate ascent and cross the outlet to Big Bear Lake. Just past this is a signed trail intersection at the trail to Lakes Basin Campground: Little Bear Lake 1/4, Cub Lake 1/4, Silver Lake 3/4, ***PCT*** 2 1/2 (all straight ahead), Gold Lake Lodge 1/2 (back). Continue straight along the north shore of Big Bear Lake to a sign: Bear Lake, Elevation 6475' Surface Area 24 acres, Maximum Depth 55' Inlet from Little Bear Lake, Populated by Eastern Brook and Rainbow Trout. There are ducks there too. Make an easy ascent past a large pile of stones and directions painted in yellow on a large boulder. Continue ascending to Little Bear Lake and a sign: Little Bear Lake, Elevation 6500'. Another easy-to-moderate ascent soon brings Cub Lake into view on the left with another sign: Cub Lake, Elevation 6550'. Continue a moderate ascent to a signed T intersection with the ***Silver Lake Trail 12E33***: Lakes Basin Campground 1 1/4, Big Bear Lake 3/4 (back); Silver Lake 1/4, Round Lake 3/4, ***PCT*** 2, Mt. Elwell 2 1/2 (all to left). The trail to the right leads to the Long Lake dam and Lakes Basin Campground.

BERGER CREEK-SAXONIA LAKE TRAIL

Elevation: 6000' to 6496'
Length: +/- 1/2 mile
Effort: Moderate
Hike Time: About 1 hour
Location: T21N R12E, sections 4,5,8,9
Quadrangle Map: Gold Lake, Sierra City **(For map see page 100)**

To reach the trailhead from the south, take the *Gold Lake Road* north from Bassett's Station on *State Route 49.* Proceed 1 1/2 miles to the Salmon Creek Bridge. To reach the trail from the north, take the *Gold Lake Road* 14 miles south from *State Route 89* at Graeagle to the same bridge. A sign points out Sardine Lakes and Packer Lake. Cross the bridge, traveling another 1/4 mile to a right on the *Packer Lake Road.* Continue about 2 miles to Berger Creek Campground. Park here, the trail begins on the left side of the campground. Make a mild rocky ascent into ground pushed around with a CAT years ago. As the trail ascends to an old ditch, bear left along the base of the hillside. The trail is poorly maintained but well blazed. It is faint and winds up through scrubby trees and brush at a moderate ascent to a bench. The northern edge of the Sierra Buttes is on the right. As the trail skirts Mud Lake it bears east through a large stand of bug-killed Jeffery pine. The trail soon becomes very steep as it winds through small trees and brush. Cross over a brushy ridge and drop to and cross an intermittent pond. Stay on the most obvious route, noting the occasional faded blue paint marks on rocks. Cross an open swale and make a level meander through a rocky area. The trail soon ascends through boulders (follow the ducks), crosses over and descends to the rocky shore of Saxonia Lake. In mid-July the water is perfect for swimming!

   Alternate Trailhead: Continue on the *Packer Lake Road* to Packer Saddle and follow the signs.

DEER LAKE TRAIL

Elevation: 6000' to 7110'
Length: +/- 3 miles
Effort: Difficult
Hike Time: About 3 hours
Location: T21N R12E, section 5 and T21N R12E, sections 30,31,32
Quadrangle Map: Sierra City **(For map see page 100)**

To reach the trailhead from the south, take the *Gold Lake Road* north from Bassett's Station on *State Route 49.* Proceed 1 1/2 miles to the Salmon Creek Bridge. To reach the trail from the north, take the *Gold Lake Road* 14 miles south from *State Route 89* at Graeagle to the same bridge. A sign points out Sardine Lakes and Packer Lake. Cross the bridge, traveling another 1/4 mile to a right on the *Packer Lake Road.* Continue about 2 1/2 miles to the Pack Saddle Campground and parking area. From the parking lot, walk across the road to the trailhead. A sign reads: Grass Lake 2, Deer Lake 2 1/2, Horse Lake 3, Upper Salmon Lake 4. The trail meanders along in old growth timber, wild flowers, and scattered aspen to a crossing of a small creek. It crosses a dry gully, then another stream, passes under the powerline to Packer Lake Lodge and past an unsigned trail intersection. The trail is a well-defined, graveled surface that makes a switchback and easy ascent. A great view back at the Sierra Buttes is part of the long, easy ascent to another switchback. Another long ascent then rounds the ridge and contours, and meanders along the east side of the ridge. Skirt the left side of a basin with a small aspen grove, and then make an easy stroll up and down. Parallel a small creek before crossing it, making two switchbacks and continuing a light ascent in open ground. Pass through a rocky area and switchback with a light ascent over the top of an old gold mining tunnel. Continue the ascent to another switchback and lots of meanders. Here and there are parts of the old trail, but please don't cut the switchbacks. Make a light winding ascent to a saddle and intersection with a sign: Grass Lake 1/4 (right), Deer Lake (ahead). (Grass Lake is about a 5-minute detour down to a marshy pond alive with waterfowl and mosquitoes). Meander across the flat, then lightly descend, cross a small basin with a meadow at right, then make a moderate ascent of the ridge onto another flat. The trail meanders to Sawmill Creek, which it parallels as it makes a light ascent up its left side. Cross the creek where it exits a marshy pond at left. A short ascent brings the trail to a 4 way signed intersection: *PCT* 1/2 (up), Deer Lake 1/4 (left), Upper Salmon Lake 1 1/2 (right),. The trail now meanders up and down in rocks, passes a pond on the right, crosses the outlet and ascends to the ridge top and a K-tag for sections 29,30,31,32. A great view of the lake is afforded from here. A short descent brings the trail to the edge of the lake and a sign: Trail Ends.

FERN FALLS OVERLOOK TRAIL

Elevation: 6200' to 6200'
Length: +/- 1/4 mile
Effort: Very Easy
Hike Time: About 1/4 hour
Location: T21N R12E, section 5
Quadrangle Map: Gold Lake **(For map see page 80)**

Don't try to follow the **Fern Falls Trail** from the Gray Eagle Lodge trailhead. It will only lead you into a brushy creek side with no view of the falls. Instead, take the much easier and sure route. Reach the trailhead by following the **Gold Lake Road** about 6 1/2 miles south from **State Route 89**. About 1/2 mile past the **Lily Lake Trail** trailhead a large sign denotes the trail and picnic area. This short trail crosses a footbridge and then ends at an overlook above the 15-foot high cascade. There is a picnic table on this short, but quite easy and pleasant walk.

FRAZIER FALLS OVERLOOK TRAIL

Elevation: 6200' to 6000'
Length: +/- 1/2 mile
Effort: Very Easy
Hike Time: About 1/2 hour

Location: T21N R12E, section 9
Quadrangle Map: Gold Lake **(For map see page 80)**

The trailhead is located on the paved ***Old Gold Lake Road*** about 6 miles from ***State Route 89*** at Graeagle. About 1 3/4 miles up the present ***Gold Lake Road***, take the signed, narrow paved access road on the left. It is about 4 miles to the trailhead from here. The road is a beautiful drive through old growth timber with great views at the top. Restrooms are available at the trailhead. This very gentle paved trail leads to the scenic fenced overlook of Frazier Falls, a 280-foot waterfall (including the cascade section at its bottom). About half way along the trail crosses Frazier Creek on a fine footbridge. You probably won't even notice that you are actually only a short distance above the falls at this point. The trailhead may also be reached via the same road, though it is graveled, from opposite the Gold Lake turnoff on the ***Gold Lake Road***, about 8 miles from ***State Route 49***. A small sign on the road notes it is 4 1/2 miles to the falls.

GRASSY LAKE TRAIL
Elevation: 6230' to 6200'
Length: +/- 3/4 mile
Effort: Easy
Hike Time: About 1 hour
Location: T21N R12E, sections 6,7,8
Quadrangle Map: Gold Lake **(For map see page 80)**

To access this short hike, take the Lakes Basin Campground turnoff and follow the road into the campground. A parking area is situated at the trailhead. Almost immediately there is a footbridge across a medium-size stream. A sign indicates Long Lake as 2 miles, Graeagle Lodge as 2 miles, and Mt. Elwell as 2 1/2 miles (corrected to 3 miles). The trail meanders with Grassy Lake on the left. This walk through the trees is quite pretty with a small spring on the trail and a meadow just below it. Just past this two small trails break off to the left and wander down to several ponds. After a bit the trail swings around with a view of Mt. Elwell, then descends along the hill with riparian brush below. The moderate descent winds through rocks and large fir trees, crosses a spring, and meanders to cross a stream and intersect with the ***Long Lake Trail*** from Gray Eagle Lodge. Several signs there read: Gray Eagle Lodge 1 1/4, Hawlsey Falls 3/4, and Long Lake 1 mile, Mt. Elwell 2 1/2 miles, and Lakes Basin Campground 3/4 mile.

GRAY EAGLE CREEK TRAIL
Elevation: 5800' to 4400'
Length: +/- 4 miles (2 miles of 4WD at NE end)
Effort: Easy
Hike Time: 3 hours (1 hour to Gold Lake Road trailhead)
Location: T22N R12E, sections 32,31,30,29,20,21
Quadrangle Map: Gold Lake, Johnsville **(For map see page 80)**

There are two trailheads, one is off the *Gold Lake Road* near Gray Eagle Lodge, the other at a signed turnout on the *Gold Lake Road* about 3 1/4 miles from *Highway 89*. The best hike here is to go to the upper or Graeagle Lodge trailhead and hike down 2 miles to the trailhead on *Gold Lake Road*. The remaining 2 miles to Graeagle is an old road. To get to the Graeagle Lodge trailhead, drive about 5 miles to the signed turnoff. Follow the paved, then gravel road a short distance to a right turn. Just before the *Smith Lake Trail* trailhead is our signed trail: Graeagle 4, Graeagle Powerhouse 2 (both ahead). The trail runs slightly down along the hill, then drops easily past a large boulder. You can hear Gray Eagle Creek to the right, but not see it. A low hanging phone line runs along the trail the entire way, and in some spots it is completely down, though operational. Descend to a wet area and meadow, then meander along to another tree-studded meadow, then an open dry area. The trail is now almost level and meanders along with a graveled tread. Light descents characterize this easy trail. A bouldery ridge is to the left, while soon the trail will enter a stand of large yellow pine. Meander along, then drop to an intersection and sign: Smith Lake 3, Gray Eagle Lodge 2 (back), Graeagle 2 ¼ (ahead). If you continue toward Graeagle, the trail will soon become a dirt road. It then drops past the Graeagle water supply, an abandoned truck cargo box, a sign pointing the way to the trail, and to a logging spur running through section 20 (which eventually hooks up with the *Smith Lake Trail*). The most pleasant hike is to go right on the 1/4-mile-long trail that crosses Gray Eagle Creek via a stout footbridge, makes a switchback, and ends at the parking area on *Gold Lake Road*.

LILY LAKE TRAIL
(and Extension to Gray Eagle Lodge)
Elevation: 6000' to 5920' (5800' at Gray Eagle Lodge)
Length: +/- 1/4 mile (1/2 mile to Gray Eagle Lodge)
Effort: Very Easy
Hike Time: About 1/4 hour (1/2 hour to Gray Eagle Lodge)
Location: T21N R12E, section 5
Quadrangle Map: Gold Lake **(For map see page 80)**

Other than Fern Falls, this is the shortest hike in the Lakes Basin region. Reach this trailhead by taking the *Gold Lake Road* about 5 1/2 miles from *State Route 89* about 2 miles east of Graeagle. The trail leaves the right side of *Gold Lake Road* and drops immediately to Lily Lake. Skirting the north side of the lake, it crosses the outlet and descends to a lodgepole pine and grassy area, which is very wet in spring. As you descend, an old unmaintained trail ascends to the *Gold Lake Road* to your left. The trail is almost level through this area, with a low phone line suspended above. At Gray Eagle Creek there is a nice footbridge to take you to Gray Eagle Lodge.

LITTLE JAMISON CREEK TRAIL
(Including Grass, Jamison and Rock lakes)
Elevation: 5100' to 6260'Length: +/- 3 1/2 miles
Effort: Moderate

Hike Time: About 3 hours
Location: T22N R11E, sections 25,36 and T21N R11E, sections 1,2
Quadrangle Map: Johnsville, Gold Lake **(For map see page 80)**

The trailhead to these wonderful little lakes is at the Jamison Mine in Plumas Eureka State Park, where several picturesque old structures are left over from the 19th century. Unfortunately, the buildings are in a state of decline. Reach the trailhead by turning south on the **Mohawk Road** off **Highway 70/89** opposite the historic and picturesque Feather River Inn. At Mohawk, turn right and proceed up the **Johnsville Road (A-14)** 4 1/2 miles to the dirt **Jamison Mine Road**. Take that road 1 1/2 miles to the gated trailhead. Signs indicate Grass Lake as 1 1/4 miles, Smith Lake 2, Wades Lake 3, and the **Pacific Crest Trail** 3 1/2. From the trailhead proceed 3/4 mile on a moderate grade enhanced with large stone steps to the **Smith Lake Trail** intersection. A sign pointing left notes that Smith Lake is 1 1/4, Gray Eagle Lodge is 2 3/4, and Mt. Elwell is 4 3/4 miles. Another sign pointing our way indicates the **Pacific Crest Trail** is 3 1/4 miles (there's those mileage discrepancies!), Mt. Washington 5 miles, and Jamison Mine is back 3/4 mile. A third sign gives Grass Lake as 1/2 mile, Jamison as 2 1/4, Wades Lake as 2 1/4, and Rock Lake as 2 1/2. Continuing up the **Little Jamison Creek Trail**, you will leave Plumas Eureka State Park, and after a bit begin to hear, but not see, the 30-foot Jamison Falls. Walk the 50 feet or so to the right to view them, but be careful of the open, loose edge. Make a slight ascent across an old mining ditch used to take water from Grass Lake to the Jamison Mine area. Soon you will pass along the east shore of Grass Lake, elevation 5842', unless you take a walk out on the hand constructed earth and rock dam. There is quite a bit of water along and across the trail through here.

Jamison Lake basin from 7812' Mt. Elwell

After leaving Grass Lake, make a slight ascent through quaking aspen and a camp area. Some of the aspen have dates of 1927, 1929 and 1930 carved in their bark, purportedly by Basque shepherds. After crossing a pretty open meadow-like area, cross Little Jamison Creek and wind along past a K-tag showing your location between sections 35 and 36, to the first **Wades Lake Trail**, to your right. A sign here notes that Wades Lake is 3/4 mile and the **Pacific Crest Trail** is 1 1/2 miles, with another sign indicating Jamison Lake as 1 and Rock Lake as 1 1/4 miles. Almost immediately, you will pass cabin ruins on your right and begin ascending about 6 switchbacks. Soon the trail crosses the creek again and reaches the second **Wades Lake Trail.** Another sign points to Wades Lake 1 mile, **Pacific Crest Trail** 2 1/2, Mt. Washington 3 1/2, Grass Lake 1 1/2, Jamison Mine 2 3/4, Rock Lake 1/2, and Jamison Lake 1/4. 50 yards from the stacked-rock Jamison Lake dam, a sign points to the ***Rock Lake Trail***. Go left here the 1/4 mile to aptly-named Rock Lake.

LONG LAKE DAM TRAIL
Elevation: 6535' to 6546'
Length: +/- 3/4 mile
Effort: Difficult
Hike Time: 3/4 hour
Location: T21N R12E, section 6,7
Quadrangle Map: Gold Lake **(For map see page 80)**

It took me quite a while to find the dam trail, and when I did I was not all that impressed with it. At the start of the last rocky ascent to Long Lake on the ***Long Lake Trail*** (see directions below), there is a vague and unsigned right fork that meanders over boulders, through brush, up small creek beds, and along the east side of Long Lake, though just far enough away to never really have a good view of the lake itself. For the most part, you follow the ducks that have been placed at intervals and keep to the more traveled-looking breaks in the brush. I suspect that this is almost exclusively a fishermen's trail, though it could be used to get to the ***Mt. Elwell Trail*** from Elwell Lodge (not recommended). I saw only one old blaze mark on a pine to indicate that there might be any age to this trail. At any rate, after meandering past several ponds, basins, over small ridge tops and down a rocky scramble, the trail ends at the concrete-faced rock Long Lake dam.

LONG LAKE TRAIL
Elevation: 6400' to 6546'
Length: +/- 3/4 mile
Effort: Moderate
Hike Time: 1/2 hour
Location: T21N R12E, section 7
Quadrangle Map: Gold Lake **(For map see page 80)**

From the Lakes Basin Campground trailhead, bear right (west) across a small stream. Side trails abound, but keep straight ahead on the easy, but bouldery and well-worn trail. The cover is typical of high elevations: lodgepole, western white pine, Jeffrey pine and white fir. The trail crosses a small stream as it continues a moderate ascent, levels, crosses another small stream, and makes a light ascent along the hill. It is a very well defined and blazed trail. Soon you will come to the signed intersection with the ***Silver Lake Trail***, which bears left. The sign points to Long Lake 1/4 mile, Silver Lake and Bear Lake 1/2 mile and the Long Lake trailhead back 1/2 mile. Stay right on the trail as it winds along at a light ascent to Long Lake. At Long Lake is a sign: Long Lake Elevation 6546. To the right is a small tin boathouse and dock with private boats.

LONG LAKE TRAIL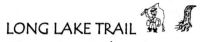

(From Gray Eagle Lodge to Mt. Elwell Trail intersection)
Elevation: 5800' to 7000'
Length: +/- 2 3/4 miles
Effort: Moderate
Hike Time: 2 hours
Location: T22N R12E, sections 31,32 and T21N R12E, section 6 and T21N R11E, sections 1,12.
Quadrangle Map: Gold Lake **(For map see page 80)**

This trail shares the same trailhead as the **Smith Lake Trail** and the **Gray Eagle Creek Trail** (or see the directions given for Big Bear Lake for an alternate trailhead at Lakes Basin Campground). A sign indicates Long Lake as 2 miles, Lakes Basin Campground as 2 1/2 miles, Mt. Elwell as 4 miles, Hawlsey Falls 1 mile, and Fern Falls 1 1/4 miles. This, more than any other trail, has conflicting mileage signs. Not only are the Forest Service signs contradictory to themselves, hikers have modified them to suit their idea of the distances. Soon after leaving the trailhead you will cross a small stream, then a 3-inch water line to Gray Eagle Lodge. Pass an unsigned trail bearing to the left and make two quick switchbacks up a rocky knob. Crest here and begin a slight descent. A sign soon appears noting that Gray Eagle Lodge is to the left 1 mile. It is actually less than 1/4 mile but the trail is closed, there being no real reason to use it. Continue on through an open area, cross a small stream, and ascend to cross a larger one where a sign points the way to Hawlsey Falls and, erroneously, Fern Falls. Continue to ascend up through a rocky area and then into trees again. The trail now contours, then makes another ascent with water in the trail. A signed intersection with the **Grassy Lake Trail** at the head of Hawlsey Falls (50 yards east) notes that the Lakes Basin Campground is 3/4 mile ahead. Stay right on the **Long Lake Trail** as it bears west. Cross a wet area and stream and make a moderate winding ascent to another sign. An old tie trail takes off here but is brushy and not maintained. Continue to ascend the small switchbacks, crest and cross a saddle. Mt. Elwell is ahead and on your left as you skirt a small pond. Ascend again along glaciated rocks. You might note a 3-foot-thick Jeffrey pine growing out of solid rock. There are also beautiful cascades (Hawlsey Falls) and, in autumn, fall colors against solid rock. Pass through a small basin and wet area and Long Lake appears. The dam is 50 yards to the left. To continue to the **Mt. Elwell Trail**, pass a huge round boulder and meander along the lake in close brush and boulders. Ascend two short rocky switchbacks and continue on a moderate grade on a very rocky tread. Because of the rocky nature of the trail you will have to stop walking to enjoy the gorgeous view of Long Lake below. The trail is not maintained and is somewhat brushy also. Near the end the trail makes a gentle ascent to a switchback and meanders along the ridgeback to a snag with a sign for northbound hikers: Hiking Trail No Horses. This is for the good of the horses. A short distance ahead is the signed intersection of the **Mud Lake Trail**, **Mt. Elwell Trail**, and the tie trail to the **Pacific Crest Trail** and **Summit Trail**.

MOUNT ELWELL TRAIL

Elevation: 7000' to 7812'
Length: +/- 3/4 mile
Effort: Difficult
Hike Time: About 1 hour
Location: T21N R11E, section 12
Quadrangle Map: Gold Lake **(For map see page 80)**

Use either the Gray Eagle Lodge trailhead or the *Mud Lake Trail* from either Lakes Basin Campground or the *Round Lake Trail* to access this trail (see descriptions of those trails and the one following). Once at the intersection of *Mud Lake Trail* and the others indicated in that trail description, begin a light ascent to a switchback, enter heavy tree cover, and make a moderate ascent with views of Long Lake below and the Sierra Buttes to the south. Continue the moderate ascent to two more switchbacks. The views are beautiful here but nothing like what awaits you from the top of Mt. Elwell! The grade becomes steeper for the next six switchbacks, then loose, rocky, and winding. It soon levels off with the actual peak at our left. Follow along its base before reaching a spot where you have to climb among the rocks to reach the summit. A sign about 50 yards from the peak reads: Mt. Elwell, Elevation 7812. Remnants of the old fire lookout lay scattered among the rocks. The view from here is magnificent! Visible is not only the Sierra in the south, but also Saddleback Lookout, Table Rock, Mt. Fillmore, Pilot Peak, Beckwourth Peak, Eureka Peak and, directly below, Rock and Jamison lakes. From this point you can continue north on the trail down to the *Smith Lake Trail* intersection and Gray Eagle Lodge, but be prepared to hike a loop or have transportation arranged.

MOUNT ELWELL TRAIL
(Smith Lake Trailhead)

Elevation: 6700' to 7812'
Length: +/- 3 miles
Effort: Difficult
Hike Time: About 2 hours
Location: T21N R11E, section 1, T22N R11E, section 36, T22N R12E, section 31
Quadrangle Map: Gold Lake **(For map see page 80)**

To reach Mount Elwell this way use the trailhead for the *Smith Lake Trail* near Gray Eagle Lodge. The trailhead can be reached by taking the *Gold Lake Road* off *Highway 89*. Proceed up this road about 5 miles to the Gray Eagle Lodge turn-off. Turn right here and continue a bit over 1/4 mile to the signed turn off to the trailhead. Plenty of parking is available here. This trailhead is shared with the *Long Lake Trail* and the *Gray Eagle Creek Trail.* Follow the *Smith Lake Trail* to about 1/4 mile north of Smith Lake, where you will see a sign pointing out the *Mt. Elwell Trail* to the left. After crossing Smith Creek the trail soon begins climbing steadily. Not far along will be an old sign on a tree pointing out an observation point 200 yards east. The trail continues through a red fir and mountain hemlock forest, makes a large switchback, and contours along a saddle with 3 small ponds and signed Hidden Lake. Begin climbing again for a distance before the trail again contours along the east side of Mt. Elwell. The trail becomes rocky and steep as it winds to the 7812' summit. Mt. Elwell provides a beautiful 360-degree view of the surrounding country: a panorama of alpine lakes, steep canyons, and forested ridges make it well worth the effort. You can descend 3/4 mile on the south side to the **Long Lake Trail, Mud Lake Trail**, and **Pacific Crest Tie Trail.**

MT. WASHINGTON TRAIL
Elevation: 6800' to 7000'
Length: +/- 2 miles
Effort: Moderate
Hike Time: About 2 hours
Location: T21N R11E, section 35 and T20N R11E, section 2
Quadrangle Map: Gold Lake **(For map see page 80)**

This trail name is somewhat misleading as it doesn't actually go to the summit of 7360' Mt. Washington. Still, it is a pleasant and rewarding hike. Reach the trailhead by taking the rough **Johnsville-La Porte Road** about 4 miles southwest of Johnsville to the **Four Hills Mine Road**. This road is well graveled and makes a distinct left off the main road. It crosses Jamison Creek via a bridge and continues about 2 miles to a saddle and the A Tree. Just before the A Tree turn left and follow the 4WD road as it winds up Luther Ridge. About 2 miles along is a sharp right-hand uphill turn into unsigned private property. If you park here you can walk about 50 yards back down the road to the trailhead that is shared with the **PCT Tie Trail** to Wades Lake. The drop is fairly loose and steep down to a timbered saddle. A signed intersection notes Wades Lake is 1/4 mile east. Continue along at an easy grade to several switchbacks then wind along onto the west side of the ridge. The red fir forest becomes taller and as the

Mud Lake from Mt. Elwell Trail.

trees give way, there are nice views up Jamison Creek canyon. As the trail makes its way along the hill Mt. Washington proper comes into view. The hillsides here are very steep so use caution. After a short distance the trail just peters out near the northwest end of the ridge. Mt. Washington is still another 300 to 600 feet of brushy scramble above.

MUD LAKE TRAIL
Elevation: 6800' to 7000'
Length: +/- 1 mile
Effort: Difficult
Hike Time: About 3/4 hour
Location: T21N R11E, section 12
Quadrangle Map: Gold Lake **(For map see page 80)**

This trail is part of a loop that can take you to Mt. Elwell, the *Pacific Crest Trail,* Long Lake, etc. Use the **Long Lake Trail** and **Silver Lake Trail** from Lakes Basin Campground, the **Round Lake Trail** from Gold Lake Lodge or the **Bear Lake Trail** from either Lakes Basin Campground or Gold Lake Lodge. At any rate, when you reach Silver Lake follow the sign indicating the route to Mt. Elwell and the *Pacific Crest Trail*. Contour along the west side of the lake, make a light ascent up the ridge between Silver and Long lakes with a view of both, and also of Bear Lake and Mills Peak lookout. The rutted trail reaches an intersection and sign: Hellgrammite Lake 1/4, Mud Lake 1/2, Mt. Elwell 2 (all to the right). Another sign for the trail headed southwest (left) reads: Silver Lake 1/4, Long Lake 1 (back down the trail), **Summit Trail** 1, *Pacific Crest Trail* 1 1/4. Stay right and within 50 yards you will reach the shores of tiny Hellgrammite Lake, elevation 7040'. Meander along the right side, then cross over the slight ridge to the Mud Lake side and begin a moderate descent to a crossing of the outlet creek from Hellgrammite Lake. Continue down to two switchbacks, make a long, rutted descent to another two switchbacks, then a lighter descent as the trail hits bottom. Cross a freshet and come to a sign: Mud Lake, elevation 6560'. Continue the meander through snow-bent pine and fir to a very light ascent and crossing of another small stream. At a Y intersection take the left and more defined fork. The right one meanders over to Long Lake and a lifetime lease cabin. Although maps show the right-hand trail reconnecting with the **Mud Lake Trail**, it doesn't. The ascent becomes steeper as the trail follows an iron water pipe up hill. After crossing a wet area the trail switchbacks at a rock face, recrosses the wet area and makes another switchback, winds up to one more switchback, then makes an eroded, moderate ascent to an intersection. From here you may continue on to Mt. Elwell, east to the Long Lake dam and Gray Eagle Lodge, or west to the *Pacific Crest Trail*. A sign at the intersection reads: Hellgrammite Lake 1/2 (should be Mud Lake), Silver Lake 2, Lakes Basin Campground 2 1/2. Another sign: *Pacific Crest Trail* 1 1/4 (left), Mt. Elwell 3/4 (ahead), Smith Lake 4 1/4 (right). 25 feet ahead is another intersection and sign: Mt. Elwell 3/4 (left), Long Lake 3/4, Graeagle Lodge 2 1/2 (both right).

PACIFIC CREST TIE TRAIL (UPPER SALMON LAKE)

Elevation: 7080' to 7400'
Length: +/- 1/2 mile
Effort: Moderate
Hike Time: About 1 hour
Location: T21N R12E, sections 29,30
Quadrangle Map: Gold Lake **(For map see page 100)**

Reach this trail by taking the **Upper Salmon Lake Trail** (see description). At the 4-way trail junction 1/4 mile north of Deer Lake, take the right hand trail. It makes a gentle meandering ascent across small seasonal creeks and through reddish rock formations to a sign reading Deer Lake 3/4 mile, Salmon Lake Lodge 2 1/2 miles, **Packer Lake Road** 2 1/2 miles, and **PCT** with an arrow. Continue ascending through the thick red fir forest another 1/4 mile or so to the junction with the **PCT**. This part of the trail was once a 4WD road but is now only used by hikers. As noted earlier in this guide, signed distances obviously do not add up.

RED FIR NATURE TRAIL
Elevation: 7040' to 7080'
Length: +/- 1/2 mile
Effort: Very Easy
Hike Time: About 1 hour
Location: T21N R12E, section 10
Quadrangle Map: Gold Lake **(For map see page 80)**

To reach the trail from the north, take the **Gold Lake Road** about 9 miles south from **State Route 89** at Graeagle. Turn left on the **Mills Peak Lookout Road** and travel about 2 miles to the trailhead. The road, though passable, is rough. At the trailhead is a log landing now used for parking. A large sign indicates where to start your walk. As soon as you begin there are arrow signs pointing to stay to the right. As you follow this short loop you will note a number of informative placards about certain features of this dense stand of red fir (abies magnifica) and white fir (abies concolor). Although many of the signs have been vandalized or are worn by weather, there are still many interesting things to see here. Of course there are the usual subjective comments made by the author of the signs (a tree that dies and rots away is therefore lost...) but on the whole it is quite educational. For instance, the number of whorl limbs on the trunk of the red fir indicates its age. Given this, a tree three inches in diameter might be 30 years old. Other than being in need of maintenance, this is a pleasant walk, especially good for children.

ROUND LAKE TRAIL
Elevation: 6600' to 6714'
Length: +/- 1 3/4 miles
Effort: Easy
Hike Time: About 1 hour
Location: T21N R12E, sections 8,17,18
Quadrangle Map: Gold Lake **(For map see page 80)**

Reach the trailhead by taking the **Gold Lake Road** 7 1/2 miles south from **State Route 89** just past Graeagle. The trailhead is off to the right in a parking lot near Gold Lake Lodge. Just out of the parking lot are two signs; one is a Lakes Basin Recreation Area information sign, the other notes Big Bear Lake is 3/4 mile and Round Lake is 1 3/4 miles. Contour along the hillside above Gold Lake Lodge on this very wide, well-defined old road/trail that originally was a wagon

Round Lake and Round Lake Mine at left.

Sierra Buttes from the Tamarack Connection Trail above the Young America Mine ruins.

road to the Round Lake Mine. Cross an intermittent spring at an intersection with signs: Round Lake 1 1/4 (straight), Bear Lakes 3/4 mile (down and to the right). Continue straight on a level walk with a view of Mt. Elwell to the right. Several small trails drop off to the right toward Gold Lake Lodge, one of which is there to avoid the lodge. Another trail climbs through a meadow to the left as a horse trail for nearby stables. Cross a seasonal creek and a big wet spot on planks, cross several draws, and then break into the open. The trail makes a light ascent up the ridge with nice views to the north of 8300' Mt. Ingalls. As it proceeds up the ridge there is a view to the right of Big Bear Lake and the rocky basin area. Cross the ridge and make a gentle descent, cross a spring, pass several intermittent ponds on both sides of the trail, and begin a rocky but easy ascent. (Note the rock walls in the trail as you approach them). As the trail ascends, pass a trail running up to a saddle on the left, and round the point of the ridge. From here is a view of Mills Peak and Smith Peak. Just above the trail are ruins of an old cabin. Begin a light descent with a view of Round Lake ahead. Ruins of the Round Lake Mine mill sit just below the trail. A sign used to give the mine's history in detail, summarized here:

Round Lake Mine, elevation 6874'. The mine was developed shortly before World War One and had a 400' incline shaft under the lake to remove gold ore valued at $1.05 per ton. The mill was built at a cost of over $100,000 by the Ready Bullion Co. of Sacramento but burned to the ground shortly after construction in 1935. The venture was then abandoned.

Just past this is a signed intersection: Round Lake, Elevation 6714', Silver Lake 3/4 (to right), **PCT** 3/4 (straight), Gold Lake Lodge 1 1/2 (back). Make a moderate, loose descent with a switchback to Round Lake and another elevation sign. From here you can return or continue on the **Silver Lake Trail 12E33** to make a loop past Bear Lakes and back to the Gold Lake Lodge. See those trail descriptions for more information.

SAND POND INTERPRETIVE TRAIL ♿

Elevation: 6000' to 6000'
Length: +/- 1 mile
Effort: Very Easy (walk), Difficult (wheelchair)
Hike Time: About 1 hour
Location: T20N R12E, section 10
Quadrangle Map: Sierra City **(For map see page 100)**

This loop trail is a very easy walk but is signed as most difficult for wheelchair use. To reach the trailhead from the south take the **Gold Lake Road** north from Bassett's Station on **State Route 49**. Proceed 1 1/2 miles to the Salmon Creek Bridge. To reach the trail from the north, take the **Gold Lake Road** 14 miles south from **State Route 89** near Graeagle to the same bridge. Take this road, cross the bridge, traveling west about 1 mile to the Sand Pond Swim Area parking lot. The signed trailhead is just east of the parking lot. Within a short distance pass the restrooms and changing rooms. After crossing a bridge you will soon be traveling along the old mining flume from Sardine Lake to Sierra City. Interpretive signs are set every so often explaining a certain feature along the trail. Several sections are somewhat narrow and have protruding boulders, but for the most part the trail is very open. After the pleasant flume route, the trail turns left onto a 4-foot-wide slightly elevated boardwalk that traverses a now almost completely dry beaver pond. A short dirt section, then board, then a bridge brings the trail's end at a nondescript spot on the road 1/4 mile east of the trailhead.

SARDINE LAKES OVERLOOK TRAIL

Elevation: 6070' to 7072'
Length: +/- 2 miles
Effort: Moderate
Hike Time: About 1 hour
Location: T20N R12E, sections 8,9
Quadrangle Map: Sierra City **(For map see page 100)**

To reach the trailhead from the south, take the **Gold Lake Road** north from Bassett's Station on **State Route 49**. Proceed 1 1/2 miles to the Salmon Creek Bridge. To reach the trail from the north, take the **Gold Lake Road** 14 miles south from **State Route 89** near Graeagle to the same bridge. A sign points out Sardine Lakes and Packer Lake. Take that road and cross the bridge, pass the **Packer Lake Road** on your right, and you will see the signed **Tamarack Connection Trail** just before the Sardine Lakes Campground. A sign reads: Sardine Overlook 2, Tamarack Lakes 3 1/2, Packer Lake 4. The trail, actually an old wagon road for several miles, makes about four gentle ascending switchbacks before reaching the ridge top, where it meanders along. A sign designates the trail as it drops gently to the left. This trail provides breathtaking views and is unique in that it dead-ends at the ore car tracks of the Young America Mine, an active producer from 1884 to 1893. Beautiful hand-stacked rock walls form the trail base.

SIERRA BUTTES TRAIL
Elevation: 7000' to 8587'
Length: +/- 2 1/2 miles
Effort: Moderate
Hike Time: About 4 hours
Location: T20N R12E, sections 8,17,18
Quadrangle Map: Sierra City **(For map see page 100)**

To reach the trailhead from the south take the **Gold Lake Road** north from Bassett's Station on **State Route 49**. Proceed 1 1/2 miles to the Salmon Creek Bridge. To reach the trail from the north, take the **Gold Lake Road** 14 miles south from **State Route 89** near Graeagle to the same bridge. A sign points out Sardine Lakes and Packer Lake. Take that road and cross the bridge, continuing about 1/4 mile to the **Packer Lake Road.** Take the right fork and go another 2 1/2 miles before turning left onto the **Packer Saddle Road**, just past the **Packer Lake Lodge Road.** Continue up the paved road to Packer Saddle. Turn left and proceed to a locked gate and parking on a 4WD road. Follow the 4WD road (now **PCT)** about 3/4 mile up a moderate ascent to a small saddle where the **PCT** bears away south along the ridgeback. Follow the trail another 1/2 mile and pass the **Tamarack Lake Trail** cut off which drops off north about 1/2 mile to Tamarack Lakes. Our trail makes a moderate ascent along the edge of the ridge, and at times is quite wide with views to the east. The old 4WD road veers west and our trail becomes cobbly but still good. Views can be seen to the west of the logged-over Yuba River canyon. The ascent steepens with winding switchbacks and lots of huge trailside boulders that get bigger as the trail goes up. Mountain hemlock begins to predominate and as the ascent becomes more moderate, the cover becomes a mixture of red fir, western white pine and mountain hemlock. After passing a large gold prospect pit and an even bigger boulder, there is a great view to the east and of the Sierra Buttes. The trail is now an old 4WD road and passes a sign indicating the trail with no motorized vehicles or bicycles allowed. Walk through the 4WD parking area for the Sierra Buttes 4WD road to the single-track trail. Continue the ascent past a sign reading **Sierra Buttes Trail 12E06**, Sierra Buttes Lookout (ahead). The gated 4WD road continues on the right. A sign also warns hikers to stay on the trail and not cut switchbacks under penalty of a $100 fine (36CFR 261.12c). The well-used trail makes a gentle ascent into a tree-studded boulder field. The ascent becomes steeper amid a number of cleared blown down trees and some very old stumps from the mining days. It is wise to pace yourself as the air is much thinner here than at the trail's beginning. Make three switchbacks, and in 20 feet ascend and intersect the 4WD road. Follow the road for six switchbacks to a sign and plaque. Five flights of steep metal stairs are not for the timid, but will take you to one of the finest views in the state!

SILVER LAKE TRAIL 12E33
Elevation: 6300' to 6688'
Length: +/- 2 miles

Effort: Moderate
Hike Time: About 1 hour
Location: T21N R12E, sections 7,8
Quadrangle Map: Gold Lake **(For map see page 80)**

The trailhead for this hike is at the Lakes Basin Campground, although you can also reach Silver Lake (or any of the lakes here) by using the **Round Lake-Bear Lakes Trailhead** at Gold Lake Lodge also. From Lakes Basin Campground use the **Long Lake Trail** to a Y intersection. Bear left here and make a moderate winding ascent with a view of Long Lake and Mt. Elwell to the right. Cross over a small ridge and descend to two signs: Silver Lake 1/4, Round Lake 3/4, **Pacific Crest Trail** 2, Mt. Elwell 2 1/2, Long Lake 1/2, and Lakes Basin Campground 3/4 (to the right). Another sign points left (east): Cub Lake 1/4, Big Bear Lake 3/4, and Lakes Basin Campground 1 1/4. Continue straight, making a light ascent and take your last nice view of Long Lake as the trail bears south. Make a short ascent, then descend to Silver Lake and a signed trail intersection: Silver Lake Elevation 6640', Surface Area 11 acres, Maximum depth 35', populated by eastern brook trout. Another sign reads: Round Lake 1/2 (left), Bear Lakes 3/4 (back), **PCT** 1 3/4, Mt. Elwell 2 1/4 (both straight). Follow the trail toward Round Lake, cross the outlet and meander along the east side of Silver Lake. To continue on to Round Lake, make a moderate ascent and two switchbacks, cross the ridge and make rocky ascents and descents to the outlet of Round Lake. Cross the outlet and continue along the east shore of the lake. The trail may be under water in sections during heavy water years. Pass around the lake side of the cement-walled tunnel that runs under Round Lake and connect with the **Round Lake Trail** at the Round Lake sign. From here you can continue on the **Round Lake Trail** to Gold Lake Lodge. See that trail description for more information.

SMITH CREEK TRAIL
Elevation: 6000' to 5100'
Length: +/- 2 1/2 miles
Effort: Moderate
Hike Time: About 2 hours
Location: T22N R12E, sections 20,29,30,31
Quadrangle Map: Gold Lake **(For map see page 80)**

It is preferable to use the **Smith Lake Trail** trailhead to access this pleasant though moderate hike, although it can be taken from the Mohawk or Graeagle end. Starting on the **Smith Lake Trail** (see description), proceed at an easy ascent for about 3/4 mile to a crossing of Smith Creek. Signs indicate the way to Smith Lake and Mt. Elwell (left). The trail heads right and passes through a marshy area as it begins a moderately steep descent along the left side of Smith Creek. After about 1/4 mile the trail makes a sweeping switchback, crosses a wet area with tiger lilies, and meanders down through a moderately heavy cover of white and red fir. The trail is lightly maintained but very well defined. A steep descent enters a pretty scene of mixed conifers comprised of pine, cedar, and Douglas fir. The trail is now cobbly and washed and descends along and across seasonal gullies. A descent to the creek and a careful fording takes the trail to the right side. Pass a

K-tag for sections 29 and 30 as the trail works along in heavy forest litter with a spring and gully on the left. Several springs and wet areas are crossed as the trail makes a moderate descent in a much more worn, ditch-like form. The smaller firs give way to big pines and a moderately easy descent. The eroded trail is now wet and continues to cross several small springs before once again crossing Smith Creek at an angle amid 1997 flood damage. Evidence of old logging can be seen on both sides of the creek now, and the trail winds as a wide, easy path through mid-size reproduction and crowding manzanita. A dead-end trail appears to cut back to the right but a propped up sign indicates the trail proper. You are now on private property. The trail continues to descend as a brush-lined old log or skid road to another fork. The left fork has a sign reading trail attached to a cedar tree. Continue down this to one last crossing of Smith Creek and the access road from Mohawk. The right fork is actually an old log spur that winds through section 20 to the access road from Graeagle to their water supply, and the north end of the *Graeagle Creek Trail*. The Smith Creek Trail is slated to be realigned to bypass the private property and hook back in with Graeagle Creek Trail sometime in the near future.

SMITH LAKE TRAIL
(From Gray Eagle Lodge)
Elevation: 5800' to 6079'
Length: +/- 1 mile
Effort: Moderate
Hike Time: About 1 hour
Location: T22N R12E, sections 30,31
Quadrangle Map: Gold Lake **(For map see page 80)**

The trailhead can be reached by taking the **Gold Lake Road** off **Highway 89**. Proceed up this road about 5 miles to the Gray Eagle Lodge turn off. Turn right here and continue a bit over 1/4 mile to the signed turn off to the trailhead. Plenty of parking is available here. This trailhead is shared with the **Long Lake Trail** and the **Gray Eagle Creek Trail.** A sign pointing to the trail indicates Smith Lake as 1 mile, **Little Jamison Creek Trail** as 2 1/2 miles, and Mt. Elwell as 4 miles. This wide, well-maintained trail makes a gradual ascent for about 3/4 mile before crossing the ridge and dropping down to a crossing of Smith Creek. Just after crossing you will see a sign pointing out the **Smith Creek Trail.** Between here and Smith Lake, 1/4 mile away are two signs both telling us Smith Lake is still 1/4 mile. Just past the Smith Creek crossing the **Mt. Elwell Trail** bears off to the left. Keep going straight for a short distance to a second crossing of Smith Creek at the outlet of the lake. All around are pleasant campsites. The trail continues on the south side of the lake another 1 1/2 miles to connect with the **Little Jamison Creek Trail**.

SMITH LAKE TRAIL
(Via Little Jamison Creek Trail)
Elevation: 6720' to 6079'
Length: +/- 1 1/4 miles
Effort: Moderate

Hike Time: About 1 hour
Location: T22N R11E, section 25 and T22N R12E, sections 30,31
Quadrangle Map: Johnsville, Gold Lake **(For map see page 80)**

To access this trail, use the ***Little Jamison Creek Trail*** description from above. Once at the signed trail intersection, follow the ***Smith Lake Trail*** on an easy uphill grade to an old mining ditch. From here the trail makes a moderate ascent through an open brush field with many nice views of Jamison Creek canyon, Mt. Washington, and Eureka Peak. As the trail levels off a bit you will enter a light cover of fir trees. Soon the trail becomes steep with winding switchbacks to a saddle on the ridge top. Stay left of the intermittent pond and proceed across the ridge to where the trail makes a moderate to steep descent to Smith Lake. Nice views of Mills Peak (right), Beckwourth Peak (left), and Smith Lake (center) are seen from the top of this grade. Continue on the right (south) side of the lake and you can take the trail to Gray Eagle Lodge, another 1 mile. (See ***Smith Lake Trail*** from Gray Eagle Lodge description).

SUMMIT TRAIL

Elevation: 6800' to 7200'
Length: +/- 1 mile
Effort: Moderate
Hike Time: 1 hour
Location: T21N R11E, section 12
Quadrangle Map: Gold Lake **(For map see page 80)**

Use the ***Mud Lake Trail*** description to reach the starting point. At the sign just east of Hellgrammite Lake make a light ascent, then descend across a marshy area. The trail is well-blazed and there is a small pond on the right. Make a descent and cross the creek below a wet basin. Begin an ascent with a view of the escarpment ahead. The trail meanders in scrub pine and hemlock and bears right toward the ridge on a light ascent. Cross the ridge to the Mud Lake side and make a light to steep descent with sweeping switchbacks and views of Mud Lake and Long Lake. Cross a small swale and make a light ascent at the bottom of a rock escarpment. The trail is quite rocky and cobbly. Continue along just below the escarpment and cross the head of a basin above Mud Lake. Beautiful views are the reward here. Cross a small freshet, make two short switchbacks, and cross a bigger freshet. Then make two winding switchbacks along the away to the ridge and an intersection with a 4WD road and a sign: Silver Lake 1 1/4 (back), Lakes Basin Campground 2 1/4 (back), ***Pacific Crest Trail*** north 1/2 (left), ***Pacific Crest Trail*** south 1/2 (right), Round Lake Trail 2 (right). An unsigned trail meanders northeast on the ridgeback. Follow the 4WD road north about 50 yards to a sign on the left: ***Pacific Crest Trail*** south 1/2 (back), ***Round Lake Trail*** 2 (back), ***Pacific Crest Trail*** north 1/2 (ahead), ***Little Jamison Creek Trail*** 2 (ahead). At this point go right or 90 degrees from the road. The trail makes a light descent with views of Mt. Elwell, and to the left a good view of Jamison Creek canyon. It then crosses back and forth over the top of the ridge, giving great vistas off both sides. Make a light descent to a trail intersection and signs for ***Mt. Elwell Trail, Mud Lake Trail***, Gray Eagle Lodge, etc.

TAMARACK CONNECTION TRAIL

Elevation: 5400' to 7050'
Length: +/- 3 1/2 miles
Effort: Moderate
Hike Time: About 2 hours
Location: T20N R12E, sections 8,9
Quadrangle Map: Sierra City **(For map see page 100)**

To reach the trailhead from the south take the **Gold Lake Road** north from Bassett's Station on **State Route 49**. Proceed 1 1/2 miles to the Salmon Creek bridge. To reach the trail from the north, take the **Gold Lake Road** 14 miles south from **State Route 89** near Graeagle to the same bridge. A sign points out Sardine Lakes and Packer Lake. Take that road and cross the bridge, pass the **Packer Lake Road** on your right, and you will see the signed *Tamarack Connection Trail* just before the Sardine Lakes Campground. A sign reads: Sardine Overlook 2, Tamarack Lakes 3 1/2, Packer Lake 4. The trail, actually an old wagon road for several miles, makes about four gentle ascending switchbacks before reaching the ridge top where it meanders along. As you ascend, you will pass an old cement water tank dated 1966. After passing the ***Sardine Overlook Trail,*** the trail winds up the ridge flanking Upper and Lower Sardine Lakes. It makes about four switchbacks up past rusting mine machinery and dirt heaps. Beautiful views of the lakes and Sierra Buttes make up for the open, hot hillside. The ascent ranges from moderate to steep with some of the switchbacks degraded by hikers cutting them. As you enter the trees and make about five more short switchbacks to the top, you will pass a K-Tag. Once on the ridgeback, there is a small meandering trail that wanders up the ridge toward the Sierra Buttes. The trail makes about seven switchbacks down through a red fir thicket, passes an old ditch on the left, and drops into a granite basin. At this point the trail again becomes an old wagon road. An old, unmaintained trail bears left (south) but soon disappears. You may note the old ***Pacific Crest Trail*** markers, used as a temporary route. After making gentle ascents and descents, the trail crosses the outlet creek for Tamarack Lakes and intersects the 4WD road from Packer Lake (about 1 1/2 miles). From here you can proceed up an abandoned spur of the 4WD road to a foot trail leading to the ***Pacific Crest Trail*** and the Sierra Buttes.

View of Lakes Basin from near the Sierra Buttes.

UPPER SALMON LAKE-DEER LAKE TRAIL

Elevation: 6500' to 7110'
Length: +/- 2 miles
Effort: Moderate
Hike Time: About 1 1/2 hours
Location: T21N R12E, sections 28,29
Quadrangle Map: Gold Lake

To reach the trailhead from the south take the **Gold Lake Road** north from Bassett's Station on **State Route 49**. Proceed 4 miles to the Salmon Lake junction. To reach the trail from the north, take the **Gold Lake Road** 11 1/2 miles south from **State Route 89** near Graeagle to the same road. A sign indicates Salmon Lake as 1 1/2 miles. Take this road to the trailhead on the right just above the parking lot. The first half is relatively level with some ups and downs and a lot of loose rocks. The trail makes a steep drop down a rocky, wet area as it skirts the west end of Upper Salmon Lake. Walk through a small grassy area and ascend past two summer cabins to a footbridge. On the other side the trail to Salmon Lake Lodge bears down to the left and is only a short walk. A sign reading **Deer Lake Trail** and Horse Lake 1/8 mile points out our trail to the right. The trail runs

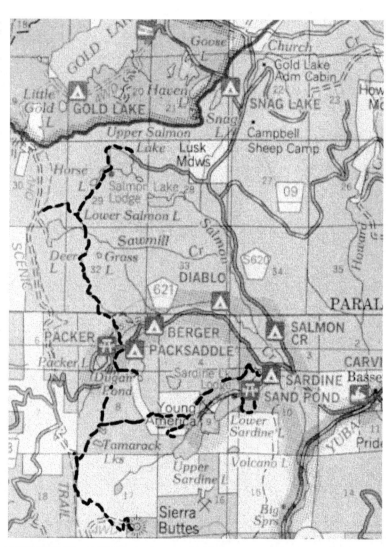

Berger Creek-Saxonia Lake Trail, Deer Lake Trail, Upper Salmon Lake-PCT Tie Trail, San Pond Interpretive Trail, Sardine Lakes Overlook Trail, Sierra Buttes Trail, Tamarack Connection Trail, Upper Salmon Lake-Deer Lake Trail.

south just past the small Horse Lake, where it begins a series of about six switchbacks up a moderately steep hill. It then meanders along to a saddle where it makes a four-way junction with the **Deer Lake Trail** from **Packer Lake Road** and a **PCT Tie Trail**. A sign indicates that Deer Lake is straight ahead 1/4 mile, the **PCT** is 1/2 mile west, and Salmon Lake Lodge is 1 1/2 miles back. The trail soon reaches Deer Lake where a small sign reads Trail Ends. In actuality the trail meanders along the west side to the 4WD road from Packer Saddle. Campsites are very limited.

WADES LAKE TRAIL
Elevation: 6200' to 6540'
Length: +/- 3/4 miles
Effort: Moderate
Hike Time: About 1 hour
Location: T21N R11E, section 2
Quadrangle Map: Johnsville, Gold Lake **(For map see page 80)**

Use the *Little Jamison Creek Trail* access and directions described earlier. When you reach the *Wades Lake-Little Jamison Creek Trail* intersection, there will be a sign pointing to Wades Lake 3/4 mile, and the *Pacific Crest Trail* 1 1/2 miles. Take this trail up a gradual to steep ascent with winding switchbacks. About halfway up, the trail becomes moderate, improving all the time. 1/4 mile from Wades Lake is the signed *Pacific Crest Tie Trail* on the right. That trail runs along at an open and easy grade for a distance before becoming steeper as it approaches the ridgeback and the *Mt. Washington Trail*. Proceed straight ahead to Wades Lake, elevation 6540'. If you like, you can return to the *Little Jamison Creek Trail* via another route. From the dam, walk down the left side of the creek about 50 feet to an obvious crossing of the stream. From here the trail parallels the stream on the right side about 1/8 mile before bearing away to the east. Wind along, down across an open rock field to a rocky gully, and cross the head of it. Proceed a short distance before dropping down a series of switchbacks. Good views of 8300' Mt. Ingalls in the distance, Grass Lake in the foreground, and Rock Lake to your right are had from this route. The trail is a bit faint here as it is not maintained. Switchback under a short rock face to the bottom of the slope where the trail levels out and quickly intersects the *Little Jamison Creek Trail*, about 1/4 mile from Jamison Lake.

Stage fording Gold Lake about 1915.

SOUTHERN PLUMAS COUNTY & NORTHEASTERN BUTTE COUNTY

Accessible by the Marysville-La Porte-Quincy Road, the only real physical difference between southern Plumas County and northern Sierra County is the county line along Slate Creek. Southern Plumas shares the same rich heritage of the Gold Rush, along with the natural splendor of Sierra County. The largest town is La Porte, population 35 in winter and 200 in summer. This seasonal increase in population is mostly due to recreational activities at Little Grass Valley Reservoir, built in 1962 to flood Little Grass Valley on the South Fork of the Feather River. The historic Quincy-La Porte Road connects this southern-most town in Plumas County to the more populated center of the county, though most La Porter's head for Oroville and Marysville, especially in winter when snow closes the Quincy road.

La Porte, originally known as Rabbit Creek, was founded in 1850. In 1857, the townspeople renamed it after La Porte, Indiana. For the next fifty years and more, it served as the major supply center for all of southern Plumas and northern Sierra counties. La Porte can also claim distinction as the cradle of competitive downhill skiing in the Western Hemisphere. It was here, in 1867 that the first organized ski races were held. For more on this wild and woolly sport, see the suggested reading section of this guide. Suffering several disastrous fires, and a general decline in mining, the town settled into semi-obscurity. It is now a favorite winter sports area. Sightseeing, OHV travel, water sports, and hiking are favorites in summer.

Six-foot diameter ponderosa pine on the Nelson Creek Trail.

To the east 25 miles by dirt road is the old mining town of Johnsville. More easily reached from the east by county road from Graeagle, Johnsville is a collection of privately owned homes that sits inside the Plumas Eureka State Park, one of California's finest, though most underused, parks. A huge, restored 1880s stamp mill, working blacksmith shop, outbuildings, and a comprehensive museum make this park an historic jewel. Nature hikes, campfire stories, and gold panning on nearby Jamison Creek are some of the activities for park campers and day users. Ski Gold Mountain, a local ski hill, provides opportunities for winter sports for county residents. Throughout the park there are also many miles of cross-country ski trails.

ABANDONED FEATHER FALLS TRAIL (Butte County)

Elevation: 3300' to 2600' (1800' if followed to end - not recommended)
Length: +/- 2 miles (4 miles if followed to end - not recommended)
Effort: Difficult (Extremely Difficult if followed to end - not recommended)
Hike Time: About 2 hours (4 hours if followed to end - not recommended)
Location: T21N R6E, sections 22,27 (34,35 if followed to end - not recommended)
Quadrangle Map: Brush Creek

This trail got some real nice press from Sunset Magazine in 1985, unfortunately it has been abandoned! I can imagine the disillusionment felt by the volunteers who worked on this trail. There are some beautiful views of Bald Rock Dome and the canyon, so it is a keen loss to the hiking community. Half of it seems to have been salvaged by attempting to hook it up with a trail from the *Watson Cabin-Feather Falls Trail* trailhead. Several problems in this area are a lack of signage so that hikers can find these trails, and the fact that at least two trails were started, but never finished. The roads are generally not maintained so you might encounter fallen trees and limbs in the roadway. To reach the trailhead for this trail, you will have to exercise acute map skills to find your way around the myriad of roads here. Some roads that the Forest Service insists on showing on their maps have been overgrown for years. Gates or berms close others. Many are not even shown on the maps. To reach the trailhead from the town of Feather Falls stay on the pavement all the way to the top of Watson Ridge. There is a cattle-loading chute on the right side of the road. Turn left onto the crushed rock road *(USFS 21N24)* and follow about 1 mile past the intersection with *USFS 21N92*. Continue another 3/4 mile to the intersection with *USFS 21N25* and take a left on that road. Follow this road past a number of unsigned intersections. It is the most obvious road and maintains somewhat the same grade with a few ups and downs. It will wind in and out, turn from crushed rock to rutted dirt, pass through an open, bouldery area and re-enter heavy pine forest. The *Watson Cabin-Feather Falls Trail* trailhead is virtually unnoticeable to the left in a ponderosa pine plantation. Ahead you will see Bald Rock Dome across the canyon. Continue about another 1 1/4 miles to a wide area at the end of the road (approximately 9 3/4 miles from the pavement). There is a small ponderosa pine plantation here and the road is closed with a dirt berm. The trailhead is unsigned but is on the northwest edge of the road (head due west). Make a gradual descent through a heavy cover of mixed conifer and skirt the bottom edge of a

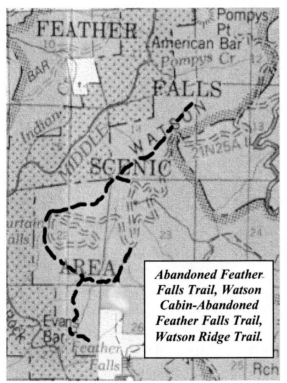

Abandoned Feather Falls Trail, Watson Cabin-Abandoned Feather Falls Trail, Watson Ridge Trail.

pine plantation as the trail opens up and offers a view down canyon and of a set of falls on the other side of the Middle Fork of the Feather River. The trail descends and then undulates in and out of seasonal draws, through a burned area, and into a large manzanita field where you must pick your way over the granite boulders in the trail. After this the trail is very good with gradual to moderate descents to a small stream. Cross and continue down to a welcome and refreshing stream and the intersection with the **Watson Cabin-Abandoned Feather Falls Trail**. This is where you should either take that trail out or return via your route in. To continue on is only to invite trouble. It is virtually impossible to reach Feather Falls on this route as part of the trail is completely washed out in a very steep canyon. In many instances you must crawl under manzanita and over logs. Although many portions of the trail are in good shape, many are not, or were never completed, and if something were to happen to you out in that mess, searchers might never find you. Besides, the best views are on the section already traveled.

BELFRIN MINE EXTENSION TRAIL (Seymour Trail)

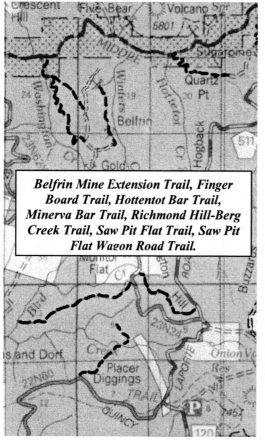

Belfrin Mine Extension Trail, Finger Board Trail, Hottentot Bar Trail, Minerva Bar Trail, Richmond Hill-Berg Creek Trail, Saw Pit Flat Trail, Saw Pit Flat Wagon Road Trail.

Elevation: 5000' to 4500'
Length: +/- 1 mile
Effort: Difficult
Hike Time: About 1 hour
Location: T23N R10E, section 19
Quadrangle Map: Onion Valley

Reach the trailhead via the **Quincy-La Porte Road (USFS 120)** to the Fingerboard and turn right on the **Washington Creek-Belfrin Mine Road**. Take this narrow road 1 mile to the **Belfrin Mine Road** turnoff and turn right again. Follow this small road almost 2 miles, past an old grown-over helicopter log landing. Just past this landing the road will swing back to the southeast. From here, you should walk as you will need 4WD to continue driving, and there is only one place to turn around. Descend the steep and winding road into Winters Creek canyon to its end at the still claimed, and maintained, Belfrin Mine. The trail begins just past the mine workings at the end of the road. It is a narrow unmaintained route that drops moderately to the old Seymour Mine, known on USFS maps as the Belfrin Extension. A spring crosses the trail about the midway point. It is a pleasant, though somewhat strenuous hike along the steep-sided, well-timbered and shaded Winters Creek.

BUTTE BAR TRAIL

Elevation: 3800' to 3000'
Length: +/- 1 mile
Effort: Difficult
Hike Time: About 1 hour
Location: T22N R8E, section 1 and T23N R8E, section 36
Quadrangle Map: Dogwood Peak

The trailhead is at the bottom of a 9-mile long, narrow, winding road. The trail is moderately steep, narrow, and under heavy cover but well used and defined. It joins the *PCT* after about 1 mile. The unsigned intersection is at a switchback on the *PCT* where nearby a refreshing spring can be found on the upper side of the trail. After an easy grade north down the *PCT* for about 1/2 mile it reaches the Middle Fork of the Feather River and the impressive Butte Bar Bridge at the mouth of Onion Valley Creek.

Butte Bar Trail, Onion Valley Creek Trail.

BUZZARD'S ROOST RIDGE TRAIL

Elevation: 6750' to 4200'
Length: +/- 3 miles
Effort: Extremely Difficult
Hike Time: About 4 hours
Location: T23N R10E, sections 22,27,28,33, and T22N R10E, section 4
Quadrangle Map: Blue Nose Mountain **(For map see page 106)**

This is an extremely difficult trail to hike, especially if you try to ascend it from Nelson Creek. Reach the trail via the shared *Pilot Peak Lookout-Poorman's Creek Road (USFS 22N84X)* about 1 mile off the *Quincy-La Porte Road* at historic and picturesque Onion Valley. When you reach the ridge crest on this road, take the 4WD road to the left, ascending quickly and steeply to the top of Buzzard's Roost. From the end of the 4WD road proceed north along the west side of Buzzard's Roost Ridge. The trail is blazed sporadically and meanders often so it is advisable to keep a sharp eye on it. A quick descent will bring you to the edge of a huge field of manzanita. From here the trail is basically non-existent until you get down to the lower end. Try to stay on the downhill and western side of the ridge for the next 2 miles. Dixon Creek canyon will be immediately below you. Again, the trail is hard to discern. About 3/4 mile from the bottom of the ridge, which ends in Nelson Creek, the brush gives way to timber. You will hit an old mining ditch, which you cross. Soon after, you will land on the *Dixon Creek-Union Creek Trail* (see below). Follow this trail left to the end of a spur road at Dixon Creek. This road will take you to the *Quincy-La Porte Road* in about 1 mile. You have to walk it as it has a locked gate at the entrance.

DIXON CREEK-UNION CREEK TRAIL

Elevation: 4200' to 4600'
Length: +/- 2 miles
Effort: Difficult
Hike Time: About 2 hours
Location: T23N R10E, sections 22,27
Quadrangle Map: Blue Nose Mountain

This hike follows an old trail-turned-narrow gauge road built in 1933 by a miner named Mr. Neher. Mr. Neher also built a small truck to carry supplies into his mine on Union Creek. It is now considerably narrower due to sloughing and is also heavily overgrown in the upper part. The first half of the trail has been replaced with a 4WD road that is kept closed to the public by some miners on Dixon Creek. You may walk the road, which is a nice hike in itself or, if you are a purist, follow the original trail, which runs close to the road. To reach the trailhead it is best to park at the Nelson Creek bridge about 10 1/2 miles south of **State Highway 70** on the paved **Quincy-La Porte Road**. Walk south about 1/4 mile to a locked gate on a 4WD road on the left. Follow this road about 1 mile to a camp on Dixon Creek, or if you prefer to take the original trail to this point do the following. Just before the locked gate is a road dropping to the right. Just opposite this road is a small ravine and stream. This is where the trail starts. It climbs at a moderate to steep grade on the left side

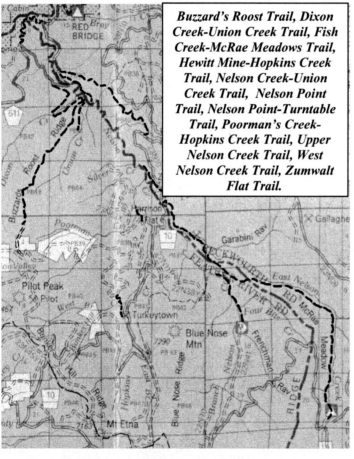

Buzzard's Roost Trail, Dixon Creek-Union Creek Trail, Fish Creek-McRae Meadows Trail, Hewitt Mine-Hopkins Creek Trail, Nelson Creek-Union Creek Trail, Nelson Point Trail, Nelson Point-Turntable Trail, Poorman's Creek-Hopkins Creek Trail, Upper Nelson Creek Trail, West Nelson Creek Trail, Zumwalt Flat Trail.

of the ravine, with overhanging brush occasionally. As it ascends past old growth firs it hits the 4WD road. Walk the road until you see the trail again above the road. Get back on the trail and follow above and parallel to the road. As it rounds the ridge point note the remnants of the old Forest Service telephone line to Pilot Peak. There is also a great view down to Independence Bar and Nelson Creek, but be careful as it is a straight-off drop here. The trail now makes an easy, though brushy descent littered with windfalls. Ultimately the trail hits the 4WD road again just a few yards from Dixon Creek. You are now back on track. Cross Dixon Creek to the east side and pick up the trail at a spring under heavy Douglas and white fir cover. From here it begins a slight ascent toward the east end of the ridge. As you round the ridge, a small, steep trail descends the ridgeback to Nelson Creek about 1/2 mile. Watch for barbed wire from past marijuana growing operations on that trail. To the right ascending the ridge is the old **Buzzard's Roost Ridge Trail** to Onion Valley. Our trail continues along at an easy ascent, though in fairly heavy brush, through a mixed conifer forest to Union Creek. Just as the trail approaches the creek it disintegrates and from here it is a scramble.

EUREKA PEAK TRAIL

Elevation: 6200' to 7447'
Length: +/- 1 1/2 miles
Effort: Moderate
Hike Time: About 3 hours
Location: T22N R11E, sections 22,23
Quadrangle Map: Johnsville, Gold Lake

To reach this trailhead take **Highway 70** east from Quincy, about 22 miles to the signed Mohawk and Johnsville turnoff on **County Road A14**. Turn right, cross the Union Pacific Railroad, pass the U.S. Forest Service Ranger Station, cross the Middle Fork of the Feather River and take a right at the signed T intersection. Proceed another 5 miles up the paved road into Plumas Eureka State Park and the town of

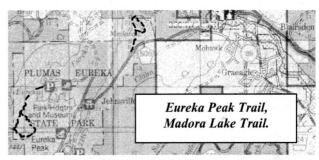

Eureka Peak Trail, Madora Lake Trail.

Johnsville. A stop at the park headquarters and museum in Johnsville is recommended for an informative and interesting visit. Pass through the town and continue to the Plumas Eureka Ski Bowl parking area. The sometimes-gated **Eureka Lake Road** is at the left of the parking lot and is signed. It is 1 1/2 miles of dirt road with some rough sections. Follow this through the ski bowl and around the mountain to a parking area and restrooms at the lake. The trail crosses the dam and overflow and begins a light ascent, passing an old road veering left. Our trail is actually an old road that ran up to the peak. It is now a footpath with a number of trail markers along the route. After a moderate ascent the conifer cover opens to give some nice views of the lake below and the false peak ahead. The trail works into rocks, brush and small trees. Ascend to a small swale where the trail makes a 90-degree left. This is the point where the trail divides to make a loop. Staying left, the trail winds faintly through the trees, ascends parallel to a small creek, passes a brass survey monument for sections 22 and 23, crosses the creek, and heads toward a rock knob. Make a sweeping switchback, ascend parallel to the creek, switchback to the left, cross a small stream (snow melt) and make a light ascent still with the creek. The trail will cross a marshy area at the top of a brush and grass field and ascend along the foot of a steep slope. Switchback left at a trail marker and make a light ascent to another switchback. Ascend on rocky ground under a small red fir, western white pine and mountain hemlock forest. Here and there are old prospect pits and tree stumps from the early mining days. Make an easterly meandering ascent to the crest of the saddle between the false peak (left) and Eureka Peak (right). A short scramble up the west side of the false peak gives a great view of the eastern and northern parts of the county. Carved into the rock are the names and initials of past hikers. One set of initials reads: S.M. Cole, M.E. Cole, Ed Richards 1911. Back at the saddle veer right along the ridge top. A steep trail drops off the front and heads down to the northeast. Our trail is now definitely an old road as it makes a moderate ascent up the ridgeback. To the left is the very steep Avalanche Chute above Jamison Creek campground. The trail levels out now and ahead can be seen a white post on the top of the peak. Note the snow-damaged shapes of the deformed trees along the way. From Eureka Peak there is an unparalleled 360-degree view of Plumas, Lassen and Sierra counties, taking in almost every major peak in Plumas County. Starting directly from the east and going clockwise is Smith Peak, Sierra Valley, Beckwourth Peak, Haskell Peak, Mills Peak, Mt. Elwell, Sierra Buttes, Mt. Washington, Luther Ridge, Florentine Canyon, the clearcuts on the south side of the North Yuba River, Rattlesnake Peak, Saddleback, Jamison Canyon, McCray Ridge, Pilot Peak, Spanish Peak, Claremont, Mt. Lassen, Mt. Hough, Indian Head, and Mt. Ingalls. After taking in this view descend along the ridge in a westerly direction. The trail is now a road still in occasional use. Follow it down and across a meadow to the Plumas Eureka State Park boundary signs. The trail drops steeply down and across a bowl to the north. Cross the head of a small draw and parallel down the right side a short distance, contour into the open, cross the head of a snowmelt draw and the ridge, and descend a small swale. The trail makes a 90-degree left (with a view of False Peak to the right) and descends a draw into a red fir forest. Continue down the hillside at a moderate grade to intersect the original trail above the lake.

Feather Falls Trail.

FEATHER FALLS NATIONAL RECREATION TRAIL
(Butte County)
Elevation: 2500' to 1900'
Length: +/- 3 3/4 miles
Effort: Moderate
Hike Time: About 3 hours (one way)
Location: T20N R6E, section 2 and T21N R6E, section 26,35
Quadrangle Map: Brush Creek and Forbestown **(For map see above)**

These waterfalls are the world's 6th highest at 640 feet. They are well worth the hike, and the trail itself is pleasant on its own. Originally a single trail, a new trail has been constructed affording the opportunity for a loop hike. Go early to beat the heat and crowds. On Memorial Day weekend it is especially busy. Reach the trailhead from Oroville by taking the **Oro Dam Boulevard (Highway 162)** to **Olive Highway (Oroville-**

Bucks Lake-Quincy Road) and follow east to the Forbestown-Feather Falls cutoff. Follow the signs toward the town of Feather Falls. Just before the town is a signed turnoff to the left. Follow this paved road ***(Bryant Ravine Road)*** about 1 1/2 miles to a large parking area with campsites and toilet facilities. I'll give the description using the older, steeper trail to get to the falls and the new, more level trail for coming back. The trail is paved for the first 25 yards, then becomes dirt. There is a sign entreating hikers to use good manners and prevent fires. Next to it is a channel iron monument in memory of Dennis Larsen, trail maintenance leader on the Plumas National Forest from 1978-1993. From here make a slight descent to the trail register where you should sign in. The trail is very wide and easy to walk. There are fleeting glimpses of Bald Rock through the oak and mixed conifer forest. Lilies, columbine, and California newts abound along the trail. At almost each set of switchbacks there is a fence to discourage hikers from cutting

Feather Falls, 640' of spectacular falling water is at the end of this moderate hike.

between them. A sign also warns that cutting switchbacks is prohibited under 36CFR 261.55d. Before this descent, the new but unsigned trail cuts away to the right. There are about four or so easy switchbacks on the descent to Frey Creek, which is crossed via a bridge reconstructed after the floods of 1997. A confluence of two creeks is just below the bridge. Make an ascent up a small set of stone steps, then begin an easy descent with the creek parallel to the trail. There is a good view down the canyon and of Bald Rock from near the 1 1/2 -mile marker (wood post). A photo opportunity is available from a granite slab, but be careful, it drops straight off. The cover has changed now to mostly live oak, madrone and brush. The creek drops well below the trail which now makes a series of easy ups and downs. Just past the 2-mile marker make a quick descent to cross a small stream. A small meadow and locust trees are on the left and the trail makes a slight ascent to cross another small stream. An abandoned water ditch runs below on the left. Contour into a small drainage and cross it, make a short rocky ascent to a switchback, then a mild ascent past another small field on the left. The cover now is ponderosa pine and manzanita with much less ground cover. Cross a dry draw and ascend a concrete path. Make a quick descent and cross a stream, make a moderate ascent and switchback into a mixed forest, and parallel a small spring before crossing it and another spring. The new trail connects about here with a sign describing the difficulty of the trails. A mild, winding ascent leads to a switchback, then another long mild ascent, some of which is concrete. As the trail rounds the ridge you can hear the falls ahead. The unsigned, steep, and unmaintained ***Jackson Ranch Trail*** cuts away to the right. Bald Rock Dome is straight ahead from an observation point on the now fenced trail. Just as you pass an iron pipe gate you get the first views of the top of Feather Falls. Descend to a switchback where cement steps also go straight and up to take you around toward the top of the falls. Follow the trail down its cement steps to a flight of wooden steps that lead down to a short bridge and the observation deck. The return along the new trail is about 1 ¼ miles longer than the original route, but it is much wider and flatter and skirts the canyon rather than going down in it. It still affords great views and winds through a number of brooks and ravines. The trail is covered with wildflowers in spring and various reptiles are always present. Even though this route is longer, the hiking time is about the same. Take plenty of water.

FINGERBOARD TRAIL (Minerva Bar)
Elevation: 5600' to 3700'
Length: +/- 2 miles
Effort: Difficult
Hike Time: About 3 hours
Location: T23N R9E, sections 24,25 and T23N R10E, section 30
Quadrangle Map: Onion Valley **(For map see page 104)**

Reach the trailhead by taking the **Quincy-La Porte Road (USFS 120)** from **Highway 70** near Quincy about 15 1/2 miles to the Fingerboard. Turn right on the **Old Cleghorn Bar Road.** Take this narrow road 1 mile to the **Belfrin Mine Road** turn, and turn right. Follow this small road almost 2 miles to an old helicopter log landing. The **Belfrin Mine Road** will continue downhill to the right (east). The trailhead to Minerva Bar is about 1/8 mile northwest of the log landing. The first 1/2 mile is faint and hard to follow but soon becomes very distinct. If you work downhill bearing to the right, you should be able to keep on the trail. There are numerous mines and prospects along the trail through this area, along with evidence of helicopter logging done in 1980. The trail consists of a number of easy switchbacks most of the distance until it nears the Middle Fork of the Feather River, where it becomes somewhat steeper. It passes the now-idle Wilson-Gomez Mine and intersects the much steeper **Minerva Bar Trail (Wilson-Gomez Route)** from the east.

An alternate approach to the trailhead is to take the **Cleghorn Bar Road** off the **Quincy-La Porte Road** about 1/2 mile north of Onion Valley. Follow this road northwest about 2 1/2 miles to the unsigned intersection with the south approach of the **Washington Creek-Belfrin Mine Road.** Follow this rutted road up a low ascent 1/2 mile to the Belfrin Mine turnoff. Continue as noted above.

FISH CREEK-McRAE MEADOWS TRAIL
Elevation: 4800' to 6300'
Length: +/- 8 miles
Effort: Difficult
Hike Time: About 6 hours
Location: T23N R10E, section 31, T22N R10E, section 1 and T22N R11E, sections 6,7,8,9,16,21
Quadrangle Map: Blue Nose Mountain, Mt. Fillmore **(For map see page 106)**

This is another of the old pack trails built by miners during the late 1800s that is still maintained by miners. Please respect their camps, claims, and property. Reach the trailhead by traveling about 13 miles east of Quincy on **State Highway 70** to the **Gill Ranch Road** and **Sloat Road** intersection. Take a right and travel about 1 1/2 miles southwest along the north side of Long Valley to Sloat. As you approach a closed sawmill-turned-feed store, turn right across the double tracks of Union Pacific Railroad, take the one lane bridge across the Middle Fork of the Feather River and continue straight, past the **Poplar Valley Road (USFS 23N08)** which is on the left. Cross Poplar Creek via a small bridge and continue on for 15 miles via the **Sloat-Gibsonville Road (USFS 23N10)** to the trailhead. This is a winding road but it does have some rather nice views of the Middle Fork canyon and Nelson Creek. The trailhead is located at a wide spot in the road at Fish Creek. If miners are camping there you can park along the road or at the Nelson Creek bridge about 200 yards farther along. The trail climbs 50 feet up a bank on the right side of Fish Creek to an abandoned water ditch. Follow the ditch 1/8 mile to where the trail begins an ascent along a rocky, brushy hillside. From here there are pleasant views of Nelson Creek below. However, keep a sharp eye out for rattlesnakes as they are

A friendly denizen of the trail.

plentiful in this area. The trail soon contours along the hillside through stands of old growth timber. In about 1 mile cross East Nelson Creek with a sign giving the distance back to Zumwalt Flat (1 1/2 miles) and ahead to McRae Meadows and the **Johnsville-La Porte Road** (6 miles). The trail continues a short distance through 19th century mining rock piles to a dry ditch. Ascend several short, steep switchbacks. Continue along a brushy, moderate but steady ascent about 1/2 mile to a saddle on the ridgeback. As the trail crosses to the west side of the ridge, West Nelson Creek is visible below with the back of Blue Nose Mountain rising sharply. As the trail dips there is another sign for McRae Meadows, Nelson Creek, and Hopkins Creek. Our trail continues southeast, dips for a time, then begins a brushy, moderate ascent of about 1 mile to the end of the closed 4WD road from the head of McRae Meadows. Follow this pleasant road 5 miles to the **Johnsville-La Porte Road**, which will take you back 7 miles to Johnsville. Along the closed 4WD road are stands of quaking aspen sporting carvings by Basque sheepherders.

GRASS VALLEY BALD MOUNTAIN TRAIL & PCT TIE TRAIL

Elevation: 5100' to 6255'
Length: +/- 2 1/4 miles (2 3/4 miles to PCT)
Effort: Easy
Hike Time: About 2 hours
Location: T22N R9E, sections 21,22
Quadrangle Map: Onion Valley, La Porte

This fairly new, heavily used trail is a very pleasant hike. To reach the trailhead on the north shore of Little Grass Valley Reservoir from Quincy take the *Quincy-La Porte Road* about 20 miles to *USFS 22N60*. Follow this semi-paved road another 10 miles to a sharp right turn onto *USFS 22N68*. Continue 1/2 mile to a 45-degree intersection with *USFS 22N57*. Proceed about 1 mile, crossing the South Fork of the Feather River, to the signed trailhead. From La Porte take the *Quincy-La Porte Road* north 2 miles, but stay on the two-lane paved highway past a right turn pointing the way to Quincy. Continue toward Little Grass Valley Reservoir, and in about 1 mile make a right turn. Signs indicate the way to several campgrounds on the east shore. Follow this road *(USFS 22N57)* along the east side, cross the South Fork of the Feather River, and in about 1/4 mile you will come to the signed trailhead. This trail is also a tie trail to the *PCT*. Begin by crossing a flat area and seasonal gully and make a moderate ascent on the well defined trail. It soon becomes an easier contouring ascent and crosses an old skid trail. On the right a wet draw parallels as the trail crosses a small flat and begins an easy ascent in heavy white fir cover.

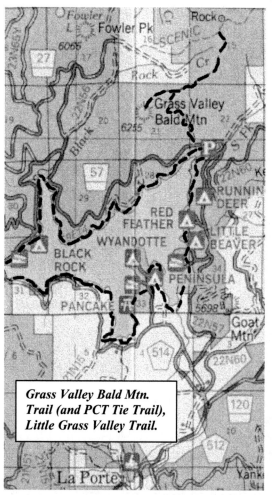

Grass Valley Bald Mtn. Trail (and PCT Tie Trail), Little Grass Valley Trail.

Evidence of old logging shows along the ascent but with all the big trees it is still quite pretty. Make a switchback and a light ascent, another switchback onto an old skid road, and a meander across the ridge top to the left side. There is a nice meander along a glade to a seasonal draw crossing. Huge white fir line the trail as it descends to a dry creek, crosses and maintains a light contouring ascent under the heavy cover. Cross three more dry gullies, make a long ascent, switchback and contour. Bracken fern covers the ground as the dying white fir cover thins. In a short distance is a signed intersection and switchback. The *PCT Tie Trail* continues to the right while the *Bald Mountain Trail* goes left. For more on the tie trail go to the end of this description. The sign indicates each one as 1 mile, but the tie trail is more like 1 1/4 miles long. Make a gentle ascent in heavy white fir, and switchback into a stand of dead white fir as the trail becomes eroded and winds up into the open. Once on the ridge top the trail is again under cover as it makes a light ascent into another stand of dead fir. Switchback and ascend into heavy cover again with views of Little Grass Valley Reservoir below. An easy ascent leads to two more switchbacks and the ridgeback. The easy ascent gives good views of Saddleback Peak, Table Rock, Mt. Fillmore, and Pilot Peak, then switchbacks to the ridgeback, and switchbacks again with a view to the north of Mt. Lassen and heavily logged stands of timber below. Another winding ascent brings the trail to the summit where there are small wind shelters built of rock by hikers. The Coast Range and Sutter Buttes can be seen on a clear day. With a map oriented to the north arrow on the brass U.S.G.S. reference marker on the summit you can pick out the different peaks in the distance.

Bald Mtn.-PCT Tie Trail: From the signed trail intersection continue northeasterly at a light ascent, then a contouring descent with fleeting glimpses of Little Grass Valley Reservoir. The corner for sections 15,16,21 and 22 and private property are just above the trail. A light ascent along the eroded trail comes to two switchbacks and a stand of dead white fir crowded by brush. The now-graveled trail winds up through small boulders and brush to the ridge top and a view of Pilot Peak, then descends in heavy white fir and bigger timber where it contours nicely to an intersection with the *PCT*. A sign points back to Little Grass Valley and Bald Mountain.

GRAVES CABIN-KENNEDY CABIN TRAIL

Elevation: 2100' to 2200'
Length: +/- 2 miles
Effort: Difficult
Hike Time: About 1 hour
Location: T21N R7E, sections 21,28
Quadrangle Map: Cascade **(For map see page 114)**

To reach the trailhead follow the directions given for the *Hanson's Bar Trail*. Starting from the Hanson's Bar cabin, the *Graves Cabin-Kennedy Cabin Trail* makes a number of minor ascents and descents as it works upstream. Be very careful, as the canyon side is precipitous. The trail passes through an extensive historic gold digging area with lots of rock piles. Graves Cabin is now just a ruin with only a few poles and the old stacked-rock fireplace surviving. A small trail drops to the river for fishing, but to continue on to Kennedy Cabin make two sharp, very steep switchbacks at a pipe pile. Continue the steep ascent a distance, then make a moderate descent. The trail becomes narrow and then makes a steep descent to a ditch and small diggings. Follow the trail/ditch along the hill to the intersection with the *Kennedy Butte Trail (7E27)*. This is a lightly blazed, unsigned intersection. If desired, continue on the *Graves Cabin-Kennedy Cabin Trail* a short distance to a small meadow, then a campsite, cross a small ravine that has some water, and follow the trail down to the river and several campsites on the bars. Above the bar is a large shut-in. It is possible to return to the Hartman Bar Ridge via the *Kennedy Butte Trail*, though that trail is not maintained and is quite steep in places. For more information see its description.

HANSON'S BAR TRAIL

Elevation: 4200' to 2100'
Length: +/- 2 miles
Effort: Difficult
Hike Time: About 1 hour
Location: T21N R7E, sections 28,29,32
Quadrangle Map: Cascade

To reach the trailhead from Brush Creek on the **Quincy-Oroville Road**, take the **Bald Rock Road** about 1/2 mile to the **Milsap Bar Road (USFS 22N62)**, then proceed south about 6 1/2 miles to Milsap Bar on the Middle Fork of the Feather River. Cross and continue 5 miles of rough road to **USFS 22N08X**. A cattle chute is on the right, and the signed road cuts back uphill under a clearcut. Proceed about 1 mile along this road to a large parking area. You may continue on another 1/2 mile or so to the trailhead but parking is very limited. Originally, a very steep foot trail dropped off the top of Hartman Bar Ridge at Mountain Spring House (since clearcut and demolished) and went into Hanson's Bar. Miners put in the 4WD road years ago, but it has since been closed and downsized to a hiking trail. Remember to give yourself ample time to come out. From the signed trailhead make a light descent that levels shortly, then switchbacks twice and contours northeast. The descent becomes a bit heavier with fleeting glimpses down and across the canyon. Make about five more switchbacks, the last of which gives a great view of Little Marble Cone across the river. The old trail is noticeable here and there in this section also. Make a long, moderate descent, switchback, and another long descent through a fine stand of black oak. Make two more switchbacks, and another long, easy-to-moderate descent to three switchbacks above a slide. The grade is steeper as the trail reaches the Wild & Scenic River zone (signed). Make two more switchbacks past old prospect holes and descend parallel to the creek. The trail would be pleasant but for the cobble. One more small switchback brings the trail out onto a flat along the river. A large pool is to the left. The trail crosses the flat

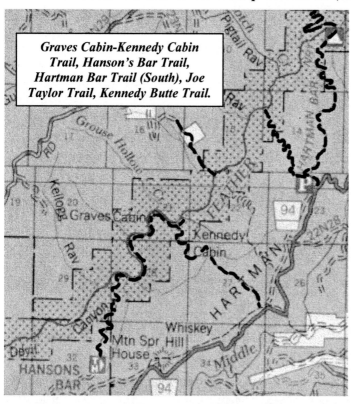

Graves Cabin-Kennedy Cabin Trail, Hanson's Bar Trail, Hartman Bar Trail (South), Joe Taylor Trail, Kennedy Butte Trail.

(note the old rock wall fence) and winds gently up to cross the creek near the grave of Martha Cahill who died there in 1936. Pass a campsite and cross a seasonal drainage to the old Hanson's Bar Cabin ruins. Several campsites are available along the river through this section. From the **Hanson's Bar Trail** the **Graves Cabin-Kennedy Cabin Trail** continues upriver about 2 miles to those two points.

HARTMAN BAR NATIONAL RECREATION TRAIL (South)
Elevation: 5000' to 2400'
Length: +/- 4 miles
Effort: Difficult
Hike Time: About 3 hours
Location: T22N R7E, sections 11,14
Quadrangle Map: Cascade **(For map see page 114)**

As far as Middle Fork of the Feather River trails go, this one and the **Dome Trail** are about the most mellow trails there are. Even so, be prepared. This is also some of the most rugged country in the north state. To reach the trailhead from La Porte, travel to Little Grass Valley Reservoir and proceed along the west side, past the dam to the paved **Hartman Bar Ridge Road**. Travel west about 15 miles to **USFS 22N42Y**. Turn right here. A crudely carved stump and tree both read **HBT**. Proceed less than 1/4 mile to the trailhead. There is a nice camp here, but the spring quite often is dry. This well-maintained trail makes a light, contouring descent for about 1 1/2 miles, with a small spring along the way. A large slide required the trail to be re-routed over the top of it several

**Hartman Bar Bridge from the north.
Sally was ready for a swim in the river.**

years ago. At the end of the 1 1/2-mile grade begins a series of about twelve short switchbacks down through old growth pine and fir cover. Occasionally you may note remnants of the original trail, a much steeper grade. The grade becomes a bit easier before again making about five switchbacks down to the ridge spine where the trail winds down, switches back and crosses an old ditch. Notice the large number of decayed Douglas fir stumps, mute evidence of the Mornington Mining Co. sawmill and mining operation that was flourishing at Hartman Bar around 1920. After crossing the ditch make another switchback, a moderate descent, cross another old ditch, make two switchbacks, cross yet another old ditch and note the old-style sign: Hartman Bar Ridge 4; Cascade 10; **Gravel Range Road** 5; Bucks Lake 11. Nearby lies a huge iron boiler, used for making steam to run equipment to log and operate the sawmill in the mining operations. According to the August 1920 Timberman magazine, The Foundation Company of San Francisco was cutting 4,000 board feet of timber per day using the old Robinson Mill brought over from Meadow Valley. The trail drops gently into a wet draw where it was recently improved and crosses to come out at the new wood and steel suspension bridge across the Middle Fork of the Feather River. Located just below the wet draw is the primitive Dan Beebe Campground. Watch for poison oak, which is thick here. For a trail description of the *Hartman Bar Trail* (North), see the Central Plumas County section.

HEWITT MINE-HOPKINS CREEK TRAIL
Elevation: 5600' to 5000'
Length: +/- 1 mile
Effort: Very Difficult
Hike Time: About 1 hour
Location: T22N R10E, section 11
Quadrangle Map: Blue Nose Mountain **(For map see page 106)**

Hopkins Creek was one of the earliest and richest gold streams discovered in Plumas County. From Quincy, travel about 13 miles to Sloat and take the *Sloat-Gibsonville Road (USFS 23N10)* about 17 miles to the *Poormans Creek Road (USFS 22N17)*. After crossing Hopkins Creek follow the road about 2 1/2 miles up hill, always staying to the left. If you come to a large log landing, you have gone about 100 yards too far. The trail starts at a muddy spring just below the spur road. This old pack trail switchbacks down the hillside to the West Branch of Hopkins Creek where mining activity was once prevalent. Modern day miners still work this creek and there are no open gold mining areas. The trail used to cross the West Branch and continue up Hopkins Creek but that portion is now almost indiscernible.

HOTTENTOT BAR TRAIL
Elevation: 4800' to 3800'
Length: +/- 1 mile
Effort: Difficult
Hike Time: About 2 hours
Location: T23N R10E, section 20
Quadrangle Map: Onion Valley **(For map see page 104)**

Take the *Quincy-La Porte Road* to the Turntable, about 1 mile past the Nelson Creek bridge and about 13 miles from the intersection of *La Porte Road* and *Highway 70* in Quincy. Bear right on the *Hottentot Creek Road* and travel about 2 miles. For more on the Turntable see the *Nelson Point-Turntable Trail* listing. The *Hottentot Creek Road* is rough and loose, and 4WD is recommended. The trailhead is at the end of the 4WD road. Parking is best about 1/2 to 1/4 mile before the road ends, at the Wild River sign. The trail drops down rather quickly through a mix of maples and conifers to an old mining ditch. Follow this ditch a short distance west and the trail will again drop down hill.

There are several switchbacks and places where large trees have fallen across the trail, but for the most part it is a pleasant hike through shaded woods. The last 200 yards is a loose, steep drop to the mouth of Hottentot Creek and the Middle Fork of the Feather River. A small cabin since burned by the Forest Service once sat here.

ILLINOIS RIDGE-CHINA BAR TRAIL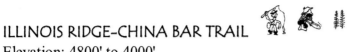
Elevation: 4800' to 4000'
Length: +/- 1/2 mile
Effort: Difficult
Hike Time: About 1/2 hour
Location: T21N R9E, section 28
Quadrangle Map: La Porte

To reach the trail go south of La Porte about 1 mile on the **Marysville-La Porte Road** and turn left onto **USFS 21N18**. Proceed about 1 mile to **Spur A,** which will take you through the historic site of Secret Diggings. Continue about another mile south of Secret Diggings to the end of the road. The last short section of road winds amongst the trees and is rather rough. There is a small area to park in the trees. There are actually two trails here, one is a very steep equipment skid trail, the other a series of about twenty-six moderate to steep switchbacks. The trail works down the ridge to Slate Creek near the mouth of Clark's Ravine. This trail to a set of mining claims is user-maintained. For the most part the trail is under fairly dense cover, and at the start is thick with mosquitoes.

Illinois Ridge-China Bar Trail.

JOE TAYLOR TRAIL
Elevation: 5000' to 2300'
Length: +/- 2 miles
Effort: Very Difficult
Hike Time: About 2 hours
Location: T22N R7E, section 14
Quadrangle Map: Haskins Valley **(For map see page 114)**

This trail utilizes the same trailhead as the **Hartman Bar Trail** (South). It was named for Joseph Taylor, a Native American who received an Indian Allotment on the Middle Fork of the Feather River in 1932. The property has since reverted to the U.S government. The unsigned trail forks off to the left of the **Hartman Bar Trail** at the U.S.F.S. signboard and is in fairly good condition though it is quite brushy and very steep. California Nutmeg, a tree whose foliage resembles the white fir, is present with its sharp needles. Upon leaving the trailhead, the trail immediately descends, making seven quick switchbacks, a steep descent, two more switchbacks and crosses a dry ravine. As the trail parallels the ravine it makes five more switchbacks, then maintains a steep descent into thick forest. It begins a more moderate descent as it works away from the drainage, but is still steep. Another switchback leads into oak and old growth timber and a winding descent along the ridge spine. Make two more long switchbacks and parallel the ravine with views of Willow Creek on the north side of the river. The trail continues steeply down, making another seven switchbacks through mixed fir and oak cover. As the route crosses an old ditch, glimpses are afforded of the river below. Switchback and cross another ditch and descend to a saddle where the trail drops to the right, paralleling a wash from another ditch. Descend into a glade-like area before descending steeply to the creek and Camp Not Responsible, a small, undeveloped spot. From here the trail runs about 50 yards to where the creek falls off into the Middle Fork of the Feather River. This section of the river is a rugged, rocky, beautiful stretch.

KENNEDY BUTTE TRAIL 7E27
Elevation: 4800' to 2200'
Length: +/- 2 miles
Effort: Very Difficult
Hike Time: About 2 hours
Location: T22N R7E, sections 21,26,27,28
Quadrangle Map: Cascade **(For map see page 114)**

This little used, poorly maintained trail is extremely difficult to find, as there is no sign or other indication of the trailhead. Reach the trailhead from the La Porte area by traveling about 3 miles east on the **Hartman Bar Ridge Road (USFS 22N94)** off the **Milsap Bar Road (USFS 22N62)**. The trailhead, which is actually a very rough, overgrown road, is located near the tip of the ridge where the **Hartman Bar Ridge Road** rounds it. Another road drops off to the right. Drive or walk up the rough road until it makes a sharp left. Take the left, meandering along in the brush and oaks, then make a slight descent into tall timber. Pass a rotted log deck and continue to where the road fizzles out and you are facing west. There will be some very rotted logs in a small pile on the left. The trail is to the right (actually an old skid road). Follow this north about 200 yards to where the footpath is faintly evident as it drops down into the trees and the skid road

Drag line bucket on the way to Kennedy Cabin.

ends. Wind down to a switchback, then sidehill shortly before making a very steep, long descent. Go sidehill again, make another steep descent, go sidehill again, and then make a long, winding descent to some nice views to the north and west. A steep descent through heavy cover with a scattering of huge ponderosa and sugar pine eventually mellows to a sidehill and more gradual descent. Wind down through very heavy cover to a seasonal ravine, switchback and cross down through it to a light ascent to an old ditch. The ditch took water out of this ravine and dropped it off the north side of the ridge to the Kennedy homestead on the Middle Fork of the Feather River. Follow the ditch around to a huge old steel drag-line bucket filled with cable, bolts and other assorted iron that never made it to the mining operations on the river. Continue up the ridgeback (Kennedy Butte Saddle) heading west a very short distance. The trail now breaks off the north side and heads down at a heavy descent through old growth timber. Make seventeen quick, steep switchbacks, make another switchback at a large ponderosa pine with an E carved in it, yet another switchback, and then a long, heavy descent to five more switchbacks. There are views of Little Marble Cone and one of the river from this section. Make a very steep descent that soon becomes more gentle, switchback, and drop steeply to the last switchback. From here the trail winds steeply down to a ditch running straight down the hill. Follow light blaze marks and cross the ditch about three times as it winds down through brush and oaks to the unsigned intersection with the **Graves Cabin-Kennedy Cabin Trail,** near the site of Kennedy Cabin.

LITTLE GRASS VALLEY LAKESHORE TRAIL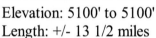
Elevation: 5100' to 5100'
Length: +/- 13 1/2 miles
Effort: Very Easy
Hike Time: About 1/2 hour
Location: T22N R9E, sections 31,32
Quadrangle Map: La Porte **(For map see page 112)**

This trail goes all the way around Little Grass Valley Reservoir, once a farming and ice producing valley for the local mines. First settled in 1850, the valley was dammed in 1962 as part of California's water resources projects. This project created a lake with 1,615 surface acres, 94,460 acre feet, and a 202' high dam. Footpaths and access ways are located immediately adjacent to campgrounds on the east and south shores of the reservoir. OHVs and motorbikes are PROHIBITED. One end of the trail takes off just south of the dam a short distance and winds along between the high water line and the road above. The trail passes through the Black Rock R.V. Campground and drops below the high water mark where it crosses private property. This is a good trail for walking small segments if you want to just take it easy. Be careful climbing up and down from the road, as traffic in summer can be heavy and fast. There is also quite a bit of bicycle traffic, and on the north side horses are allowed.

MADORA LAKE NATURE TRAIL
Elevation: 4850' to 5000'
Length: +/- 1 1/2 miles
Effort: Very Easy
Hike Time: About 1 hour
Location: T22N R12E, section 7
Quadrangle Map: Johnsville **(For map see page 107)**

This is a beautiful family stroll with many interesting things to see. To reach this trailhead, take **Highway 70** east from Quincy about 22 miles to the Mohawk and Johnsville turnoff on **County Road A14**. Turn right, cross the Union Pacific Railroad, pass the U.S. Forest Service Ranger Station, cross the Middle Fork of the Feather River, and take a right at the signed T intersection. Proceed another 2 miles to the east boundary of Plumas Eureka State Park. There is a signed turnoff into a paved parking area with a picnic table and restrooms. Starting at a sign by the picnic table, the trail makes a very light descent to the Lundy Ditch, which runs water into Madora Lake. Follow the trail along this pleasant watercourse to a small footbridge, cross the ditch, and meander along through a heavy pine forest. There is a profusion of plant life along this trail, especially in late spring and early summer. The lake soon comes in sight, the trail working along its west shore. At the dam is another picnic table. From here the trail continues around the east side of the lake, hugging close to the shore. Many different species of waterfowl can be observed from here. As the trail reaches the south end of the lake it crosses a small wet meadow via a plank walkway, and soon completes a loop when it connects at the Lundy Ditch footbridge. No camping, fires, or dogs (except seeing-eye dogs) are allowed on the trail.

MINERVA BAR TRAIL (Wilson Gomez Route)
Elevation: 5100' to 3700'
Length: +/- 1 miles
Effort: Very Difficult
Hike Time: About 2 hours
Location: T23N R9E, section 24, T23N R10E, section 19
Quadrangle Map: Onion Valley **(For map see page 104)**

Reach the trailhead via the **Quincy-La Porte Road (USFS 120)** to the Fingerboard and turn right on **Old Cleghorn Bar Road**. Take this narrow road 1 mile to the **Belfrin Mine Road** turnoff and turn right. Follow this rough road almost 2 miles to where it splits. The **Belfrin Mine Road** swings downhill to the right. Stay on the upper road, passing an old helicopter landing and the trailhead for the **Finger Board Trail** (southern route) to Minerva Bar. About 1/2 mile past this point the road becomes a definite 4WD route. Follow this road down the back of the ridge another 1/2 mile or so to a split in the road. The right hand fork drops steeply. Stay on the left fork for approximately another 1/4 mile to the end of the road. From here the **Wilson Gomez Route** to Minerva Bar drops steeply down to the river. Though this route is shorter than the southern route, it is much more strenuous.
Alternate trailhead: Take the **Cleghorn Bar Road** off the **Quincy-La Porte Road** about 1/2 mile north of Onion Valley. Follow this road northwest about 2 1/2 miles to the unsigned intersection with the south approach of the **Washington Creek-Belfrin Mine Road**. Follow this rutted road up a low ascent 1/2 mile to the Belfrin Mine turnoff. Proceed as noted above.

NELSON CREEK BRIDGE-UNION CREEK TRAIL

Elevation: 4000' to 4600'
Length: +/- 1 mile
Effort: Easy
Hike Time: About 1 hour
Location: T23N R10E, section 22
Quadrangle Map: Blue Nose Mountain **(For map see page 106)**

Young hikers on the trail.

Nelson Creek is one of the premier mining and fishing creeks of Plumas County. It is rich in history as well as gold, so please leave the artifacts of its mining heritage where they are. The entire creek is also under current mineral claims, so panning, sluicing, or any kind of digging is illegal without permission of the claim holders. Please respect their rights. To reach this trail, park at or before the Nelson Creek bridge on the ***Quincy-La Porte Road***, about 10 miles from the ***State Highway 70-La Porte Road*** intersection. The trailhead is cut into the road bank at an angle. For the most part it is fairly level, dipping up and down under cover of live oak, then black oak, then manzanita. After about 1/2 mile a secondary trail cuts down to the right to Independence Bar, just opposite the mouth of Dixon Creek. Staying on the main trail, continue until opposite the mouth of Union Creek where it drops almost to creek level. From here the trail continues along the side of the hill and in several places you must pick your way among the rocks. The trail ends at a stacked rock campsite.

NELSON POINT-LA PORTE ROAD TRAIL

Elevation: 4000' to 3500'
Length: +/- 1/2 mile
Effort: Difficult
Hike Time: About 1/2 hour
Location: T23N R10E, section 16
Quadrangle Map: Blue Nose Mountain **(For map see page 106)**

Take the ***Quincy-La Porte Road*** about 10 miles from the intersection of the ***La Porte Road-Highway 70*** in Quincy. Turn right on the short, dirt spur road that drops quickly to an unimproved parking area. In summer try to park under the locust trees for shade as it gets quite hot here. The trail is very obvious as it drops quickly along the side of the ridge to Nelson Creek and the site of the wickedest gold camp in California. Gold was discovered here in early 1850 and before long the entire creek was crowded with miners. Nothing remains of this once wild town. A swim in the Middle Fork of the Feather River, or much cooler Nelson Creek, is a welcome refresher before hiking back out. Across Nelson Creek is the *Nelson Point-Turntable Trail*.

NELSON POINT-TURNTABLE TRAIL
Elevation: 4895' to 3500'
Length: +/- 1 mile
Effort: Very Difficult
Hike Time: About 1 1/2 hours
Location: T23N R10E, section 16
Quadrangle Map: Blue Nose Mountain **(For map see page 106)**

This trail is a portion of the historic pack and passenger trail to Nelson Point from Marysville, La Porte and Onion Valley. Thousands of gold-hungry argonauts passed down and then back up this trail in 1850 and the ensuing years. Diaries tell of mules and other livestock falling off the sides of this route. One such entry tells of a steer rolling down the hillside and becoming lodged between the rear of a store and the dirt bank. A wall had to be taken out of the store in order to free the animal. When using this route, it is advisable to have someone drop you off at the trailhead or have a car at each end. Start at the Turntable on the *Quincy-La Porte Road*, about 13 miles from the *La Porte Road-Highway 70* intersection in Quincy. One story on the Turntable is that the switchback in the road was so sharp that a revolving table had to be built to turn wagons so that they could make the turn. This seems pretty fanciful but it makes some folks happy, so there you have it. To find the trail, drop straight off the point of the road and down the spine of the ridge. The trail is faint and brushy for a time but soon becomes quite discernible. Many switchbacks work this historic mule packing trail down the mountain. The last 100 yards is a loose scramble. Once at the junction of Nelson Creek and the Middle Fork of the Feather River, a fording of Nelson Creek is required before the steep 1/2-mile climb to the *Nelson Point Trail-La Porte Road* parking area. This is at the end of a 1/4-mile spur off the *Quincy-La Porte Road.*

ONION VALLEY CREEK MINE TRAIL
Elevation: 4600' to 4000'
Length: +/- 1 mile
Effort: Extremely Difficult
Hike Time: About 1/2 hour
Location: T22N R9E, section 4
Quadrangle Map: Onion Valley **(For map see page 126)**

This trail is one of the most toe jamming routes I have ever had the displeasure to use. The mine shown at the terminus on maps is no more a mine than many others that are not shown. To reach the trailhead from Quincy, take the **Quincy-La Porte Road** about 17 miles to the **Cleghorn Bar Road (USFS 23N24)**. If you reach Onion Valley you have gone about 1/2 mile too far. Turn right, and take the **Cleghorn Bar Road** about 6 miles to its intersection with *23N67Y* and turn left. Follow this crushed black rock road about 3 miles to its dead end at a large turn-around. A good view of Dogwood Peak and the ill-conceived road below it are had from here. No Mining signs adorn a few trees as the trail begins its descent. Only occasionally does it go sidehill, and then usually at a steep grade. Near the bottom is a large natural boulder pile, a good place to keep an eye out for snakes.

ONION VALLEY CREEK TRAIL
Elevation: 3000' to 3200'
Length: +/- 1 mile
Effort: Very Difficult
Hike Time: About 1 hour
Location: T22N R8E, sections 1,6
Quadrangle Map: Dogwood Peak **(For map see page 105)**

The trailhead is reached from Quincy via 4WD road to Butte Bar and Deadman Springs. From here take the **PCT** south across the Middle Fork of the Feather River to the **Butte Bar Trail** intersection. Follow the Butte Bar Trail a short distance and soon the **Onion Valley Trail** will head east. This old and faint, yet well constructed, miners' trail is still used, and since there may be valid mining claims along it, please respect any items you might run across. The trail works along the south side about 50 to 100 feet above Onion Valley Creek. There are a number of easy ascents and descents, but there are also quite a number of obstructions and some heavy brush. Big trees and interesting rock formations above the pools and gravel stream bed make this a very pretty part of the trail. Cross several small rock fields and two seasonal drainages between which is an open area with big trees and a view of the brushy, rocky, north side of Onion Valley Creek canyon. A light descent under bluffs gives views of beautiful pools in the creek before landing at a treed flat and modern miner's camp. A homemade table has names and dates carved in it dating to 1980. Sadly, users have also left their garbage at this pretty spot. From this spot the trail continues upstream about another 3/4 to 1 mile, but it becomes quite faint, irregular and hard to follow. It is not recommended, but if you decide to continue, the trail crosses the flat and steeply ascends the short ridgeback to contour along past a large rock slab overhang at least eight feet in diameter. Thimbleberry, mid-sized Douglas fir, maple, and oak trees dominate the steep hillside. A moderate descent gives another view of the rocky north side of the canyon, crosses a seasonal draw, makes a short ascent and descent, then an easy cruise along a very straight and level portion of the creek. It's now out of the shade and into the open, then a dense fir thicket (watch for trimmings), a descent to cross a wet draw, then a steep ascent to the right and a sharp left to contour across a small rock field and ledge on a bluff. From here it is very loose and obstructed. There is a 3-foot drop off a rock and lots of up and down in rocks before the trail dwindles away to the creek. This creek, much like Nelson Creek, has several small, user maintained trails between various sections, but has no continuous trail its entire length.

OVERMEYER TRAIL

Elevation: 5200' to 4300'
Length: +/- 1 1/2 miles
Effort: Very Difficult
Hike Time: About 1 hour
Location: T21N R8E, sections 3,10,11
Quadrangle Map: American House

To reach the trailhead from Little Grass Valley Reservoir, take **USFS 94** from near the dam about 1 1/2 miles to its intersection with **Lumpkin Ridge Road (USFS 22N27)**. Follow this paved single-lane road about 4 1/2 miles to McNair Saddle. This is the original trailhead. To cut off half the trail distance, continue on the road another mile to a left turn onto graveled **USFS 21N65**. Follow this somewhat rough road 2 miles to the spot indicated later in the description. Following the maps, I wasted an entire day and evening trying to locate and follow this trail. On the east end (south side of the South Fork of the Feather River) near Lexington Hill, it is traceable a short distance before it completely disappears in the trees along the very steep hillside above the South Fork of the Feather River. At McNair Saddle on Lumpkin Ridge is the encouraging, though rodent-gnawed, sign proclaiming: **Overmeyer Trail**, South Fork Feather 2.

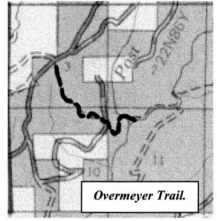

Overmeyer Trail.

Recent logging wrecked the first 1/4 mile, and it appears no work has been done to the trail in years. Head southeast and veer left, looking for blazes. It is quite difficult to see the trail because of logging, but keep on the flat along the hillside. It is still quite passable for almost 1 mile until you come to a 100-foot-wide by 200-yard-long clearcut strip that wipes out the trail for that width. Look for rocks set on the tree stumps to show the way across. A steep descent leads to a drop down the road bank onto **USFS 21N65A**. Cross the road at an angle to a painted sugar pine. Drop straight down a short distance to the obvious trail and begin a light-to-moderate descent along the hillside under old growth. The trail is better defined than above the road and seems to get more use. Shortly, what appears to be a trail is actually a firebreak running away from the trail to the south. Make a light descent with a sweeping switchback, skirt a huge blown down white fir at a switchback, and descend in semi-open ground with huge trees. Continue to descend sixteen switchbacks, occasionally glimpsing the river and its pools below. Near the last three switchbacks Post Creek is seen at left, and soon an access trail bears right. Cross Post Creek at a huge sugar pine and a bit upstream of its confluence with the South Fork of the Feather River. As for the rest of the trail shown on the map, I was unable to locate a trace of it from either end, and though I hate to argue with old maps, it sure doesn't seem to exist. As a matter of fact, the trail on the map does not follow very closely the entire trail in reality.

POORMANS CREEK ROAD-HOPKINS CREEK TRAIL
Elevation: 4800' to 4550'
Length: +/- 1/2 mile
Effort: Extremely Difficult
Hike Time: About 1 hour
Location: T22N R10E, section 2 and T23N R10E, section 35
Quadrangle Map: Blue Nose Mountain **(For map see page 106)**

Reach this trail by taking the **Poormans Creek Road (USFS 22N17)** off the **Sloat-Gibsonville Road (USFS 23N10)**, about 18 miles south of Sloat. After crossing Hopkins Creek follow the road about 1/2 mile to a fork. Stay right on the lower road **(USFS 23N45X)** and go another 1/2 mile to a point on the ridge. The unsigned trail drops off steeply on the left side of the point, and switchbacks down to the confluence of Hopkins Creek and Poormans Creek. The trail is very brushy and not maintained.

Blue Nose Mountain and the headwaters of Hopkins Creek.

RICHMOND HILL-BERG CREEK TRAIL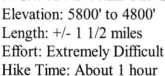
Elevation: 5800' to 4800'
Length: +/- 1 1/2 miles
Effort: Extremely Difficult
Hike Time: About 1 hour
Location: T22N R9E, section 1 and R10E, section 6
Quadrangle Map: Onion Valley **(For map see page 104)**

This historic trail is one that mapmakers insist on showing, but is now so faint and overgrown it hardly exists. To access it one must cross private land and then search the manzanita for the faint trace of trail. Once located, it meanders down the ridgeback, alternating between open expanses and heavy brush and timber. A steep brushy descent brings the trail onto a saddle on the ridgeback above Onion Valley Creek, before dropping steeply to the right toward Berg Creek and oblivion. I have listed this trail only for its historical significance, as there are now much easier ways to access Onion Valley and Berg creeks.

SAWMILL TOM TRAIL

Elevation: 5200' to 3100'
Length: +/- 2 1/2 miles
Effort: Very Difficult
Hike Time: About 2 hours
Location: T23N R9E, sections 33,28,29
Quadrangle Map: Onion Valley

This is an old pack trail that is a <u>very</u> strenuous hike back out. The trail itself is pretty well defined but is very steep, loose and not much fun for hiking. One way to avoid climbing back out is to carefully work your way down river to Cleghorn Bar and walk out the **Cleghorn Bar Road.** This option all depends on the weather, river level, your swimming ability, etc. If you are lucky you might even catch a ride out with a returning fisherman. Aspects of this trail are very similar to the **Kennedy Butte Trail**, although this one is steeper. To reach the trailhead, take the **Cleghorn Bar Road (USFS 23N24)** off the **Quincy-La Porte Road (USFS 501)**. The trailhead shown on maps is about 1/4 mile past the intersection of a spur road turning left off **Cleghorn Bar Road** (near the site of Barker's Cabin). There

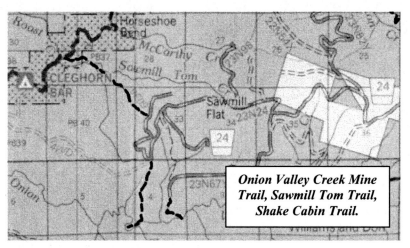

Onion Valley Creek Mine Trail, Sawmill Tom Trail, Shake Cabin Trail.

is nothing to indicate the trailhead other than a small pile of rocks on the road shoulder. The trail was logged over, but if you head straight down the hill following an open skid trail you will soon encounter the unmaintained pack trail. It is quite wide and becomes more discernible as it rounds the ridge and descends sidehill into and across a dry ravine. It continues at a moderate descent down to an intersection with **USFS 24N66Y.** For practical purposes this is now the trailhead. To reach this spot by road, pass the above-described trailhead and continue about 1/2 mile to the intersection with **USFS 24N66Y.** Turn right on that road and follow it just over a mile to where you see a small primitive road to the left. This is where the old trail hits **USFS 24N66Y** and crosses. The trail parallels the small road about 1/10 mile before crossing it and dropping steeply down the ridge. Continue paralleling the 4WD road. Old maintenance on the trail is noticeable. As the road veers right and over the ridgeback, the trail continues a moderate descent along the top and left side of the ridge. Pay special attention to the overgrown blaze marks, as the trail is quite faint in this section. Mixed conifers and oaks make a pretty setting here. As the trail enters a thick understory with a large overstory, it also becomes a much more distinct and gentle walk. Continue along the right side of the ridge then cross over to the left and begin a very steep descent. This is one trail where the map does not lie. The descent is straight down the mountain with only a slight attempt at switchbacks. The trail is under heavy cover, affording only one view of the opposite side of Last Chance Creek. As the trail steepens it begins to wind a bit more, makes a sweeping switchback, enters the live oak belt, and descends onto the ridgeback. Both sides drop off steeply, and from here you can hear Sawmill Tom Creek on the right. Continue steeply down the rocky ridgeback crossing back and forth. Make about four short, steep switchbacks, cross an old ditch, and drop to the confluence of Last Chance and Sawmill Tom creeks. A nylon rope has been tied to a tree to help make the ascent back out. Cross Sawmill Tom Creek and ascend sidehill to the west to the ditch. Follow the ditch west to where it makes a deep cut in the ridgeback and crosses to the right side of the ridge. A faint trail also splits off here and drops down to a point on the river upstream of our destination about 1 mile. Our trail continues along the ridge top before beginning a steep, winding descent down the ridgeback. There is a very nice view from a point on the ridge top just off the trail. Follow the trail back and forth across the ridgeback in rocks and manzanita, making a very steep descent to two switchbacks and a quick drop to the river. There is a nice campsite just upstream from where Last Chance Creek empties into the Middle Fork.

SAWPIT FLAT TRAIL
Elevation: 5477' to 6400'
Length: +/- 1 1/2 miles
Effort: Moderate
Hike Time: About 1 1/2 hours
Location: T22N R10E, sections 5,6 and T23N R10E, section 31
Quadrangle Map: Onion Valley **(For map see page 104)**

Reach this obscure trail and trailhead by taking the ***Quincy-LaPorte Road*** south from ***Highway 70*** to the ***Cleghorn Bar Road (USFS 23N24)*** just before Onion Valley. To find the trail, walk across the open field on the right side of both roads to the base of the hill slope. The trail at this point is actually an old wagon road. It passes just beneath a modern-day snow gauge as it also parallels the ***Cleghorn Bar Road.*** As the wagon road nears a mule ear patch, it begins dropping away toward the present road. The trail continues at an almost indiscernible ascent out of the trees and now across the mule ear patch, touching a stand of timber in its center. In this section the trail is almost non-existent. Upon entering the trees at the opposite side of the field, the trail becomes evident again, though faint. There are no blazes but the trail soon resembles a wagon road again. Make a gradual ascent through open, rocky ground with a number of ancient stumps along the way. Make a light descent and cross another large mule ear patch with scattered trees and five or six dry freshets to cross. Look for ducks along the trail here. The much narrower, but well-defined trail makes a slight dip, then a light ascent as it passes out of small trees and into another mule ear patch. A moderate ascent brings the trail to the ridgeback where it gradually rounds it under shade of larger trees. Note the very old and very tall stump below the trail, a remnant of logging for the mines in deep snow. Continue at a light descent along the hillside. As you descend you might notice a second trail paralleling just above. The two soon connect, then the trail makes a slight ascent, levels out, then lightly descends past a left-hand switchback, and after one more small mule ear patch reaches a private property line and heavily logged parcel. A skid road runs along the property line, and if you follow it down it will take you right to the **Cleghorn Bar Road (USFS 23N24)**.

SAWPIT FLAT WAGON ROAD TRAIL
Elevation: 6280' to 5800'
Length: +/- 1 1/2 miles
Effort: Very Difficult
Hike Time: About 1 1/2 hours
Location: T22N R10E, sections 6,7
Quadrangle Map: Onion Valley **(For map see page 104)**

This wagon road was abandoned just after construction of the **La Porte-Quincy Road** in 1867. It is now very overgrown with brush and trees, and the original surface has eroded to a cobbly finish. In several places it is so overgrown it is easy to lose. I list it as I have others of its type because of its historical significance. The trail starts at a logging spur near the west line of section 7 on **USFS 22N60**. It works through a logged off area to a swale at the head of a fairly steep draw. From that point the road drops down the draw, crosses at an angle, and works sidehill and onto the flat top of the ridge. It then descends to a wet area overgrown with bushes, crosses through, and continues down the ridge to make a right turn and drop to Onion Valley Creek. A bridge built of cedar logs once spanned the creek here. After crossing it makes a moderate ascent on a rocky, open face up Ohio Ravine to the old Sawpit Flat and Richmond Hill mines.

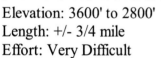

SEVEN FALLS TRAIL (Butte County)
Elevation: 3600' to 2800'
Length: +/- 3/4 mile
Effort: Very Difficult
Hike Time: About 1/2 hour
Location: T21N R7E, section 6
Quadrangle Map: Cascade

This does not really qualify as a true trail, but rather as a scramble. The redeeming feature here is the spectacular falls (actually a series of nine falls of 60 to 100 feet each). Though it is a tough hike, the short, steep path down to Seven Falls is well worth the effort. Be extremely careful because in some spots it is only a scramble among boulders. To reach the trailhead from Brush Creek, take the **Milsap Bar Road** off the **Oroville-Quincy Road** 7 miles into the Middle Fork of the Feather River. Cross the Middle Fork and climb out 3 1/2 miles of very rough road to a flat spot on the ridge about 2 1/4 miles north of **Hartman Bar Road**. Look for a slight turnout on the west side of the road with an old log. The trail begins here. A very steep descent of about 3/4 mile will take you to the falls. Be careful here, one slip and it can be all over. The thunder and the spray are really quite exhilarating. Pompey's Point, a chunk of granite, overlooks the pools of Seven Falls. Native American Maidu legend says Pompey was a shaman who drew his spiritual strength from these falls. If you would rather view the entire set of falls without the effort and danger of going right to them, there is an alternative. A very short distance before the above trailhead is a large wide spot in the road where it rounds the ridge. Park here and walk west along the sidehill a short distance, and then drop steeply down the ridgeback (there may be orange ribbons to guide you) to a spot in the manzanita with a spectacular view. If you are coming from Oroville and Feather Falls, follow the paved

On the edge of one of the Seven Falls.

road past the Cascade cutoff about 3 miles to a sharp switchback. Veer right on the dirt road skirting an old clearcut. Follow this road about 3 miles on a gradual descent to the trailhead mentioned above.

SHAKE CABIN TRAIL
Elevation: 5000' to 3700'
Length: +/- 1 mile
Effort: Very Difficult
Hike Time: About 1 hour
Location: T22N R9E, section 4
Quadrangle Map: Onion Valley **(For map see page 126)**

This is another user-maintained trail that demands your respect of property rights. The trailhead is near the center of section 4, T22N and section 33, T23N R9E along the **Cleghorn Bar Road.** To reach this point, take the **La Porte-Quincy Road** about 17 miles south of Quincy, or 15 miles north of La Porte to the signed turnoff. Follow the **Cleghorn Bar Road** about 7 miles west to the above trailhead (the **Cleghorn Bar Road** bears right and down, and an overgrown log landing can be seen to the left). Go through the landing and follow the narrow 4WD road down to where it turns to a single track and crosses the old Last Chance water ditch. A steep descent through small trees gives way to heavy old growth, then winds more moderately into the open. The limestone bluffs above Limestone Creek are visible to the right as is a limited view down Onion Valley Creek canyon. To the south is Dogwood Peak and Stag Point. The descent continues along the ridge spine to a switchback. An equipment skid trail continues steeply and straight down. Make a long descent through live oaks to another switchback, another long descent that crosses the equipment skid trail, five more switchbacks under live oak and big conifers, and cross a dry ravine at another switchback. A steep descent takes the trail past the ruins of a log cabin used until the 1960s, crosses the same ravine again, and finally becomes a very pleasant, gentle walk down Onion Valley Creek. In a short distance the trail comes to a small one-room shake cabin built before the 1940s. It is maintained as a storage facility for small-scale mining. The trail now passes it and gently climbs to the top of the ridge behind the cabin. From here the trail drops steeply and is a lightly maintained bar-to-bar access trail.

UPPER NELSON CREEK TRAIL
Elevation: 4174' to 4800'
Length: +/- 4 miles
Effort: Very Difficult
Hike Time: About 6 hours
Location: T23N R10E, sections 22,23,26
Quadrangle Map: Blue Nose Mountain **(For map see page 106)**

The unsigned trailhead is about 11 miles up the paved **Quincy-La Porte Road** from the intersection of that road and **State Highway 70** in Quincy. As you round the last point about 1/2 mile north of and before the Nelson Creek bridge, the trail takes off to your left. Recent road construction has destroyed the trailhead. If you can pick it up above the road, the faint trail traces a few switchbacks up the south side of the ridge to just short of a saddle. Here the trail becomes more distinct, although it is very brushy. Views of Nelson Creek far below are glimpsed occasionally. The trail base is very wide in parts, a reminder of its use as a pack trail. It continues to work its way in and out of small ravines and gullies before descending across Golden Creek. After climbing out of Golden Creek it passes into an overgrown burn from 1934, making it difficult to follow. As the trail works around into Coldwater Creek it becomes lost entirely. The **Sloat-Gibsonville Road (USFS 23N10)** is not too far above the trail at this point.

WATSON CABIN-ABANDONED FEATHER FALLS TRAIL (Butte County)
Elevation: 3400' to 2600'
Length: +/- 1 mile
Effort: Very Difficult
Hike Time: About 1 hour
Location: T21N R6E, sections 22,23
Quadrangle Map: Brush Creek **(For map see page 103)**

Some folks in this area have a propensity for tearing down trail and road signs. You will have to exercise acute map skills and common sense to find your way around the myriad of roads here. Some roads that the Forest Service insists on showing on their maps have been overgrown for years, others are closed by gates or berms. Many are not even shown on the maps. This trail is an extremely steep path that ends up connecting with the never finished **Abandoned Feather Falls Trail.** It seems to me to be a trail thrown in to mitigate some of the loss of that trail (built by volunteers). If you want to hike this trail down to the **Abandoned Feather Falls Trail** and then return by hiking that trail out to its trailhead, it is only a little over a mile back by road to the start. This trailhead is shared with the ***Watson Cabin-Feather Falls Trail.*** To reach the trailhead from the town of Feather Falls stay on the pavement all the way to the top of Watson Ridge. There is a cattle loading chute on the right side of the road. Turn left onto the crushed rock road ***(USFS 21N24)*** and follow about 1 mile past the intersection with ***USFS 21N92.*** Continue another 3/4 mile to the intersection with ***USFS 21N25*** and take a left on that road. Follow this road past a number of unsigned intersections. It is the most obvious road and maintains somewhat the same grade with a few ups and downs. It will wind in and out, turn from crushed rock to rutted dirt, pass through an open, bouldery area and re-enter heavy pine forest. The trailhead is virtually unnoticeable. When you see Bald Rock Dome across the canyon and ahead of you, you have gone about 50 yards too far. My odometer gives me a distance of 8 1/2 miles from the pavement to the trailhead. After all this, park in any one of the several wide spots on the road. The trail begins on the south in a ponderosa pine plantation that has been well cleared. As you leave this short section, the ***Watson Cabin-Feather Falls Trail*** drops straight down the hill. Our trail swings to the right and begins a moderate descent through a controlled burn area. What were switchbacks have now been almost totally obliterated by hikers cutting through them. The trail winds down the ridgeback under ponderosa pine cover with occasional open areas, then makes a very steep descent, then a short easy grade, then steepens and moderates off and on and suddenly drops steeply to the right. Cross an old mining ditch and you are at a refreshing little stream. You have also just connected with the ***Abandoned Feather Falls Trail.*** From here it is a nice hike out to that trailhead. See the ***Abandoned Feather Falls Trail*** for a description of that route.

The 1880's Harrington Cabin on Poormans Creek.

WATSON RIDGE TRAIL (Butte County)
Elevation: 3300' to 3700'
Length: +/- 1 1/2 miles (3 1/2 to Pompeys Creek area - not recommended)
Effort: Difficult (Very Difficult to Pompeys Creek area - not recommended)
Hike Time: About 1 hour (3 hours to Pompeys Creek area - not recommended)
Location: T21N R6E, sections 22,23 (13,14, to Pompeys Creek area - not recommended)
Quadrangle Map: Brush Creek **(For map see page 103)**

For the most part this is a pleasant hike, though there are some rough and dangerous spots, hence the difficult rating. The section to Pompeys Creek area is definitely not worth the effort at this writing. What starts out with promise ends up a real fistfight. Not only is it a moderate downhill grade almost the entire distance, it is covered with windfalls and there are no views. Although maintenance has been performed recently, it has only been on the first section. In addition, the trail is not completed and ends in a dangerous rock cliff area. Leave it go until it is completed. To reach the trailhead for the more pleasant and first mile of the trail, take the route described for the *Abandoned Feather Falls Trail*. Once there, the trailhead is directly east and about 50 yards from the other trail. It, too, is unsigned, but with a little looking around you will see it. It begins with a gentle, shaded walk that soon becomes steeper. There are fleeting views of the Middle Fork of the Feather River, the *Milsap Bar Road*, and some houses on the north side of the river. You might also notice the scars on some of the black oaks, a result of girdling the tree in an attempt to kill it. The Forest Service, back in their intensive timber managing days, did this. The trail now becomes steeper and runs into small black oaks, gets steeper still and very poor due to erosion. Shortly, the trail levels out again as it descends to a slight saddle and a large rotted stump on the right. A short distance before the saddle you will notice evidence of logging from years past. At the stump, the trail makes a right angle turn and gently drops down to the closed *Watson Cabin Road*. You will realize you have missed this turn if you continue down a nice trail at a bit steeper grade. This means you are on your way toward Pompeys Creek area. Turn back! Either direction you take on the *Watson Cabin Road* will take you back to *USFS 21N25A,* although if you are parked at the trailhead, you will be better off to walk south toward the *Watson Cabin-Abandoned Feather Falls* trailhead and follow the road back around.

The historic Cascade Hotel, located in Plumas County's southernmost town.

WEST BRANCH NELSON CREEK TRAIL
Elevation: 5300' to 4900'
Length: +/- 1 1/2 miles
Effort: Very Difficult
Hike Time: About 2 hours
Location: T22N R11E, sections 7,18
Quadrangle Map: Blue Nose Mountain **(For map see page 106)**

This trail takes off of the end of *USFS 22N41*, 2 miles from the *Johnsville-La Porte Road*, about 12 miles west of Johnsville, or about 8 miles east of Gibsonville. There are a number of old cabin ruins and mining claims at the trailhead. This old mining trail has become more of a fisherman's trail and is quite difficult to follow. It is also intermittent and very faint as it descends along the east bank of West Nelson Creek. It begins by dropping steeply to cross Frenchman Ravine, then continues down across Four Bits Creek, both names reminiscent of gold rush days. Please respect the two old cabins that are private property along the creek. At trail's end you may ford the creek and take the 4WD road about 1 1/2 miles to the *Sloat-Gibsonville Road (USFS 23N10).*

ZUMWALT FLAT-NELSON CREEK TRAIL

Elevation: 4600' to 4400'
Length: +/- 1/2 mile
Effort: Moderate
Hike Time: About 1/2 hour
Location: T23N R10E, sections 35,36
Quadrangle Map: Blue Nose Mountain **(For map see page 106)**

Reach the trailhead via the *Sloat-Gibsonville Road (USFS 23N10)*, about 15 miles south of Sloat. Sloat is east of Quincy about 14 miles via *Highway 70.* The trail starts at a modern day miner's camp, about 1/2 mile north of the Nelson Creek Bridge. Walk around a locked gate at the entrance to the camp road on the west side and descend past the camp. The trail runs at a nice descent to Nelson Creek, just below the mouth of Hopkins Creek. This trail is a miner-maintained trail. Again, please respect their property.

Mt. Etna at the head of Hopkins Creek.

CENTRAL PLUMAS COUNTY
Including Bucks Lake Wilderness and a Portion of Butte County

Bounded on the south by the Middle Fork of the Feather River and on the north by the East Branch and North Fork of the same stream, this region is more populated, has more roads, and therefore, is more developed than the southern part of the county. However, the beautiful countryside contains many trails, a wilderness area, and other intriguing features, one of which is Quincy, the county seat, and largest community in Plumas County. By making Quincy a base, hiking and sightseeing opportunities are available in all directions. The Middle Fork of the Feather River is one of the most rugged, wild, native trout fisheries in the state. Designated a Wild & Scenic River in 1964, it is off limits to motorized vehicles except in designated areas. The East Branch and North Fork share a rich history of gold mining. For more on that aspect of the area read The Shirley Letters, Fariss & Smith's 1882 History of Plumas County, and other titles listed in the beginning of this guide. The area is accessible from the Sacramento Valley by traveling to Oroville and then taking either the Bucks Lake Road or State Route 70, a National Forest Scenic Byway, east into the mountains. Another route from Sacramento is to take interstate 80 to California State Route 89 (another Scenic Byway) at Truckee and proceed north. Travelers from Reno may take U.S. 395 to State Highway 70 and proceed west.

Bald Rock Canyon from the north rim.

BIG BALD ROCK TRAIL (Butte County)
Elevation: 3100' to 3270'
Length: +/- 1/2 mile
Effort: Easy
Hike Time: About 1/2 hour
Location: T21N R6E, section 30
Quadrangle Map: Brush Creek

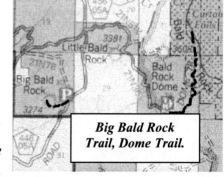
Big Bald Rock Trail, Dome Trail.

Reach the trailhead via the ***Oroville-Bucks Lake Road (Highway 162)*** about 24 miles from Oroville. At Berry Creek, turn right on ***Bald Rock Road*** and follow the dirt road about 1 1/4 miles to the parking area. From Quincy, travel about 45 miles west on the ***Oroville-Quincy Road*** to the Brush Creek Work Center. Take ***Bald Rock Road*** approximately 4 miles south to ***USFS Road 21N33Y*** (old Big Bald Rock Picnic Area). This road is not signed so look carefully for the road turning back into the trees. Just opposite the turn off is a

Forest Service seasonal billboard. This trail starts up a seasonal creek then quickly reaches the open granite monolith of Big Bald Rock. Nice granite, bad graffiti. As you leave the creek, bear left up the granite. It is a quick, easy climb to the top of Big Bald Rock. There are great views of the Sacramento Valley and Coast Range, as well as evidence of the Maidu Indians in the form of grinding bowls worn into the rock. The monster Uino, of Maidu folklore, protects the Middle Fork of the Feather River, far below.

BUCKHORN MINE TRAIL
Elevation: 4400' to 4000'
Length: +/- 1/2 mile
Effort: Difficult
Hike Time: About 1 hour
Location: T23N R10E, section 7
Quadrangle Map: Blue Nose Mountain

In the 1850s, gold miners scoured the rivers and streams of this area. The Buckhorn Mine is a remnant of those days, but is now under private ownership. To reach the trailhead take **State Highway 70** about 12 miles east of Quincy to Lee Summit.

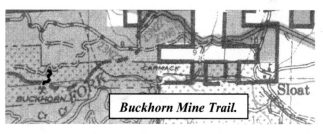
Buckhorn Mine Trail.

Turn right on **USFS 23N22** at the summit and travel about 1 mile to **USFS 23N22A**. Follow this spur about 1 1/2 miles to the Middle Fork of the Feather River Wild and Scenic boundary. The trail switchbacks steeply to the Middle Fork. In summer it can be quite hot.

BUCKS CREEK TRAIL
Elevation: 5520' to 5200'
Length: +/- 2 miles
Effort: Very Easy
Hike Time: About 1 hour
Location: T24N R8E, section 31 and T24N R7E, section 36 and T23N R8E, section 6 and T23N R7E, section 1
Quadrangle Map: Bucks Lake

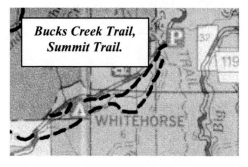
Bucks Creek Trail, Summit Trail.

From Quincy, take the **Bucks Lake Road** west about 14 miles to Bucks Summit where there are restrooms and a parking area. Walk west on the pavement about 1/4 mile to the trailhead, which is on the left, or south side, of the road. The trail parallels Bucks Creek at a distance as it descends through meadows and forest. It is not too well marked so keep a sharp eye out for the path. At one point it touches the **Bucks Lake Road** at a parking spot. As the trail nears White Horse Campground it crosses Bucks Creek over a washed out culvert. Enter the campground and if desired, go left through the campground where the trail resumes for a short distance before intersecting the **Bucks Lake Road** opposite the trailhead for the **Mill Creek Trail.** This hike combined with the **Summit Trail** makes a nice loop hike.

CAMP RODGERS SADDLE TRAIL

Elevation: 2200' to 5200'
Length: +/- 3 miles
Effort: Very Difficult
Hike Time: About 3 hours
Location: T24N R6E, sections 2,11,12
Quadrangle Map: Storrie

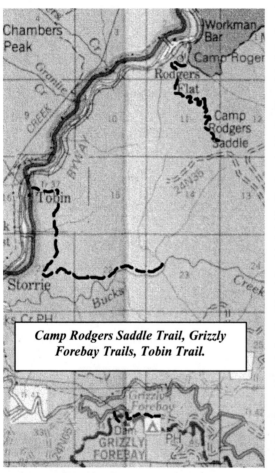

Camp Rodgers Saddle Trail, Grizzly Forebay Trails, Tobin Trail.

Unfortunately, this trail suffered fire damage during the Storrie Fire of 2000. But, as noted previously, the chance to observe Mother Nature recovering should not be overlooked. This would be a good trail for an ambitious and enthusiastic trail group to adopt. It has some nice views, particularly in spring and fall when the oak leaves are off the trees. The trail base for the most part is in good condition, but brush and trees are taking over again. The last mile to Camp Rodgers Saddle is also indiscernible. However, I enjoyed the hike up to where I lost the trail. The trailhead is about 32 miles west of Quincy on **Highway 70**, just past Belden. Camp Rodgers is a P.G. & E. facility with a gated bridge that is locked weekends and nights. (They really do lock it, I know from experience.) It is best to park across from the bridge along the highway and walk the 1/2 mile or so over to the trailhead. To find the trailhead cross the bridge and go left past the P.G. & E. buildings and parking lot to a dirt road paralleling the Union Pacific Railroad. Follow this to a locked gate at a cement underpass. Walk through the underpass and about 100 feet after exiting it, you will see a decayed and illegible sign and post on the right side of the road. The trailhead is eroded away here so scramble up where you can. The trail heads left at a slight ascent along an iron water pipe. On the left about 50 yards from the first switchback is a USDA survey monument. As the trail hits a small dry ravine make the switchback. The trail base is very good, but the brush is quite heavy. The trail now winds moderately up a grassy, black oak studded-knoll to the ridgeback. From here there is a nice view of Milk Ranch Creek and the **Three Lakes Road**. The trail makes a moderate ascent on the ridge back with glimpses of the P.G. & E. station through the trees below. The ascent becomes heavier under mixed conifers and oaks. There are also overgrown blazes on some of the larger trees now. Cross the ridge onto the southeast side and break into the open. Make a steep ascent to a short switchback at a dry gulch and then almost immediately make another steep switchback. Pass an old sawn cedar stump, cross a dry ravine, and ascend along the rocky slope to a good view of the Feather River, **Highway 70,** and the Union Pacific Railroad. The trail base is good through this section as you continue to ascend and cross another dry ravine. It is also well shaded here. As the trail ascends into a live stream it becomes rocky and brushy. Cross the stream (which has a pretty 10-foot fall) and continue contouring and ascending to a large ponderosa pine where the trail makes a light descent through scrub oak to another live stream. Cross and make a moderate ascent in an easterly direction to a switchback, make another switchback at a seasonal stream, and then make a moderate-to-heavy ascent. Great views of the canyon and the rocky mountainsides on the north side of it can be had here. You might also notice large amounts of bear scat on the trail. As you ascend note the small rock wall on the high side of the trail. The ascent becomes somewhat steeper and the trail makes a series of five switchbacks. A long, moderate ascent leads to a switchback that is almost non-existent. It is in a group of old growth trees and is where you can look down into the rocky canyon of the last stream crossed. Make another seven switchbacks, one with a view of the **Three Lakes Road,** which is considerably closer now, before the trail soon disappears in the brush. There are several rotted pine snags with old blazes evident, but due to brush and snowdrifts, I was not able to locate the last mile of trail.

Looking north across the North Fork Feather River from Camp Rodgers Saddle Trail.

CASCADES TRAIL
Elevation: 3200' to 3250'
Length: +/- 2 miles
Effort: Easy
Hike Time: About 1 hour
Location: T25N R9E, sections 25,26
Quadrangle Map: Crescent Mills, Quincy **(For map see page 138)**

To reach this trail, take **State Highway 70** north from Quincy about 6 miles to the **Old Keddie Highway**. Follow this paved one lane road about 1 mile east to where it makes a switchback. At this point drive straight ahead on the rough dirt road about 1/2 mile to ample parking. The trail is a wide, smooth, almost level walk to the set of five small but impressive falls on Spanish Creek. This trail was originally built in 1876 as the Maxwell Mining Co. Ditch to take water over ten miles or so down the Feather River Canyon to a hydraulic mine. 30 years later it was converted by the Utah Construction Co. as a supply road for building the Western Pacific Railroad. After reaching Cascades you can continue

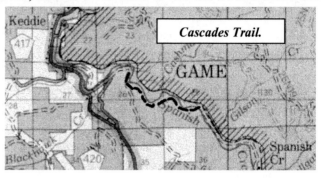

Cascades Trail.

upstream about one more mile to the lower end of Oakland Camp, a summer camp operated by the City of Oakland. In summer a bridge is set across the creek to access the dead-end dirt road from the camp, about one mile above. This road is rough with protruding rocks. Be very careful at the Cascades as the small bridge across a declivity has only one handhold, though the bridge is strong. This trail has some very impressive scenery and was featured in the national magazine <u>Walking</u> in 2000. It is ideal for a family picnic outing. Good swimming holes are also available.

DEADMAN SPRINGS TRAIL

Elevation: 3600' to 3000'
Length: +/- 1/2 mile (1 1/4 miles if using old trail)
Effort: Difficult
Hike Time: About 1 hour (1 1/2 hours if using old trail)
Location: T23N R8E, section 35 (also 26 if using old trail)
Quadrangle Map: Dogwood Peak

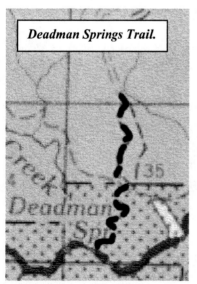

Deadman Springs Trail.

To reach the trailhead travel west from Quincy about 10 miles to the **Big Creek Road** (new **Bucks Lake Road**). Follow it several miles to **USFS 24N28**. Follow this road about 8 miles to the unsigned **Butte Bar 4WD Road**. Take the 4WD road about 2 1/2 miles down to Deadman Springs. (If you are walking and want to hike about 3/4 mile of trail on the way down the 4WD road, look for a blazed ponderosa pine on the right about halfway down the road. The trail makes a moderate drop along the side of the ridge above Bear Creek and though it is not maintained, it is well defined. After crossing several swales it reconnects with the 4WD road at a large switchback). Near here you will cross the **Pacific Crest Trail** running from Onion Valley to Bucks Summit. A right-hand fork in the road takes you to the desired trail, an old steam engine boiler, and a parking area. The left fork takes you to private property. From Deadman Springs there is a graded incline that was used for hauling mining equipment down to the river. A series of switchbacks also works down to the Middle Fork from the springs. Good fishing is to be found at Bear Creek, which flows into the Middle Fork here.

DOME TRAIL (Butte County)
Elevation: 2800' to 1000'
Length: +/- 2 miles
Effort: Moderate
Hike Time: About 1 hour
Location: T21N R6E, sections 21,28
Quadrangle Map: Brush Creek **(For map see page 134)**

This is one of the easiest and most pleasant Middle Fork hikes I have ever made. If it weren't for the stairs being so steep, I would rate this trail as easy. The railings and stairs have been installed due to several very serious mishaps over the past several years. Spring is a very good time to do this trail because it is cooler, the oaks are not in full leaf yet (giving better views), and the river is quite impressive at high water. Reach this trail by taking the *Oroville-Bucks Lake Road* to Brush Creek, about 24 miles northeast of Oroville, or 45 miles west of Quincy (via the *Oroville-Bucks Lake-Quincy Road*). Turn right on the *Bald Rock Road (USFS 21N50Y)*. After about 1/2 mile pass the *Milsap Bar Road* on the left and continue on *Bald Rock Road* 2 miles to a four-way intersection with *Zink Road* and *USFS 21N51Y*. Turn left on *21N51Y* and follow this winding road through a small portion of private property about 1 1/2 miles to a three-way intersection with a sign pointing to the trailhead 0.3 miles ahead. Continue the short distance to ample parking at the trailhead. The trail begins as a closed 4WD road and makes an easy descent under a mixed forest complemented with huge manzanita (a hallmark of this region). After a short distance the old and overgrown road continues down the ridge to the right while our now single-track trail drops to the left at a group of granite boulders. Make an easy descent through three switchbacks to a small stream, switchback onto an old ditch, cross another small stream and round the ridge into another drainage. Make four more switchbacks, cross a stream and, as you round the ridge, hear the river thundering below. Make two more switchbacks under live oak and through a small burn started by careless smokers in the fall of 1995. Make two more switchbacks, cross a creek with a nice set of falls, descend to another switchback and a slight view of the canyon. Make eight switchbacks and get the first good view of the river and falls upstream. Please don't cut through the switchbacks, others already have and it has created an erosion problem. Another switchback gives a great view of Bald Rock Dome, then a series of six easy switchbacks take you right under the shadow of the Dome. Make a slight ascent across a small rocky freshet (with falls above), an easy ascent with guardrails and a nice view of the river, then a light descent with two switchbacks to yet more guard rails. Cross a spring running off the granite face with a great view of the river directly under the trail. A stairway of rock descends to a very steep wood stairway, then levels out with railings. Wind down a boulder patch with more rock steps, yet more steep, winding rock stairs to a switchback, and cross a small stream. The trail then winds among rocks and brush, descends more steps to a closer view of the river thundering past, and then descends to an extremely narrow declivity in the rock and the end of the trail.

FIVE BEAR MINE-BACH CREEK TRAIL 10E16
Elevation: 4400' to 4800'
Length: +/- 3 miles
Effort: Moderate
Hike Time: About 3 hours
Location: T23N R10E, sections 17,18
Quadrangle Map: Onion Valley

Bach Creek was originally named Bachelder's Creek for J.B. Bachelder, builder of the first sawmill in Plumas County. He constructed his water-powered mill at the mouth of this creek on the Middle Fork of the Feather River to supply lumber to the miners of Rich Bar, just upstream. Rich Bar was the site of large fluming operations in the summer of 1851, baring the bed of the river to the gold seekers. Over the years the name of his creek was shortened to Bach Creek. Reach the trailhead by taking **La Porte-Quincy Road** about 7 miles to signed **USFS 23N92**. Go 2 miles to a Y and continue left on **USFS 23N92A** for 1 mile to Lost Cabin Springs. The trailhead is about 1/2 mile down the road from Lost Cabin Springs proper. 4WD is recommended. The trail contours along the canyon side, while the **Lost Cabin Springs-Sugar Pine Mine Trail** drops steeply to the left. A moderately level trail, it is somewhat narrow in spots, especially as it passes under the shoulder of the limestone formation known as Little Volcano. Several springs cross the trail about midway to Bach Creek. The first 2 miles are mostly through oak and brush-covered slopes, so it can be usually pretty warm in summer. At Bach Creek the crossing is obvious, but the trail on the other side isn't. Keep your eyes open as you make a moderately steep ascent out of Bach Creek. There are numerous smaller blazed trails made by campers and hikers that can confuse you. The trail tends to work its way southwest along and around the ridge to the Five Bear Mine where it connects with the **Claremont Peak-Five Bear Mine 4WD**

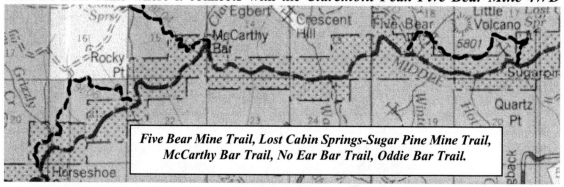

Five Bear Mine Trail, Lost Cabin Springs-Sugar Pine Mine Trail, McCarthy Bar Trail, No Ear Bar Trail, Oddie Bar Trail.

Road from Quincy. There are many nice views of the Middle Fork of the Feather River from this trail, and at Five Bear Mine the river is nice for swimming.

GRIZZLY FOREBAY GAUGING STATION TRAIL
Elevation: 4200' to 4100'
Length: +/- 1/4 mile
Effort: Easy
Hike Time: 1/4 hour
Location: T232N R6E, section 2 and T24N R6E, section 34
Quadrangle Map: Storrie **(For map see page 136)**

The trail begins at the ***Grizzly Forebay Trail*** trailhead (see description below). It leaves the road west of the parking area and meanders along under the road to the dam and the gauging station. Be careful as the banks are steep.

GRIZZLY FOREBAY TRAIL
Elevation: 4300' to 4300'
Length: +/- 3/4 mile
Effort: Easy
Hike Time: 1/2 hour
Location: T23N R6E, section 2 and T24N R6E, sections 34,35
Quadrangle Map: Storrie **(For map see page 136)**

Reach the trailhead at Grizzly Forebay by taking the ***Oroville-Bucks Lake-Quincy Road*** 2 1/2 miles west of Bucks Lake from the ***Big Creek Road*** intersection. A sign at the right turn gives the distance as 10 miles. Follow this narrow but paved road about 7 miles to a signed left turn and rough gravel ***(USFS 24N34)***. Continue about 2 1/2 miles to another left ***(USFS 24N34Y)*** that is paved and heads steeply down about 1/2 mile to the Grizzly Forebay parking lot, heliport, and restrooms. A sign near the ADA accessible restroom reads: Grizzly Forebay Walk-in 3/4 mile. Drop three flights of stairs to a flat above the water and turn left past the icon signs indicating the direction to the campground. (An alternative is to go to the east end of the parking lot and drop one flight of stairs and a moderately steep pitch to connect with the main trail. From here the trail makes moderate but short ascents and descents, crosses a small stream, then winds down to the lake level and high water mark. As it meanders it passes four campsites, crosses another small stream, and forks three ways. The right fork continues at lake level, the middle fork climbs up and over a short ridge to reconnect with the right fork, and the left fork runs uphill to (strangely enough) ADA restrooms that are somewhat inaccessible, except possibly by boat. The campsites are pleasant and sport tables and fire pits and seclusion. The drawback is the annoying siren-like noise that the hydro facility at the head of the lake makes. Where the middle trail and the left trail reconnect is the end.

HARTMAN BAR TRAIL (North)

Elevation: 5200' to 2400'
Length: +/- 4 1/2 miles
Effort: Moderate
Hike Time: About 2 hours
Location: T23N R7E, section 34 and T22N R7E, sections 2,3,11,14
Quadrangle Map: Haskins Valley

The road signs to this trailhead at least point in the correct direction, even if the distances are all balled up. Reach the trailhead by traveling about 10 miles west from Quincy on the **Bucks Lake Road** to the **Big Creek Road** (new **Bucks Lake Road**). Follow it about 8 miles to a left turn on the signed **Hartman Bar Road** and climb about one mile to an offset five-way intersection. Stay to the right following the Hartman Bar signs. Follow this well-graveled road about 4 miles to a four-way signed intersection. Go left about 2 miles to another signed four-way intersection. Continue following this road another mile to a T intersection. A sign will direct you left on **USFS 23N60** 1 mile to the trailhead road. The last 1/2 mile of road can be slippery if the weather is wet, so if you don't have 4WD you may want to park on the main road. A sign at the trailhead notes that the Middle Fork is 4.4 miles and Hartman Bar Ridge is 8.4 miles. This extremely well maintained trail descends gradually the entire way to the Middle Fork of the Feather River. In the first mile you will make seven very gradual switchbacks. Also note the **California Riding & Hiking Trail** signs from the 1940s-50s. About 1/2 mile down the trail is a small spring with a pipe. Although it is a closed source spring, it is recommended that you carry your own water. As the trail continues to drop it passes

View of Middle Fork Feather River from near Willow Creek.

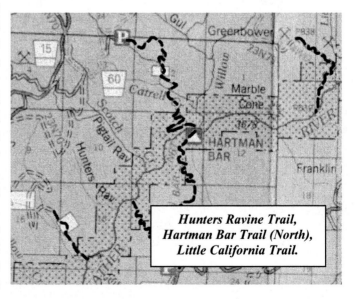

Hunters Ravine Trail, Hartman Bar Trail (North), Little California Trail.

through a beautiful mixed old growth forest. Soon after crossing a low saddle it passes along a hillside covered with black oak. After making a switchback in this section note the vandalized sign pointing out the tallest ponderosa pine in the United States (or world). It is about 100 feet east and above the trail. Here are the particulars on this mammoth: 334' tall, 24' circumference, 7 1/2' diameter, and approximately 25,000 board feet. Just past this the trail passes through private property and the site of an old home and apple orchard. Again, please respect the property owner's rights. The trail makes about three more switchbacks, crosses Catrell Creek, and then

Overgrown Riding & Hiking Trail sign from the 1940s.

makes another six switchbacks along its route down the oak-covered hillside. Glimpses of Marble Cone and the river below are seen from here. About 1/2 mile from the river a good view of the Hartman Bar Bridge is afforded from an opening in the brush. Shortly before reaching the river the trail makes two more switchbacks. At the river is a new steel suspension bridge replacing the old wood one. The Dan Beebe Campground on the south side of the river has several nice campsites. The large cut in the bedrock at the bridge was made in the early 1900's by miners working the bed of the river. The ***Hartman Bar National Recreation Trail*** ascends the hill on the south side, approximately 4 miles to ***USFS 22N42Y*** off the ***Hartman Bar Ridge Road***, accessible from Little Grass Valley Reservoir. As with many lower-elevation trails, watch out for poison oak. For more on the ***Hartman Bar Trail (South)***, see the Southern Plumas County section.

HEINZ CREEK TRAIL (Butte County)

Elevation: 1380' to 2800'
Length: +/- 1 3/4 miles
Effort: Moderate
Hike Time: About 2 hours
Location: T23N R5E, sections 32,33
Quadrangle Map: Pulga

Heinz Creek Trail.

This short trail winds quickly up the canyonside to a long ridge and the end of a 4WD road. A small explanation attached to the ***Heinz Creek Trail*** sign informs hikers that the trail is maintained as an access in case of forest fire. The beginning has some erosion damage from heavy rains in 1997. Adopted some years ago by the students of Concow School, they spent many hours clearing and cleaning the trail and erecting posts with identifying signs of nearby plants. There is somewhere in the neighborhood of two-dozen of these markers. The trail is very well-maintained, and a pleasant, though somewhat exerting hike. The trail is actually a bit longer than the 1 1/2 miles the sign indicates. Reach the trailhead by traveling about 48 miles west of Quincy on ***State Route 70*** to Poe Dam, or 28 miles east from Oroville. Just before the dam itself you will see a small area to park at the trailhead. The trail winds quickly up a small draw making about five switchbacks, contours for a time, then makes three more. For a few moments the trail breaks into the open, gently ascends west and passes the 1/2-mile marker. Occasionally you will get a fleeting glimpse up the Feather River canyon, but for the most part the trail is under a heavy canopy of mixed oak and Douglas fir. The trail rounds the ridge into the Mill Creek drainage, passes an old phone line, makes about seven short, easy switchbacks up and over the ridge back, and then begins a long, gradual ascent to the east. Along this section is the 1-mile marker. Not far from here the trail utilizes an abandoned road, makes a switchback on the road (where a faint trail crosses the road and continues easterly), leaves the road on and off again, passes the 1 1/2-mile marker, makes two more switchbacks and reaches the ridge top and end of a 4WD road. There is a nice view of the upper end of Mill Creek from here. An old mine site off to the south 1/2 mile or so holds nothing of interest.

HUNTER'S RAVINE TRAIL
Elevation: 3600' to 2100'
Length: +/- 1 mile
Effort: Very Difficult
Hike Time: About 1 hour
Location: T22N R7E, sections 15,16,22
Quadrangle Map: Haskins Valley **(For map see page 142)**

Please note that some USFS maps have Hunters Ravine incorrectly located. The map in this book is one of those. To reach the trailhead travel west from Quincy about 10 miles on the **Bucks Lake Road** to the **Big Creek Road**, proceed about 8 miles to the **Hartman Bar Road,** then on that road 7 miles to a four-way intersection. Go right on **USFS 22N29** (graveled road) about 1 1/2 miles to a signed Y and turn left on the pavement. Descend about 1 1/2 miles to a three-way intersection and take the left fork *(USFS 22N77)*. The sign reads **Hunter Ravine Trail** 3, but it is actually 4 1/2 miles. The road winds down to the south end of private property and a log landing and meadow. The unmaintained trail is past some logging slash at some oak trees with overgrown blazes, and logs cut out of the path. It is a steep, brushy drop to the river with lots of poison oak and mosquitoes.

JACKSON CREEK–MIDDLE FORK FEATHER RIVER TRAIL
Elevation: 4400' to 4200'
Length: +/- 1/2 mile
Effort: Easy
Hike Time: About 1/2 hour
Location: T23N R12E, section 19
Quadrangle Map: Johnsville

Jackson Creek Trail.

From Quincy travel about 16 miles east on **Highway 70** to the **Jackson Creek Road** turnoff near Mt. Tomba restaurant. Park across from the Jackson Creek Picnic Area (an old campground). There is a sign: **Jackson**

Creek Trail, Middle Fork Feather River 1/2 mile. Walk under the highway via a cement pedestrian tunnel. The trail will wind gently up and parallel to **Highway 70** on the west side under powerlines and along a wire fence. It soon comes to the edge of the hillside with a good view of the Middle Fork of the Feather River and the Union Pacific Railroad below. A gradual descent through the Camp Layman fire of the early 1990s has three switchbacks that soon drop you to the river and the railroad tracks. The river looks very pleasant through here.

LITTLE CALIFORNIA MINE TRAIL
Elevation: 5100' to 2400'
Length: +/- 2 miles
Effort: Difficult
Hike Time: About 2 hours
Location: T22N R8E, sections 6,7
Quadrangle Map: Haskins Valley, Dogwood Peak **(For map see page 142)**

All but the last 1/2 mile of this trail is 4WD. I've included it here because it is a very popular route into the Middle Fork. Reach via **USFS 23N60** and **23N75** off the **Big Creek Road** (new **Bucks Lake Road**) about 9 miles south of Meadow Valley and 15 miles west of Quincy. Park at the Greenbower Mine and proceed down the rough, rocky 4WD trail. There are many switchbacks to the end of the 4WD trail, then the last 1/2 mile drops quickly. Poison oak abounds in this area. Still, it is an interesting and scenic area to visit.

LITTLE NORTH FORK TRAIL
Elevation: 4100' to 4800'
Length: +/- 2 miles (3 to Robinson Mine)
Effort: Easy (to Robinson Mine, Difficult)
Hike Time: About 2 hours (to Robinson Mine, 3 hours)
Location: T22N R6E, section 1 and T23N R6E, section 36
Quadrangle Map: Haskins Valley, Soapstone Hill **(For map see page 136)**

Reach the trailhead by taking the **Oroville-Quincy Road** to Merrimac, about 34 miles from Quincy. Take **USFS 23N15** east 4 miles to the Little North Fork Campground. If you park at the campground you will need to walk back across the bridge over the Little North Fork to the unsigned but obvious trail intersection. This is an easy going walk for the first 2 miles as the trail works in and out of a number of dry gullies and several wet ones. There is also a small rock wall at one draw. A little over halfway along you will get your first real view up and down the canyon. The trail here is rocky, and as it rounds a point, it begins making a gradual descent toward the Little North Fork. Be sure to look east across the canyon to a small but picturesque set of falls. Just as the trail approaches the creek it makes a short switchback to the water. This is were you should turn around and return. If you decide you must continue on, cross here and crash the brush up and to

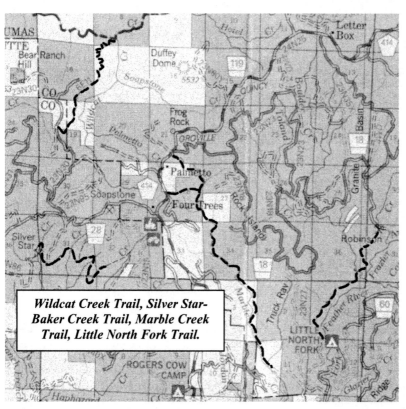

Wildcat Creek Trail, Silver Star-Baker Creek Trail, Marble Creek Trail, Little North Fork Trail.

the right. Once you regain the trail, it is well-defined and sports a rock wall, but is brushy. It makes five quick but easy switchbacks in the first 1/4 mile before leaving the open and entering the heavy cover of old growth timber. From here the trail makes a gradual ascent high above the Little North Fork drainage, becoming less obvious and, in one spot, seemingly vanishes altogether. Keep on the same grade though and it soon reappears. Just past an open area it begins rounding the hill into a saddle with a heavy white fir thicket. The trail is almost a road here it is so wide. It soon intersects a rough, unmapped road with many small spurs. Follow the main road up, or northeast for about 1/2 mile to **USFS 23N12X** and a K-tag for sections 25 and 36. From here it is a short drop to **USFS 23N35Y**. South about 1/2 mile is the Robinson Mine where there were once a number of old buildings and mining features, including a cemetery.

LONG VALLEY TRAIL
Elevation: 4400' to 5500'
Length: +/- 3 miles
Effort: Moderate
Hike Time: About 3 hours
Location: T23N R12E, sections 18,7,8,9
Quadrangle Map: Johnsville and Mt. Ingalls

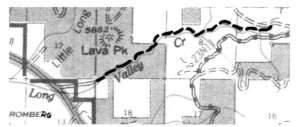

This is an old pack and livestock trail that until recently was maintained by a local riding club. Reach the trailhead by going east about 14 miles from Quincy on **State Highway 70** to a left-hand turn just before Long Valley Creek and Cromberg. Take **Bixler Road** and pass through private property for about 1/2 mile to the trailhead. There are several small cabins at the trailhead that are also private property. I can't stress enough the need to respect the property owner's rights. From the signed trailhead the trail makes a very easy ascent on a wide tread to a dry ravine. Once this is crossed the still-wide trail becomes somewhat narrower. Grizzled old growth Douglas fir, ponderosa pine and cedars line this refreshing, fast-running creek. In spring the wildflowers abound along the trail. There are some nice rock walls as the trail continues its easy ascent through large rock outcrops and boulder patches. Evidence of ground fires is noticeable as is an old K-tag in the SE 1/4 of the SW 1/4 of section 7. For about one mile the trail makes gradual ascents and descents to the creek, probably so that the cattle that used it could always be near water. The trail is also well blazed and in brushy areas marked with ducks. For the most part this section is shaded with occasional open areas. After rounding a point with rock projections on each side, the trail descends to the creek and begins to work into an open area with lots of manzanita and whitethorn. Shorts are not advised from here on. Soon the trail passes through an open, grassy bowl that was burned after logging years ago. Make a gradual ascent to a small flowing spring and a block of wood carved TRAIL with an arrow. The trail continues a light ascent through open country with brush crowding the way. Boulders are

Old cabin on private property along the Hartman Bar Trail (North). Please do not disturb these historic sites.

nestled all about, producing a heavy soil of decomposed granite. Make a short, heavy ascent in a large rock pile and pass an old gatepost. A short, winding switchback brings the trail on a contour and then a light descent to a small stream. Follow this down to the remnants of an old dam on Long Valley Creek. Across the creek is a fairly large meadow. The trail parallels Long Valley Creek staying on the base of the hillside on the left side of the creek. After a short distance begin a gradual ascent on the hillside, still paralleling the creek. The trees here are mostly second growth white fir, Jeffrey pine, and some red fir. The trail ambles along to a small campsite at the crossing of Bull Run Creek. After crossing this small stream the trail continues to wander up the left side of Long Valley Creek, and though it is faint, it is still apparent. As you enter yet another meadow, note the metal post and triangular metal marker attached to it. From that post contour along with the creek and the trail will again show itself. Wild strawberries are profuse in this area. From here it alternates between trees and small meadows and willows to another large open area that is marked with ducks. Continue along the edge of the hill, then ascend into a recently logged area. The trail has been used for skidding logs but is still pleasant. As you continue, note the blazed trees, mostly pine, and follow them back onto single-track trail. The trail is now below and parallel to *USFS 23N12*. In a short distance it will intersect that road with a short climb up the bank. This end of the trail is also signed. Not far to the east is a beautiful meadow on Missouri Gulch Creek, but it is private property and posted No Camping.

LOST CABIN SPRINGS-SUGAR PINE MINE TRAIL
Elevation: 5000' to 3800'
Length: +/- 1 mile
Effort: Difficult
Hike Time: About 1 hour
Location: T23N R10E, section 17
Quadrangle Map: Onion Valley **(For map see page 140)**

Reach the trailhead by taking **La Porte-Quincy Road** from **Highway 70** about 7 miles to signed **USFS 23N92**. Go 2 miles to a Y and continue left on **USFS 23N92A** for 1 mile to Lost Cabin Springs. The trailhead is about 1/2 mile down the road from Lost Cabin Springs proper. The **Five Bear Mine-Bach Creek Trail** bears off to the right as the **Lost Cabin Springs Trail** heads steeply down to the Middle Fork of the Feather River. Along the way the trail passes the abandoned Sugar Pine Mine. This trail is extremely loose near the bottom.

MARBLE CREEK TRAIL
Elevation: 5200' to 3600'
Length: +/- 5 miles
Effort: Difficult
Hike Time: About 3 hours
Location: T23N R6E, sections 27,28,34 and T22N R6E, sections 3,11
Quadrangle Map: Soapstone Hill **(For map see page 146)**

Reach this pretty, but unmaintained trail by taking the **Oroville-Bucks Lake-Quincy Road** 31 miles west of Quincy, and about 1 1/2 miles north of the **Four Trees-Coyote Gap Road (USFS 23N28)** intersection. The one-mile-long road to the trailhead is unsigned and on the south side of the intersection of **Oroville-Bucks Lake-Quincy Road**, **23N48X** and **23N18**. The trailhead is on timber company property, as is about 1 1/2 miles of trail, and is one reason it is not maintained. A sign informs the hiker that the trail is maintained by a Boy Scout troop from Oroville; however, it has not been worked on in some years. Nice campsites are found along the creek and about five miles down the trail at its end. The first fifty yards of trail is on an old skid trail that drops quickly across a small draw. The trail is somewhat faint and descends quickly through old growth timber about 1/4 mile to the head of Marble Creek. Parallel the creek to its first crossing at a confluence. Continue on the east side to another confluence and cross to the west side, then almost immediately, cross again. A slight ascent and descent soon bring you to another confluence. Cross the left one staying on the east side and ascend along the hillside. The trail is good here, crossing several dry ravines and climbing up over the low ridge to make four quick switchbacks down to a flat on the creek. At the bottom of the flat cross the creek and walk along it a short distance, cross again to the east side and make a short, steep ascent. You will soon pass a K-tag for sections 27 and 34 and cross

Little Volcano from the Middle Fork Feather River near the mouth of Winters Creek and Five Bear Mine. Because volcanoes were thought to be a source of gold, early-day miners scoured its slopes in search of gold deposits. Actually a limestone formation, it is one of many beautiful sights in the Feather River region.

on to private property. Turn into a small drainage and cross a small creek making a descent along the east side to cross Marble Creek yet again. You are now off private property. The faint trail wanders along a flat, so keep an eye out for old blazes. Cross a small, wet ravine and soon the country becomes more open and rocky. Make some ups and downs and then ascend the hillside, drop and cross the creek, walking down the east side to a major washout. Work through this and ascend the trail along the hillside, then through a flat, across a dry ravine and past a small natural rock shelter. The trail winds along, then crosses the creek, ascends the right side, then descends again to cross the creek for the last time. It now makes lots of ups and downs through flats and campsites to another set of private property markers. Pass an old cabin site, then ascend and cross a dry ravine with a small rock wall, cross another dry wash at its mouth, and meander along the creek bed fifty yards or so. Ascend the left side, contour along and descend quickly to cross a wet draw where the trail is now well above the creek. Descend quickly and soon the trail wanders along an old mining ditch past another set of private property markers, where it passes into and off of national forest quickly. The trail soon drops from the ditch to cross dry Truck Ravine and connect with a small road leading to the main road *(USFS 22N80)*.

McCARTHY BAR TRAIL 9E04

Elevation: 5500' to 3600'
Length: +/- 2 miles
Effort: Very Difficult
Hike Time: About 2 hours
Location: T23N R9E, section 15
Quadrangle Map: Onion Valley **(For map see page 140)**

To reach this trailhead travel west from Quincy 4 miles on the **Bucks Lake Road** to the **Slate Creek Road (USFS 24N28).** Turn left on this road and travel about 8 3/4 miles, passing Deanes Valley Campground, to the ridge top. From here take the left fork *(USFS 23N99)* about 2 1/2 miles, passing the shared **Oddie Bar-No Ear Bar Trails** to the signed trailhead. This trail has beautiful views that make up for the effort required coming out. It is a strenuous hike back up and somewhere in the neighborhood of forty switchbacks, I lost count. Cross a dry ravine, then seasonal Claremont Creek, then make a steep descent to the river. McCarthy Bar is actually across the Middle Fork and was named for prospector Thomas McCarthy who was active in the area around 1917. Later, in the 1930s, a miner died there and was packed out to be buried elsewhere.

MIDDLE BRANCH MILL CREEK TRAIL

Elevation: 3800' to 4400'
Length: +/- 1 mile
Effort: Very Difficult
Hike Time: About 2 hours
Location: T24N R9E, section 25,36
Quadrangle Map: Quincy

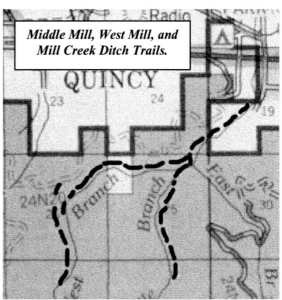

Middle Mill, West Mill, and Mill Creek Ditch Trails.

To reach the trailhead, take **South Redburg Avenue** in East Quincy about 1/2 mile to a locked gate. Park off the road and follow the left-hand road past several houses. You are passing through private property so show due respect. The road is rough and sometimes washed out but continue on to the government line. The road leads through a meadow area to the confluence of the West, Middle and East branches of Mill Creek and the site of Hymer's Cabin. When you reach Hymer's Cabin site, cross Mill Creek and start up the left side of the Middle Branch. The trail soon becomes apparent. It is fairly distinct until about half way up where it seems to disappear. Keep working in and out of the small gullies and the trail will soon reappear. It then works gradually down onto the creek and the old Hefty Mine camp. Anything of value has already been pilfered from this site.

MILL CREEK DITCH TRAIL
Elevation: 4650' to 4800'
Length: +/- 1/2 mile
Effort: Easy
Hike Time: About 1/2 hour
Location: T24N R9E, section 26
Quadrangle Map: Quincy **(For map see page 150)**

To reach the trailhead, take the ***Quincy Watershed Road (USFS 24N20)*** opposite the ***Plumas County Fairgrounds Road***, about 1 mile east of the courthouse in Quincy. Follow this road about 4 miles to a saddle where the road crosses into the Boyle Ravine drainage. Park at the saddle. The trail is to the left of the road and is actually on the old Mill Creek-Hungarian Hill Mine Ditch. It was made into a trail so that loggers could access their work above the ditch. There is one washout to be careful at, but otherwise it is a very easy, almost level walk. About halfway into the West Branch of Mill Creek the trail ends but you can follow the ditch the rest of the way to the creek. The ditch crosses the creek, but don't bother following any further as it was never completed and soon peters out on a brushy hillside.

MOUNTAIN HOUSE CREEK TRAIL (Butte County)
Elevation: 3500' to 1960'
Length: +/- 2 miles
Effort: Difficult
Hike Time: About 2 hours
Location: T21N R6E, sections 3,4 and T22N R6E, section 34
Quadrangle Map: Brush Creek

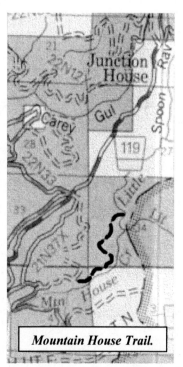

Mountain House Trail.

Reach the trailhead via the ***Oroville-Bucks Lake-Quincy Road*** at Mountain House. About 1/2 mile north of Mountain House, take a right on dirt road ***USFS 21N36Y*** for 1/4 mile to a Y intersection of our road and ***USFS 21N37Y***. A sign pointing toward the trailhead still exists. Take the right fork *(36Y)* and follow this east for about 1/2 mile to ***USFS 22N54***. Just after you make an angled intersection with this road, the trailhead is apparent on the right side of the road, though the sign has been cut down. The trail starts as a closed logging spur. This is contrary to what is indicated on the map, as is another feature of this trail. Make an easy descent down this shaded road, cross a small stream with a culvert, and a bit further a short trail drops to the right to the creek. Our trail makes a short ascent, then drops with Mountain House Creek below on the right. Pass through the very corner of private property and the trail now becomes a definite single track. The descent now becomes somewhat steeper but is still a nice walk. The character of the land begins to change now from heavy forest to rockier ground and open slopes. Make a steep descent to two switchbacks, a moderate descent, then level out with a view across the canyon. By now the creek has dropped far below. Gradually descend to a switchback, then a moderate descent through five more. The cover is heavy again with madrone, oaks and fir. Make a switchback at the head of a steep grassy slope with a view to the north of the **Oroville-Quincy Road** and the Little North Fork of the Middle Fork of the Feather River. Descend to three

Mountain House Creek Trail and Little North Fork Trail sign.

more switchbacks and make a gradual descent to a small creek and another switchback. It is here that the map indicates the trail crosses and continues to the Little North Fork. Although there does appear to be a trail just below, I could find no trace of it on the other side of the small creek. Continue on our trail parallel to this small stream and gradually make a long, contouring descent away and toward Mountain House Creek. At the switchback at that creek is a sign propped up: Mountain House Creek (to right); Little North Fork 1.2 mile (to left). Scratched into this sign is Washed Out. To continue, gradually descend through four switchbacks and cross a small stream. The trail is faint here but descends parallel to the stream just crossed. Make a steep descent along the foot of the hill, there is a blazed birch, then a blazed cedar. The trail all but disappears, so is careful picking your way down the rocks. Soon you will reach a campsite on the bank of the Little North Fork, just up from where Mountain House Creek joins it. A huge madrone tree has been used as a fireplace and garbage dump. Please carry your trash (and any other's) out.

NO EAR BAR TRAIL 9E06
Elevation: 5000' to 3600'
Length: +/- 1 1/2 miles
Effort: Difficult
Hike Time: About 2 hours
Location: T23N R9E, sections 16,21,22
Quadrangle Map: Onion Valley **(For map see page 140)**

I don't know the story behind this colorful name, but an 1892 map shows it as "No Earred Bar." One can imagine a miner losing his ear in a knife fight, or maybe having a grizzly bear chew it off. To reach the shared trailhead with the **Oddie Bar Trail**, travel west from Quincy 4 miles on the **Bucks Lake Road** to the **Slate Creek Road (USFS 24N28).** Turn left on this road and travel about 8 3/4 miles, passing Deanes Valley Campground, to the ridge top. From here take the left fork *(USFS 23N99)* about 1 1/2 miles to the signed trailhead on private property. This hike is a series of winding switchbacks and straight descents, occasionally passing in and out of private property the 1500 feet or so that it drops. It is quick going in, but watch the return climb out. It is quite demanding, especially in summer. The trail stops at the Middle Fork and a wet crossing is required to reach No Ear Bar proper. For a good hike, take this trail down to the Middle Fork of the Feather River, work down river approximately 1 1/2 miles to Oddie Bar, and hike out the ***Oddie Bar Trail*** back to the trailhead. Some wading or swimming of the river is required to make this loop.

ODDIE BAR TRAIL 9E08
Elevation: 5000' to 3500'
Length: +/- 1 1/2 miles
Effort: Difficult
Hike Time: About 2 hours
Location: T23N R9E, sections 16,20,21
Quadrangle Map: Onion Valley **(For map see page 140)**

To reach the shared trailhead with the *No Ear Bar Trail*, travel west from Quincy 4 miles on the **Bucks Lake Road** to the **Slate Creek Road (USFS 24N28).** Turn left on this road and travel about 8 3/4 miles, passing Deanes Valley Campground, to the ridge top. From here take the left fork *(USFS 23N99)* about 1 1/2 miles to the signed trailhead. This is an easy hike in, but beware the climb out. Beautiful scenery and a well-defined trail make it a very pleasant hike in. As the trail reaches the Middle Fork of the Feather River it crosses Grizzly Creek, then takes you out onto Oddie Bar, site of once-active mining operations, first during the Gold Rush and later around the turn of the century. A trail continues downstream to Horseshoe Bend about 1/2 mile or so. For a good hike, take this trail down to the Middle Fork of the Feather River, work up river approximately 1 1/2 miles to No Ear Bar, and hike out the ***No Ear Bar Trail*** back to the trailhead. Some wading or swimming of the river is required to make this loop.

SILVER STAR MINE-BAKER CREEK TRAIL (Butte County)
Elevation: 4200' to 4100'
Length: +/- 3 1/2 miles
Effort: Moderate
Hike Time: About 2 hours
Location: T22N R6E, section 6 and T23N R6E, sections 31,32
Quadrangle Map: Soapstone Hill **(For map see page 146)**

Reach the trail via the **Coyote Gap-Four Trees Road (USFS 00)** from near Pulga on **State Highway 70,** about 30 miles east of Oroville or 45 miles west of Quincy. Follow the forest road about 7 miles to Coyote Gap. Another way is to take the **Four Trees Road**

(**USFS 23N28**) off the **Oroville-Quincy Road** (27 1/2 miles from Quincy) about 5 miles to Coyote Gap. Once at Coyote Gap take **USFS 23N86** almost 2 miles to a washout and dead end. This spur and the trail you will walk were once part of the Swayne Lumber Co. logging railroad. The railbed works in and out of Rody Creek, Little Rody Creek, and Baker Creeks. It is somewhat brushy in spots but is an interesting hike along a long-abandoned logging railroad. For more information on the Swayne Lumber Co. operations see the suggested reading section of this guide.

SUMMIT TRAIL

Elevation: 5520' to 5200'
Length: +/- 2 miles
Effort: Very Easy
Hike Time: About 1 hour
Location: T24N R8E, sections 31,32 and T24N R7E, section 36 and T23N R8E, sections 5,6 and T23N R7E, section 1
Quadrangle Map: Bucks Lake **(For map see page 135)**

From Quincy take the **Bucks Lake Road** west about 14 miles to Bucks Summit, where there are restrooms and parking. The trail starts just west of the summit on the left (south) side of the road. Make a light descent to cross a road connecting **Bucks Lake Road** with the **Big Creek Road**. The trail continues along the forested hillside as a closed-off logging spur for a distance, before dropping to run along the upper edges of several meadows and brush patches. Part of a meadow washed out requiring the trail to be relocated above. For the most part it is in red fir and lodgepole pine cover with some open areas. About halfway along it becomes more trail-like and pleasant, and in spring there is a profusion of wildflowers. The trail ends at the **Bucks Lake Road** on the west side of the Bucks Creek Bridge. From here you can cross the bridge and take the **Bucks Creek Trail** back to the summit.

TOBIN TRAIL

Elevation: 2000' to 3000' (5200' to Rodger's Saddle)
Length: +/- 3 1/2 miles (5 1/2 miles full length)
Effort: Very Difficult
Hike Time: About 3 hours (5 hours for full length)
Location: T24N R6E, sections 23,22,21,16 (13,14 full length)
Quadrangle Map: Storrie **(For map see page 136)**

The following trail is another that suffered damage during the Storrie Fire of 2000. I have not rehiked it since, but am relatively sure that the description should be about the same. This hike is a hot one in summer, although it makes a gradual ascent out of the Feather River Canyon. Keep a sharp eye out for rattlesnakes and the magnificent poison oak that abounds in the area. On an April hike I saw a number of alligator lizards, newts, gopher snakes, and a covey of quail. The trail seems to be frequented mainly by fishermen, and though it is likely the trail does continue to Rodger's Saddle, I stopped the hike upon reaching Bucks Creek. From Quincy take **State Route 70** west about 38 miles to Tobin

Resort. From Oroville travel east on the same route about 38 miles. It is advised to park at the post office and walk up the road to the signed trailhead. A sign on the way notes that the private road is closed in 1/4 mile while also pointing out the **Tobin Trail**. There are several houses along the route and at the trailhead, so beware of their dogs and respect their property. The dogs came out to greet me but didn't bite me. The trail contours and makes a light ascent above the houses, passes through an area of moss-covered boulders, then crosses a brushy flat studded with large ponderosa pines. Make a light ascent under black oak and live oak, then cross the head of a wet draw and lightly descend to a small switchback crossing of a large unnamed stream. Make two small switchbacks and contour along the steep hillside under heavy cover of live oak, cedar, and Douglas fir. The unmaintained trail is narrow but well-defined. There are some fifteen-foot high falls in the canyon below the trail, while blowdowns, a small spring, larger trees, and no sounds from the highway far below accent the light, winding ascent. Cross a small

North Fork Feather River from Bucks Lake Wilderness. Except for the highway and railroad, this is much the same view Dame Shirley had on her ride into Rich Bar.

stream and make another light ascent with a view of the canyon, the railroad, and P.G. & E's Rock Crest housing facility. The rocky peak to the northeast is Ben Lomond. Cross another small stream with lush moss, make a light ascent and contour along. There are also several large blowdowns across the trail. A good view of the bridge on the highway at Storrie is had from here. Soon the trail crosses a dry ravine, while the tread becomes rockier and less sure. The trail makes a split, but stay right. Make two switchbacks and begin a moderate-to-steep ascent to the ridgeback. From here there is a good view of the Bucks Creek watershed and an old railroad grade contouring along the hillside. It was used in the 1920s for construction of the Bucks Creek hydroelectric power project. As the trail descends, it also becomes brushier on this warmer side of the mountain. The tread becomes sloughed and hard to negotiate, though the trail is still obvious. Make a short, steep descent to a wet stream, cross, and continue the light descent. The trail disintegrates even more and several blowdowns add to the fun. Tantalizing glimpses of Bucks Creek are had through the brush and thickets that cover the trail. A view of Rodger's Saddle is ahead as the trail makes several short steep pitches, descents, and contours. An easy descent on the well-defined trail leads to another spring crossing. Ascend over a hump into another shaded wet draw, cross, and contour along. There are some great falls across the canyon from this point. Continue making light ups and downs, round a ridge, descend into another wet draw, cross, contour and descend along the hillside just above Bucks Creek to a brushy, treed flat with several campsites. The trail crosses the flat and continues in a thicket to the creek itself, which it follows a short distance, then climbs the bank and begins a brushy ascent toward Rodger's Saddle. I gave it up at this point due to the brush and the fact that there was a large snow pack to encounter far before trail's end.

WEST BRANCH MILL CREEK TRAIL
Elevation: 3800' to 4400'
Length: +/- 1 1/2 miles
Effort: Difficult
Hike Time: About 2 hours
Location: T24N R9E, sections 25,26
Quadrangle Map: Quincy **(For map see page 150)**

To reach the trailhead, take **South Redburg Avenue** in East Quincy about 1/2 mile to a locked gate. Park off the road and follow the left-hand road past several houses. You are passing through private property so show due respect. The road is rough and sometimes washed out but continue on to the government line. The road leads through a meadow area to the confluence of the West, Middle and East branches of Mill Creek and the site of Hymer's Cabin. Stay to the right along the West Branch and soon you will see the trail ascend the bank. From here it continues past numerous old mines, tunnels and diggings to a cabin site that is frequently used for camping. The trail is rough in places and somewhat brushy, but is mostly a very gradual walk.

WILDCAT CREEK TRAIL
Elevation: 4760' to 2750'
Length: +/- 2 1/2 miles
Effort: Very Difficult
Hike Time: About 2 1/2 hours
Location: T23N R6E, sections 8,17,18,19
Quadrangle Map: Soapstone Hill **(For map see page 146)**

(Just a note about the following description. I was told that this trail has had some maintenance work done to it in the last year or so, but I have not hiked it again to see if this is so.) I suspect this trail to be one of those constructed during the Civilian Conservation Corps (CCC) days in the 1930s. It would still be a great trail if it were maintained. Nearly every one of its switchbacks has a down tree on it, resulting in cut and eroded trail segments. A lot of effort went into constructing it, and it would be a shame to lose it. The other drawback is that most of it is on private property. To reach the trailhead take the *Oroville-Bucks Lake-Quincy Road* about 27 1/2 miles west of Quincy. Take the **Four Trees-Coyote Gap Road (USFS 23N28)** (passing the OHV warming hut) about 2 1/2 miles to an old cattle pen and chute. The **Bear Ranch Hill Road (USFS 23N30)** bears right. A sign reads: *Highway 70* 10; Bear Ranch 5; *Wildcat Trail 6E11* 3. Continue about

1/2 mile to another signed intersection and turn right. Follow this road around and down, across a creek, and into Butte County (about 2 miles). The road drops into a swale, which is now a log landing. The trailhead itself is on private property and was logged over in 1994. There are remnants of an old cattle pen where the trail drops to the east. Follow an old skid trail downhill and to the right where you will soon hit the well defined though unmaintained trail. At this point there is a small gurgling spring to the left. The trail makes a moderate to heavy descent and seven steep switchbacks to a live creek. Parallel

A group of surveyors for the Western Pacific Railroad construction project masquerading as prospectors in the Feather River canyon about 1903.

the creek that rapidly descends while the trail stays at a gentle descent. The tread is fairly good but brush is taking over. Washington lilies, mock orange, currants, and other plants are all vying for trail space. As the trail works along the hillside there is soon a dramatic view of Rodgers Saddle across the canyon to the north. The trail is quite rocky and the hillside very steep so be careful. The cover is now mostly black oak with some large old cedars here and there. Along this section the trail crosses two dry ravines, another with a spring, and another seven dry ravines. It becomes very rocky under the live oak cover though the grade remains gentle. As the trail rounds a point, note the ponderosa pine with many initials in its bark. There are several small-to-medium rock walls along the trail here also. Glimpses through the oaks reveal the rugged Grizzly Creek canyon to the right and Wildcat Creek below. You can hear the falls on Wildcat Creek and in several places catch a view of them. Make a moderate descent and round the ridge. The trail is quite brushy with poor tread. Now comes the fun. From switchback number one to number fourteen the grade is fairly moderate. From number fourteen to number nineteen the switchbacks are shorter and somewhat steeper. At number twenty cross a spring, hitting it again for the next three. At switchback number twenty-seven the trail makes a long, gradual descent and is the best section of the entire trail. At switchback twenty-eight you can hear the creek below. Make another three and you are at the confluence of Wildcat Creek and Grizzly Creek. In all, there are thirty-one switchbacks on this section alone (about one mile's worth). There are several nice camping sites between the creeks.

Ferry boat on the East Branch of the North Fork Feather River between Soda Bar and Iron Bar, now Paxton. This was one of the first ferries to operate in Plumas County.

BUCKS LAKE WILDERNESS
No Motorized Vehicles

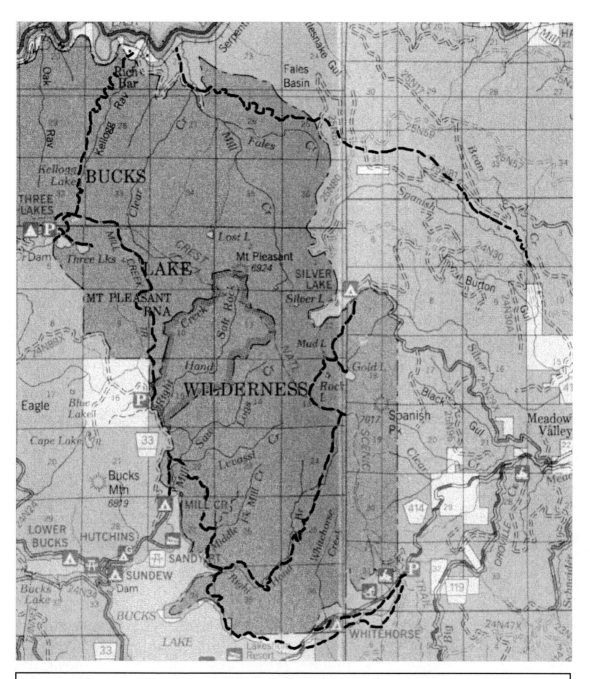

Granite Gap Trail, Mill Creek Trail, Right Hand Branch Mill Creek Trail, Silver Lake-Gold Lake Trail, Spanish Ranch-Rich Bar Trail, Three Lakes-PCT Tie Trail, Three Lakes-Rich Bar Trail, Three Lakes Trail.

This 21,000-acre wilderness near Bucks Lake has a broad diversity of plant life, trees, and landscape features. Ranging from 2,000 feet to 7,017 feet in elevation, the Bucks Lake Wilderness includes gentle slopes, steep canyons, and sheer cliffs. **The Pacific Crest Trail** crosses the wilderness and is accessible at Bucks Summit or Belden, or by several trails that tie into it. Within Bucks Wilderness are a number of small lakes and ponds, streams, meadows, and historic sites. Through this area poured the gold seekers intent on reaching Rich Bar, Mountain House, and other gold-rich placers during the 1850s. Self-registration is required, and according to the Forest Service there are registration boxes at all the trailheads. The trails located in the wilderness are alphabetized in this subsection. No bicycles or motorized vehicles or equipment are allowed.

GRANITE GAP TRAIL 7E12
Elevation: 5800' to 6200'
Length: +/- 1 mile
Effort: Moderate
Hike Time: About 1 hour
Location: T24N R7E, sections 12,13
Quadrangle Map: Bucks Lake **(For map see page 158)**

This signed trail departs the *Gold Lake Trail* (see directions). The steep, but fairly easy trail will take you to Mud Lake, Rock Lake, and the *Pacific Crest Trail* between Spanish Peak and Three Lakes. For this reason it is sometimes used as a *PCT* Tie Trail. A sign on the *PCT* says it is 2 miles to Silver Lake, a tired hiker added 1/2 mile to that.

MILL CREEK TRAIL
Elevation: 5100' to 6400'
Length: +/- 10 miles
Effort: Moderate
Hike Time: About 6 hours
Location: T23N R7E, sections 1,2 and T24N R7E, sections 4,9,10,15,22, 27,34,35
Quadrangle Map: Bucks Lake **(For map see page)**

This trail is one of the old *California Riding & Hiking Trails* network, though it may predate that program. Numerous painted tin signs are nailed to the trees, copious blaze marks are present, and every so often, halves of 1938 California license plates are nailed to trees, over 20 feet off the ground. This is a very pleasant hike with many beautiful meadows, streams and tall trees. There are three trailheads: Mill Creek Campground; along the *Mill Creek Road;* and this trailhead on the *Quincy-Bucks Lake Road*, about 1/2 mile west of the Whitehorse Campground at Bucks Lake. It is shared with the *Right Hand Branch Mill Creek Trail* trailhead. The first 4 miles amble along the northeast shore of Bucks Lake with the first mile of trail on Pacific Gas & Electric ground. The trail begins a moderate ascent near the mouth of Mill Creek opposite Mill Creek Campground. Cross Mill Creek and make a short ascent to the Mill Creek Campground trailhead. Head north 1 1/2 miles and intersect the *Mill Creek Road*. Just before this point an abandoned trail heads east across Mill Creek and up a ridge between Levassi Creek and an unnamed tributary of Mill Creek. After intersecting the *Mill Creek Road* the trail crosses the road, then runs a distance back to the road. Follow the road about 1/2 mile to a large white fir with overgrown blaze marks on it on the east side of the road. The trail runs under the road and crosses Mill Creek. On the opposite side of the creek is a huge jumble of granite boulders. The trail is not maintained through this section. In less than a mile you will intersect the *Mill Creek Trail* trailhead access. The trailhead is on the *Mill Creek Road* on the west side of Mill Creek. A sign here informs the hiker that the *Pacific Crest Trail* is 3 miles and Three Lakes 4 miles. Heading north, pass through a pretty meadow marred only by a snow measurement instrument. The trail gradually ascends the last 2 1/2 miles to the *Pacific Crest Trail.* A sign here reads: Mill Creek Trailhead 3 1/2, Bucks Lake 5 1/2, Mill Creek Campground 5 1/2. There are several old trails that veer off the main trail, none of which are maintained.

A plethora of signs is found at this intersection on the Mill Creek Trail. A PCT diamond at left, an overgrown "Y" at center, a newer sign, and an old California Riding & Hiking Trail sign.

RIGHT HAND BRANCH MILL CREEK TRAIL
Elevation: 5100' to 6800'
Length: +/- 5 miles
Effort: Difficult
Hike Time: About 3 hours
Location: T23N R7E, sections 1,2 and T24N R7E, sections 24,25,26,34,35
Quadrangle Map: Bucks Lake **(For map see page 158)**

This trail is better appreciated if you can start at the top and work down. And though it is tempting to cut through the switchbacks when going this direction, ***please refrain*** from this practice. These features help maintain the trail for others behind you. Reach the shared trailhead with the main *Mill Creek Trail* via the *Quincy-Bucks Lake Road* about 15 miles west of Quincy. The first mile is on Pacific Gas & Electric ground as it meanders along the northeast shore of Bucks Lake. Another 1 1/2 miles brings you to the mouth of the Right Hand Branch of Mill Creek. Cross the creek to a post with directions given vertically. The trail ascends the left side of the creek for about 1 1/2 miles. Not far from the beginning is a huge granite boulder sitting on another rock. Just past this is a nice spring and several not so nice boggy spots in the trail. This section is a beautiful walk through some very tall, very large old growth timber. Several well-maintained campsites can be found in this area. Soon you will ascend two switchbacks and cross to the other side of the Right Hand Branch of Mill Creek. Ascend along a tributary of this creek, up two more switchbacks, cross a tributary again, and then climb about nine more switchbacks. After again crossing a tributary you begin the ascent of about sixteen more switchbacks. These were installed a few years ago to lessen the grade of the original pack trail. Gradually ascend along the side of the hill, crossing a tributary about one mile before again reaching the Right Hand Branch of Mill Creek. Cross the creek and ascend moderately. The top portion of this trail is faint. As you enter a sloping meadow, stay to the left edge and you will again pick up the trail. From the Right Hand Branch of Mill Creek the *Pacific Crest Trail* is about 1 mile. A sign here will inform you that the trail is 4.9 miles long. From the *Pacific Crest Trail* junction it is about 1/2 mile northeast to Spanish Peak.

SILVER LAKE–GOLD LAKE TRAIL 8E04

Elevation: 5800' to 6200'
Length: +/- 1 1/2 miles
Effort: Easy
Hike Time: About 1 hour
Location: T24N R8E, sections 7,18
Quadrangle Map: Bucks Lake **(For map see page 158)**

This trail provides access to the 21,000-acre Bucks Wilderness and *PCT*, besides being a fine hike. Reach the trailhead by going west 9 miles on the *Quincy-Bucks Lake Road*, then turn right at the signed intersection and proceed 6 1/2 miles on the rough *Silver Lake Road (USFS 24N29X)* to the dam at the lake. Here there are campsites and toilets. Once at Silver Lake go east across the dam. In a short distance you will leave the lake and proceed on a very well-maintained trail

Silver Lake from the south near Spanish Peak.

along a brushy ridge. Near the beginning you will cross the Gold Lake Ditch, a remnant of former mining days when Gold and Silver lakes were water supply reservoirs for the hydraulic mines of the Spanish Ranch area. The trail is an easy grade to Gold Lake. Along the way you will intersect the signed *Granite Gap Trail*, a tie trail to the *Pacific*

Crest Trail about 1 mile south on top of the Spanish Peak escarpment. There is one section that is a scramble as the trail drops to Gold Lake. There is not much shade along this trail, but at this higher elevation the temperatures do not normally get too hot, except in mid-summer.

SPANISH RANCH-RICH BAR TRAIL
Elevation: 4000' to 3000'
Length: +/- 9 miles
Effort: Very difficult
Hike Time: About 6 hours
Location: T24N R8E, sections 3,4,10 and T25N R8E, sections 31,32,33 and T25N R7E, sections 21,22,25,26,27
Quadrangle Map: Meadow Valley, Bucks Lake, Caribou **(For map see page 158)**

This is one of the earliest and most famous of Plumas County's historic trails. Used by miners and packers to access the gold rich East Branch of the North Fork of the Feather River, it saw continuous use from 1850 until around 1920 when automobile roads began to penetrate the canyon. Dame Shirley, in The Shirley Letters, used this trail on her trek into American Valley in October of 1852. If you are interested in California history, her book is a definite must to read. The last four miles of this trail are included in the Bucks Lake Wilderness, hence its position in this guide. To reach the trailhead take the *Bucks Lake Road* west 7 miles from Quincy to Spanish Ranch. Pass through this once-bustling supply camp by going west through the T intersection onto the graveled road. Follow the gravel about 1/2 mile to a Y intersection and keep right. The road turns to dirt. Proceed about 1 mile past two more right turns to an intersection with the left-hand road

Shimmering aspens at Bucks Lake on a warm autumn afternoon.

blocked by a dirt berm. Proceed to the right. You will see a great mass of white quartz gravel to your left. These are impounded tailings from the once-rich Bean Hill Hydraulic Mine. About 50 yards before the wet crossing of Spanish Creek take the rough, narrow road to your right. This is the *Green Flat Road.* Follow it to the end, about 1 mile. From here begin a slight ascent along the hill and you will pick up the trail contouring along about 75 feet above Spanish Creek. Proceed about 1/4 mile to Bean Creek, carefully crossing on the boulders. The trail now makes a series of very deeply worn switchbacks. At the top of these it then maintains a moderate ascent along the canyon side. Nice views of Spanish Creek are seen from this section. Halfway up the canyon is a blazed cedar that indicates the old *Bean Hill Trail*. This trail climbs up and over the ridge, dropping steeply to Bean Creek and the Bean Hill Mine. As the *Rich Bar Trail* nears the summit of Red Hill, cross the old Spanish Ranch Water Ditch, which once carried water over 20 miles from the head of Spanish Creek to Gopher Hill, Badger Hill, and Elizabethtown area mines. The trail braids out a bit here, but keep on the most worn path as it makes a moderate ascent to Red Hill. As it comes out in the open the trail begins to bear left along the back of the hill. Round the shoulder of the hill and work through the 1962 Virgilia burn. The trail is faint here. Soon you will hit the **Fales Hill Road (USFS 25N17)** on the right. Almost immediately there is a Y intersection. Keep left and, after about 50 yards, drop off the road to the left side and pick up the trail again just below the road. It now parallels the road for one mile or so before crossing a seasonal gully, climbing up across the road, and continuing at a moderate ascent through Smith's Flat Diggings. Here it has been converted to an old logging road for a short distance. It soon resumes as trail to climb up to the old **Mountain House-Spanish Ranch Wagon Road.** Follow this for 1/2 mile to and through the Mountain House Diggings to the site of Mountain House and the high point of 5200'. From here to Fales Hill the wagon road/trail runs parallel on the left of the main road. It is easiest to just proceed on to Fales Hill, where you pick up the wagon road again as it drops off the main road down along the south side of the diggings. The road soon becomes trail again as it switchbacks and descends down the north side of Mill Creek canyon. Great views of the canyon can be seen from here. The trail makes a number of switchbacks, crosses a few springs, and ends at Mill Creek at the Bud Lee Mine. Carefully cross the creek here and follow the road to its gated end at Rich Bar, or at the Shenandoah Mine and Hamrick's cabin, take the trail again as it drops off the point to the right and works down the open, brushy hillside to the Union Pacific Railroad. From here it is about 1/2 mile to Rich Bar along the tracks.

THREE LAKES-PCT TIE TRAIL
Elevation: 6200' to 6250'
Length: +/- 1/2 mile
Effort: Easy
Hike Time: About 1/2 hour
Location: T24N R7E, section 5 and T25N R7E, section 32
Quadrangle Map: Bucks Lake **(For map see page 158)**

The trailhead is at the lower of the Three Lakes and utilizes the same trailhead as the ***Three Lakes Trail*** (see description). It is an easy stroll over to the ***PCT*** from here.

THREE LAKES-RICH BAR TRAIL (via Kellogg Lake)
Elevation: 6200' to 2500'
Length: +/- 4 1/2 miles
Effort: Extremely Difficult
Hike Time: About 5 hours
Location: T24N R7E, section 5 and T25N R7E, sections 21,28,29,32

Quadrangle Map: Bucks Lake, Caribou **(For map see page 158)**

Even though this trail was burned over in the summer of 2000's Storrie Fire, it is historically important due to the fact that it is well described by Louise Clappe in her famous Shirley Letters and was a major route to the mining camp of Rich Bar. Reach the trailhead from Quincy by taking the **Bucks Lake-Quincy Road** to Lower Bucks Lake, a distance of about 23 miles. Follow the rough 13-mile-long **Three Lakes Road** from Lower Bucks Lake to the Three Lakes Dam. The 1/2-mile-long **Three Lakes-Pacific Crest Trail-Tie Trail** will connect you to the **PCT,** and once on it travel east approximately 1/2 mile to the **Kellogg Lake Trail.** This trail rises quickly to a saddle with a beautiful view of Rich Bar on the East Branch of the North Fork of the Feather River. From here it is almost indiscernible and drops quickly to Kellogg Lake, more a lily pond than a lake. The trail down the hill to Rich Bar leaves to the west of the lake's outlet, near the north end of a small flat and the foot of the hill slope. The trail is now much more visible than before the fire of 2000, but care must still be exercised not to lose it. It also makes several switchbacks that drop it about 300 feet in elevation. After this the trail becomes more evident as it follows the hogback of the ridge for quite a distance before making a series of switchbacks down the ridge. Most of the way through the forested section the trail is adorned with fallen trees and debris, particularly since the fire. After crossing the historic Utah Construction Company Road used in the building of the Western Pacific Railroad, it ends up at the Rich Bar Cemetery. About one mile from this end, the Smith Point fork bears left and down the ridge to that old mining camp. Though this trail was used by mule-packers during the Gold Rush, it is not suitable for equestrians today. As a matter of fact, until it is rebuilt, it is hardly suitable for hikers. About 1989 when I was 32, Jim Young, then 55 and 80-year old Bill Penland hiked it down, and boy did we have a day! Of the brush field Dame Shirley remarked on September 13, 1851:

Small lakes dot the Bucks Lake Wilderness. These granite-bound lakes are near the head of Mill Creek above Rich Bar. The view is from the PCT.

"Of a ghastly whiteness, they at first reminded me of a plantation of antlers, and I amused myself by fancying them a herd of crouching deer; but they grew so wan and ghastly, that I began to look forward to the creeping across a *chaparral* – (it is no easy task for the mules to wind through them,) with almost a feeling of dread…But what a lovely sight greeted our enchanted eyes, as we stopped for a few moments on the summit of the hill leading into Rich Bar. Deep in the shadowy nooks of the far down valleys, lay half a dozen blue-bosomed lagoons, glittering and gleaming and sparkling in the sunlight, as though each tiny wavelet were formed of rifted diamonds."

According to a document archived at the Plumas County Museum, "In the spring of 1852, a man named Hubord made a new trail from Bucks Ranch to Rich Bar…and induced miners and pack trains to go the trail. They drove beef cattle down it, then a Mexican with a pack train who lost a load of six cases of claret into French Ravine, then Bob Love's mule train followed and lost a case of brandy. Love declared 'he would not go that route again.'" Despite the trouble mule trains had with the trail, miners on foot utilized it heavily for many years.

Kellogg Lake, on the route down to Rich Bar. Red Hill is in the background. A small dairy ranch was operating near the lake during the 1850s to supply the miners on the river with milk.

THREE LAKES TRAIL
Elevation: 6200' to 6300'
Length: +/- 1 mile
Effort: Moderate
Hike Time: About 1/2 hour
Location: T24N R7E, section 5
Quadrangle Map: Bucks Lake **(For map see page 158)**

These lakes were the site of the Milk Ranch, a supply point for Rich Bar and the Feather River mines. Great Western Power Company, who installed a large supply pipe carrying water along the road to Lower Bucks Lake, dammed the lower valley around 1928. Reach the trailhead from Quincy by taking the **Bucks Lake Road** to Lower Bucks Lake, a distance of about 23 miles. From here travel 13 miles via the rough **Three Lakes Road** to the dam. Once at the dam this nice trail ascends gradually along the north side from the trailhead at Lower Three Lakes, past the middle lake, to Upper Three Lakes.

NORTHERN PLUMAS & SOUTHERN LASSEN COUNTIES
Including the Caribou Wilderness and Lassen National Park

This region forms the transition zone between the Sierra and the Cascade ranges. On the north is towering 10,457' Mt. Lassen with its semi-active volcanic attractions. Lassen's last eruptions were in 1914, 1915, and 1917. Near Chester, the largest town in northern Plumas County, is Stover Mountain Ski Area, a community run ski hill. Winter sports and summer water recreation provide residents and visitors with a plethora of activities. To the south are the North Fork and the East Branch of the Feather River. To the east are the high valleys of Clover Valley, Squaw Queen Valley and Dixie Valley, where dairying and cattle ranching once played an important part in Plumas County's economy. There are a number of lakes in this region also, including large Lake Almanor, dammed in 1914 for hydro-electric power, Antelope Lake, a relative newcomer of 1962, Butt Valley, another hydro reservoir, and Round Valley, a product of the mining days of the 1860s. Besides these, many smaller ponds and lakes provide fishing and recreation. Long, winding streams, and short, rushing freshets empty into the North Fork and East Branch of the Feather River, adding their contribution to the waters of Lake Oroville. Included in this section is the Caribou Wilderness, Mt. Lassen, and at least one trail just inside Tehama County.

Spring Valley Mountain in the High Lakes region above the Feather River.

The area is accessible by State Highway 70 from the Sacramento Valley, State Highway 89, State highways 32 and 36, and from the east, U.S. 395.

ANTELOPE LAKE NATURE TRAIL
Elevation: 5000' to 5100'
Length: +/- 1/4 mile
Effort: Very Easy
Hike Time: About 1/4 hour
Location: T27N R12E, section 15
Quadrangle Map: Antelope Lake **(For map see page 168)**

This paved, short trail has a number of interpretive signs along it, but sadly, it never evens goes by the lake itself. To reach the trailhead at Lone Rock Campground take the Taylorsville turnoff on *Highway 89*, 1 mile south of Crescent Mills or 16 miles north of Quincy. In 5 miles the road passes through the little town of Taylorsville, and in another 6 miles passes the historic Genesee Store. Continue on this road, passing the Beckwourth turnoff. Follow the road up Indian Creek canyon to Antelope Lake, staying to the left, where signs give directions to the Lone Rock and Boulder Creek campgrounds. A canopied display board exhibits photos of plants of the area.

ANTELOPE LAKE-TAYLOR LAKE TRAIL
Elevation: 5000' to 6803'
Length: +/- 10 miles
Effort: Moderate
Hike Time: About 5 hours
Location: T27N R12E, sections 20,21,22,29,30 and T27N R11E, sections 25,36,35
Quadrangle Map: Kettle Rock, Antelope Lake

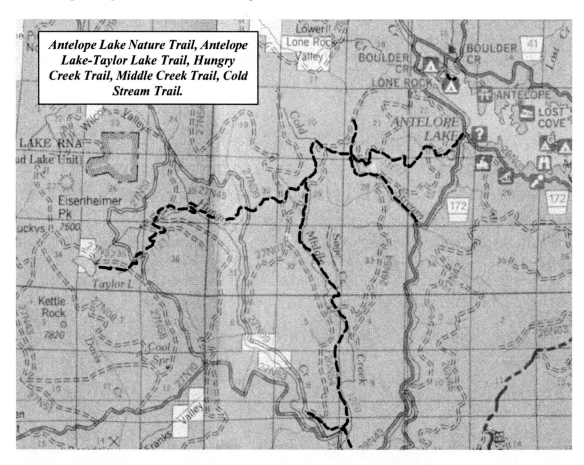

Antelope Lake Nature Trail, Antelope Lake-Taylor Lake Trail, Hungry Creek Trail, Middle Creek Trail, Cold Stream Trail.

This is a relatively new trail that was completed in 1999. By connecting with either the *Cold Stream Trail* or *Middle Creek Trail*, you can make several pleasant shorter streamside hikes. See those trails for their descriptions. To reach the trailhead, take the Taylorsville turnoff on *Highway 89* one mile south of Crescent Mills, or about 16 miles north of Quincy. In 5 miles you will pass through the little town of Taylorsville. Another

6 miles will take you past the inviting and open historic Genesee Store. Continue on this road, passing the Beckwourth turnoff. Follow the road up Indian Creek canyon to just south of Antelope Lake. On the left is a short spur that leads to the equestrian trailhead. There is a pen and loading chute here. If you like, you may continue to the intersection of the road and one that crosses the dam. Park here and you will note the unsigned trail taking off to the left and up the hill. Follow the trail along the hill above and parallel to the *Antelope Lake Road* as it swings around and down past the equestrian trailhead. Begin a light, winding ascent in large ponderosa pine and mixed small pine and white fir. Wind in and out and up and down through small swales and gullies. Watch for barbed wire near a downed gate on a wire range fence as the trail enters a more broken country. Evidence of recent logging dots the landscape. Cross a skid trail and make a light descent along the hillside and under *USFS 26N54*. The trail now makes a light, winding descent and crosses a flat studded with huge old growth Douglas fir and pine and blowdowns. Pass through a log landing and cross *USFS 26N54* diagonally (at the same time crossing a small stream). The trail parallels the creek along the left side under shady cover. This ends soon as it enters the devastation of a clearcut on both sides of the creek. The barren landscape is dotted with huge granite boulders, thistles, mullen, and large, charred stumps. As the trail departs the clearcut it makes a more moderate ascent onto an old skid road. It is now an easy ascent to the crossing of a spur road off *USFS 27N07*. Bear right and make a light ascent crossing several old, steep skid trails. Make a light descent to a contour and then ascend through bouldery ground on a steeper hillside. The clearcut that was just passed through is somewhat visible from here. The trail swings down to cross a draw, then winds along, makes a switchback and ascends lightly. From this point is our first view of Antelope Lake. The trail ascends lightly to another switchback and lots of boulders, crosses another skid trail, makes a switchback, crosses another skid trail and the ridgeback, and then makes a moderate, winding descent through big ponderosa pine and Douglas fir to a gentle descent through two switchbacks. Contour along to the top of a small draw with *USFS 27N07* just above and to the right and descend under and parallel to the road. A view of snow-covered peaks in the distance may be had here. The road and salvage logging are also very evident here. The trail crosses a dry ravine with large granite boulders and contours along to four switchbacks that make a quick ascent to again contour along to the intersection with the *Cold Stream Trail.* From here these two trails share the same route. Once the trail intersects *USFS 27N07* the *Antelope Lake-Taylor Lake Trail* crosses that road, then crosses Cold Stream, ascends gently through three switchbacks to a skid road, which it follows a short distance before veering away to the right. Make a gradual ascent through logged ground, then up and down, then along a steep hillside with heavy young white fir cover. Make two switchbacks, then contour into the open where there are large rounded granite boulders above the trail. These are accented by old growth ponderosa pine and on the left of the trail is a collection of three large boulders with a hole through the center. An easy descent comes to a switchback and a sign Rocky Point, then another three switchbacks all on the ridgeback. As you bear right and contour along the hillside, the easy-but-loose descent comes to another switchback, makes another easy descent with a view of *Middle Creek Road* below, then switchbacks and descends onto a flat and old logging activity. The trail passes under cedar and white fir cover with a lush meadow on the left. A trail bears left to the *Middle Creek Trail* and a sign points the way to Taylor Lake. Cross an old logging road and

begin a moderate ascent under shady cover. Cross another old road and begin a long, easy ascent under predominately white fir cover. You may even see a low flying hawk in these woods. A switchback heralds a moderate ascent, then levels out on the ridgeback before winding through old logging, manzanita and whitethorn. A very mild descent through mixed forest brings the trail into a lodgepole pine basin. The trail is raised above the wet floor by short logs covered with dirt. Delphinium, snow plants, tiger lilies, Bracken fern, forget-me-nots, quaking aspen and other pretty bushes and flowers highlight the route. What may sound like running water is actually quaking aspen rustling in the breeze. A long, winding walk in Douglas fir and lodgepole pine with a meadow at left soon runs into an overgrown road, which the trail follows through willows before making a light ascent, and then a level walk across an old landing to a road crossing. Continue on a level course to what looks like a fork in the trail. Bear right and make a moderate ascent. The new trail appears to be a firebreak constructed for fuel burning. As the trail reaches the ridge top it crosses the firebreak again and continues over the ridgeback. As you begin a moderately easy descent, there are views of Eisenhiemer Peak to the right and the back of Kettle Rock through the trees. The moderate descent is accented by four switchbacks, then a long descent onto an overgrown logging road, a switchback off the road, another long descent, then three more switchbacks. Continue on the moderately winding, sandy descent to another

Early trail building on the national forest was often done with Civilian Conservation Corps.

old logging road. Cross, descend to a switchback and a moderate meandering descent to another switchback, then a final soft descent under heavy forest cover to a crossing of **USFS 27N56**. After crossing the road pass through an old log landing to a wet area with a sign proclaiming Water Hole. Nearby are several large ponderosa pine. Cross the stream over a culvert and bear left on an old logging road. The trail is faint but keep going forward through an old log landing. The road is our route for quite some distance now. This level walk works through mixed forest with occasional brushy openings and, for me, the opportunity of following huge bear tracks, and seeing several dusty depressions where the bruin had rolled in the dirt. The road also affords good views of old clear-cuts from the 1980s that are slowly growing over with brush and some small trees. Occasional diamond-shaped tags on trees indicate the route as it crosses several small, dry draws and old landings. As the road encounters some willow bushes, our single-track trail drops gradually to the left. It levels out under a mixed canopy and crosses a creek on the fine plank and timber bridge. The trail then makes a gradual, winding ascent onto another old logging road. The easy-but-sandy ascent in brush comes to a switchback (watch out for the old logging cable poking out into the trail). The route is now back to single-track with a long, pleasant sidehill ascent that brings us to yet another old logging road. The route levels out and crosses a dry draw, then begins a light descent on single track with a creek on the left below. It is still a nice sidehill walk that winds in and out of some small dry ravines under heavy timber with the small refreshing stream below. An occasional stately old growth Douglas fir or sugar pine accents the route. A light ascent brings the trail onto a road. Cross it and the creek, and head south to the other side. The trail's light ascent in trees, with a huge clearcut on the left and the creek on the right, soon becomes faint as it enters the clearcut. Continue the light ascent in grass away from the creek and into the clearcut. As the trail starts along the sidehill it becomes more distinct. In spring this part of the trail is covered in Indian paintbrush, delphinium, lupine, thimbleberry, and numerous other wildflowers. A switchback and light ascent comes to two more switchbacks and a road. Follow the road east about 100 feet to a sign indicating the route to Taylor Lake. There is now a long sidehill ascent in timber, then a moderate ascent in a clearcut. The once-loose soil is now a reddish brown and sports heavy wildflower growth. A switchback and winding ascent give glimpses of the back of Kettle Rock. Pass a rotted log deck and wind through old stumps to a moderate ascent under timber. The well-cut trail skirts the clearcut on the right, then makes a long, moderate ascent across it with more views of Kettle Rock. Eventually the trail intersects **USFS 27N10**, where a sign indicating Taylor Lake points your walk 100 feet west to the trail. Riparian growth on the right, and the winding ascent through columbine and other colorful plants is a pleasant walk. Soon the route is sidehill under white fir with the road visible and parallel below. A light, winding ascent to a switchback on the ridge back bears the trail to the right with a light ascent through timber and old logging. When the trail hits the **Taylor Lake Road**, follow it about 300 feet to where the trail bears left and uphill. The trail is an old jeep road for a short distance, then becomes single track under a red fir forest. The road comes into view below on the right as the trail meanders sidehill into open, low-growing manzanita and views of Kettle Rock at left. A short wander takes the trail to its unsigned conclusion on the shores of pretty Taylor Lake and a small dirt parking area.

BELDEN-SODA CREEK TRAIL
Elevation: 6100' to 6300'
Length: +/- 5 1/2 miles
Effort: Moderate
Hike Time: About 3 hours
Location: T26N R6E, sections 21,28,29,31,32 and T26N R5E, sections 35,36 and T25N R5E, section 1 and T25N R6E, section 6
Quadrangle Map: Jonesville **(For map see page 172)**

Sadly, this trail also suffered from the Storrie Fire of 2000. When I hiked it, there were views of miles of untouched old growth timber. In all my wanderings in Lassen, Plumas and Sierra counties, I doubt I have ever run across this much untouched mixed conifer forest in one area. The only road visible was the historic **Humbug Valley-Belden Road** built in 1911, and it is clear across Yellow Creek canyon. From points on this trail you can see Claremont barely poking up to the left of the Spanish Peak escarpment, Red Hill and its lookout, and undulating green-carpeted canyon sides. Reach the unsigned trailhead either by taking the *Indian Springs Trail* from Belden (see description), or *USFS 26N08 spur L* 8 miles south of the Lemm Ranch in Humbug Valley. Reach that trailhead by about 11 miles of gravel road south of *State Route 89* about 38 miles north of Quincy, or 7 miles south of Chester. A sign at a five-way intersection just past the Lemm Ranch notes *Belden Trail* 8 miles. The description here will assume you are starting from the *Indian Springs Trail* (about 3 miles from its beginning at Belden). To determine that you are at the *Soda Creek Trail* intersection with the *Indian Springs Trail*, look for a stand of about four large sugar pine (each about 4 1/2 feet to 5 feet in diameter), two of which have overgrown blazes. If you pass them into a brush field, go back, you have gone about 50 yards too far west. The *Soda Creek Trail* breaks off to the north (right) and gently descends through a wooded basin, then gradually ascends through a thick, mostly small-to-medium white fir forest. The trail here is very wide, almost resembling an old road. After a bit you will begin a gentle descent along the hillside with the small dry ravines becoming progressively deeper. The hillside also becomes much steeper, so care should be exercised as the trail is now narrow. There is much forest debris and fallen wood across the trail, but there are also beautiful views of the timber-covered canyons and ridges to the east. Cross a small stream, then a dry ravine, then a small spring in the trail. Soon the trail descends to an unnamed tributary of Squirrel Creek, where a campsite sits on the north side, just above the creek. The trail ascends parallel to, and about 30 feet from, Squirrel Creek, crosses a small, fast-running stream, and continues for about 1/3 mile to a wet crossing of Squirrel Creek. From here it is a gentle ascent up a swale to a low saddle covered with mixed conifer and small black oaks. The trail again widens out and begins a gradual descent to a small, dry ravine where the descent becomes somewhat steeper. Make three switchbacks, the second at a large washout created by the 1986 floods, and wind down the right side of the washed-out gully to a switchback and Soda Creek. Here it is a wet crossing to the north side of this large creek. Though many

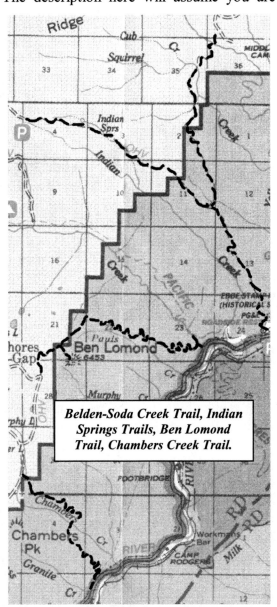

Belden-Soda Creek Trail, Indian Springs Trails, Ben Lomond Trail, Chambers Creek Trail.

large logs are scattered about, it is not recommended they be used to cross. Pick up the trail directly across the stream and follow it downstream a short distance where it begins ascending, making about five switchbacks up the rocky, timbered hillside to **USFS 26N08L** from Humbug Valley.

BEN LOMOND TRAIL
Elevation: 2400' to 6400'
Length: +/- 5 miles
Effort: Very Difficult
Hike Time: About 7 hours
Location: T25N R6E, sections 21,22,23
Quadrangle Map: Jonesville **(For map see page 172)**

Another casualty of the Storrie Fire of 2000, this trail still affords great views of the Feather River canyon. Reach the trailhead via **State Route 70** approximately 1 1/4 miles below Belden, or 29 1/2 miles west of Quincy. The trail begins at the mouth of Chipps Creek on the south side and climbs 4,000 feet with numerous switchbacks. It is a very strenuous hike, but well worth the spectacular scenery. Ben Lomond Peak, though only 6453' high, gives great views up the canyon. From here you can connect with the trails in the High Lakes Region. Besides Morris Lake and Lott Lake, there are a number of smaller lakes dotting the countryside.

BIZZ JOHNSON TRAIL (Lassen County)
Elevation: 5085' to 4258'
Length: +/- 26 miles
Effort: Very Easy
Hike Time: About 9 hours (for the 18 mile hike segment)
Location: T28N R9E, section 5 and T29N R9E sections 4,5,7,8,17,18,2029,32 and T30N R9E, sections 22,25,26,27,28,33,36 and T30N R10E, sections 31-35 and T29N R10E, sections 1,2 and T29N R11E, sections 2-6 and T30N R11E, sections 35,36 and T30N R12E, section 31.
Quadrangle Map: Westwood **(Map not available in this guide)**

I have not had the good fortune to use this trail yet, but have included the following information from another source that I think pretty well covers this popular trail. The Bizz Johnson Trail is one of Lassen County's most scenic, accessible and tranquil recreational offerings. It is built on one of the most significant historical sites in Lassen County, with roots dating back to the turn-of-the-century development of Westwood and Susanville. The trail is named after former Congressman Harold T. Bizz Johnson who was instrumental in getting the trail going. The trail begins in the high-desert terrain at Susanville and climbs into the Sierra and Cascade mountain forest. The 18-mile segment along the Susan River from Susanville to Westwood Junction is the most scenic portion. It is an easy hike with a maximum three-percent grade ascent to the west. A variety of day hikes are possible from the many trailheads along it. Horseback riding is encouraged with the eleven bridges and two tunnels being easily passable. Riverside trails provide alternate routes around the tunnels. Mountain biking is also enjoyed on the trail, but watch for planking on the decked bridges and for the unlighted tunnels. Camping is allowed outside the trailheads, and there is a U.S.F.S. campground at Goumaz, at the approximate mid-point of the trail. There is a very interesting history to this railroad that you can read more about in the Lassen County Visitor's Guide available at most visitor centers in the county.

BLUE LAKE-RIDGE LAKE TRAIL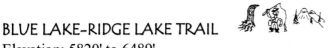

Elevation: 5820' to 6489'
Length: +/- 2 1/2 miles
Effort: Moderate
Hike Time: About 1 1/2 hours
Location: T29N R5E, section 6 and T30N R5E, section 31
Quadrangle Map: Mt. Harkness **(For map see page 184)**

The trailhead is about 20 miles northwest of the town of Chester. To reach it take the ***Juniper Lake Road*** out of Chester, and within a mile turn left onto the ***Drakesbad Resort Road.*** Follow the paved road to the next left indicating the town of Mineral 22 miles away. You might notice the fish ladders on Willow Creek as you cross the bridge. After 8 1/2 miles the pavement ends and the road is very rough, though suitable for low-clearance autos. Follow the Upper Rice Creek signs, staying on ***USFS 29N18***. About a mile from South Arm Rice Creek is ***USFS spur 29N02Y***, which is an alternate trailhead to Blue Lake. From the parking area at its end it is a short, steep ascent through scrub manzanita over the ridge to the lake. For hiking purposes we will pass this and continue on the main road to the South Arm Rice Creek. The trailhead is unsigned and is immediately on the right side of the creek and road. There is a small parking area on both sides of the road. Make a steep ascent on an eroded trail past recent logging. A small set of falls is just to the left. After the short ascent, pass the ***Blue Lake Tie Trail*** to ***Spencer Meadow Trail*** intersection at left and make a switchback, then another up onto another bench. There is a nice view of Mt. Lassen from here. Wind up and down with a mild ascent over a hump, then wind down along a bench with a view of Duck Lake below and to the right. Make a winding ascent to another bench and soon you will come to signed Blue Lake, elevation 6279'. Read on if you would like to continue to the far side of the lake or on to Ridge Lake. A trail seems to go along the left side, but continue straight

Small, high mountain lakes afford wonderful fishing opportunities.
Photo by Suzi Brakken.

ahead along the south end of the lake. The trail meanders about 50 feet from the water, passes a campsite, and makes a short ascent as it goes along the east side of the lake. Just before the outlet, the first mentioned access trail heads uphill, to the right. Follow our trail across the outlet and gently ascend a small ridgeback. Keep an eye out for blazes on some of the bigger Jeffrey pine. Ascend into the trees, then veer right on the sidehill to a short steep ascent between two rock formations. Once on the ridgetop veer left of the obvious rock formation straight ahead. Meander in heavy lodgepole pine at a slight ascent. At times the trail is faint, but obvious. Continue the meander on a descent to Ridge Lake. It is probably a good idea to stop here. If not, and you decide to continue from the east end of this grassy, shallow lake, the trail is unmaintained but discernible if you watch for old cuttings. It drops along a drainage and hits the **North Arm Rice Creek 4WD Road/Trail**, which is bermed some distance downstream. You can either follow this trail down to **Spur A** off of **USFS 29N18** or continue upstream to Spencer Meadow. See **North Arm Rice Creek Trail** description for that route.

BLUE LAKE-SPENCER MEADOWS TIE TRAIL
Elevation: 6000' to 6200'
Length: +/- 3/4 mile
Effort: Moderate
Hike Time: About 1/2 hour
Location: T29N R4E, section 12 and T29N R5E, sections 6,7
Quadrangle Map: Mt. Harkness **(For map see page 184)**

Take either the **Blue Lake-Ridge Lake Trail** (see description above), or take **USFS spur 29N40** off of **USFS 29N18** about 1/4 mile to access this trail. If using the former, ascend past the small falls, and upon hitting the level, take a hard left, cross South Arm Rice Creek, then cross **USFS spur 29N40** and make a rocky, moderately steep ascent on the open ridge. The trail levels a while, then winds up, then levels again on a sidehill course, all in old logging. Cross the top of a spring, enter the trees and make two switchbacks to the ridgeback. A short, winding ascent in scrub manzanita takes the trail over the ridgeback to a mild descent in Jeffrey pine and white fir and finally leads the trail onto a flat and a signed intersection with **Spencer Meadows Trail.**

CHAMBERS CREEK TRAIL
Elevation: 2000' to 6100'
Length: +/- 4 1/2 miles
Effort: Moderate
Hike Time: About 5 hours
Location: T24N R6E, sections 3,4,10 and T25N R6E, sections 29,30,32,33
Quadrangle Map: Storrie **(For map see page 172)**

This trail has had its share of bad luck. Not only did it burn in 1973, it recovered only to suffer the same fate in the Storrie Fire of 2000. But remember, Nature is a master at recovery, and this one will be no exception. This cascading stream was named for Plumas County pioneer Robert Craig Chambers by county surveyor Arthur W. Keddie while surveying a wagon road for Mr. Chambers in 1864. Reach via **State Route 70** at the now-closed James Lee Campground 6 1/2 miles below Belden, or 35 1/2 miles from Quincy. The trailhead is opposite the campground and has a large cedar to provide some shaded parking. The trail starts on an abandoned P.G.& E. maintenance road and climbs quickly to a small sign marked Trail with an arrow pointing right (north). At this point you will ford Granite Creek, pass under the powerlines and proceed along the abandoned road. About 1/2 mile from the beginning the trail proper leaves the road. An old Douglas

Fog on an early spring morning on the Chambers Creek Trail.

fir stump with a small wood sign marked 6EO6 is just above the trail on the left. The ascent up the mountain through the 1973 Chambers Creek burn and the 2000 Storrie Fire is steady, with four switchbacks. Wildflowers and flowering shrubs were abundant and beautiful in the spring and shared the trail with the ever-present poison oak. At the end of the fourth switchback you will enter Chambers Creek canyon. You can hear the creek roaring far below, but can't see it until rounding the bend just before reaching the creek. Suddenly, an iron bridge and spectacular scenery greet you. This is the last you will see of the creek until you are about another 2 miles up. After crossing the bridge, the trail makes a series of ten switchbacks over the next 2 1/2 miles to the top, though many are more of a winding climb than real switchbacks. The ascent through here is steady and fairly steep. You can see the character and features of the land change from the river to the top. The last time you break over into the Chambers Creek side you will see and hear the cascading water far below. The trail now becomes brushier and rougher. Several seasonal creeks run in the trail and many small windfalls make walking difficult. At the top of the ridge is a fairly flat, wet, swampy area of fir, cedar and lodgepole pine. From here you can cut over to the left toward Chambers Peak, or go ahead to Ben Lomond Peak and various small lakes in the High Lakes region.

COLD STREAM TRAIL
Elevation: 4800' to 5400'
Length: +/- 2 miles
Effort: Easy
Hike Time: About 2 hours
Location: T27N R12E, sections 21,27,28
Quadrangle Map: Kettle Rock, Antelope Lake **(For map see page 168)**

Cold Stream Trail and *Middle Creek Trail* combined make a great hike if you have transportation at both ends. Both trails are fairly easy except for the trees and debris in the trails. It is easiest to hike up the *Cold Stream Trail*, follow *USFS 27N07* 1 1/2 miles around to Middle Creek and walk down that trail. If you want you can take the newly completed *Antelope Lake-Taylor Lake Trail* from the *Cold Stream Trailhead* to Middle Creek. That trail is above and roughly parallels *USFS 27N07* around to the head of Middle Creek. Reach the *Cold Stream Trail* trailhead by taking *Plumas County A-22* to Taylorsville 1 mile south of Crescent Mills, or about 16 miles north of Quincy on *Highway 89*. In 5 miles you will pass through the small town of Taylorsville. In another 6 miles you will see the historic Genesee Store. Continue on this road, passing the *Beckwourth Road* turnoff. Follow the road up Indian Creek canyon toward Antelope Lake, about 4 1/4 miles, passing the *Middle Creek Trail* trailhead (small sign depicting a hiker). Turn left on a small dirt road on the left side of the creek. A parking area is just ahead. Just past this is a sign for the trail. The trail parallels the creek, while on the right side are huge granite boulders peppered with ponderosa pine. The walk is an easy, almost level grade with occasional evidence of helicopter logging. Soon the trail crosses a small creek, then passes through a well-timbered flat. After a bit it makes a light-to-moderate ascent. The tread is

View to the west off the Dixie Mountain escarpment.

decomposed granite and in very good condition. The overgrown blazes indicate this trail as of rather old vintage. After crossing a dry ravine the trail passes along the west edge of an old log landing. Working through the thick young pine trees, the small creek now runs right down the trail. This is a tributary of Cold Stream, which bore away to the southwest a while back. Walk up a grassy wet area with horses tails and woodland strawberries past a trail sign 50- feet below the road. Cross *USFS 26N54* and pass another trail sign. The trail wanders through old logging, parallels the creek, and makes a gradual ascent before crossing the creek. The cover here is very thick white fir and Douglas fir with some larger pine and cedar. Make a switchback and ascend gradually to a wet area, make two quick switchbacks and meander gently along the ridge side through old logging. As the trail crosses the ridge, make a gradual descent out of the logged area and into a nice forest and Cold Stream. The trail parallels the creek and makes a light ascent to an old sign reading: **Cold Stream Trail.** Here the **Antelope Lake-Taylor Lake Trail** intersects the **Cold Stream Trail**. Continue upstream, passing along the base of a huge clearcut with a number of wet marshy areas along the trail. As the trail leaves the clearcut, it parallels the creek to a heavily timbered flat and utilizes an old skid trail, though it is still nice walking. The trail soon intersects a closed road with a sign reading: Wilcox Valley 5 (to left) and **Boulder Creek Road** 3 (to right). Go straight ahead and to the left of the sign and continue upstream. In a little bit the trail intersects **USFS 27N07**. A sign points out the **Cold Stream Trail.** Officially, this is the end of our trail. However, it is possible to continue along the **Antelope Lake-Taylor Lake Trail** to Middle Creek. See that trail description for more information, or walk **USFS 27N07** the 1 1/2 miles or so to Middle Creek.

DIXIE MOUNTAIN TRAIL

Elevation: 8040' to 6400'
Length: +/- 1 mile
Effort: Difficult
Hike Time: About 1 hour
Location: T24N R15E, sections 11,14,15
Quadrangle Map: Dixie Mountain, Frenchman Lake

To reach this trailhead, take **State Highway 70** east from Quincy about 50 miles, or 28 miles west from Reno to the small town of Chilcoot. From Chilcoot head north on **Highway 284** for 8 miles to Frenchman Dam. Proceed along the

west side of Frenchman Lake on **USFS 25N11** for 6 miles to the signed junction with **USFS 24N02Y**, where the road to Dixie Mountain Lookout is indicated. Take this rough road 7 miles to the upper trailhead. While near the peak, it is worth it to take a walk up to the lookout. There are spectacular views from this lofty 8327' perch. If you prefer hiking the trail from the bottom up, continue past **24N02Y** on **25N11** another 2 miles to the junction of **USFS 25N03 (Lookout Creek Road)**. Follow this to the signed trailhead.

HOMER LAKE-DEERHEART LAKE TRAIL

Elevation: 6800' to 6139'
Length: +/- 2 1/2 miles
Effort: Easy
Hike Time: About 2 hours
Location: T27N R9E, sections 4,8 and T28N R9E, section 32,33
Quadrangle Map: Greenville **(For map see page 179)**

Homer Lake-Deerheart Lake Trail.

To access the trailhead, travel north of Greenville on **State Route 89** about 3 miles to **County Road 201**. Make a right onto the unsigned paved road. It quickly turns to dirt. About 2 miles up take a right at the signed intersection on **USFS 28N38**. From here it is 10 miles to Homer Lake. Continue past another signed intersection to Greenville Saddle. The somewhat barren landscape is a result of the Williams Valley fire in the 1980s. Bear left at the saddle on **USFS 28N68** and continue to another left **(USFS 28N60A)**. Follow this about 2 miles to the end of the road where there is ample parking. The unsigned trail starts on the right side of the parking lot and makes about ten very easy switchbacks down to Homer Lake. The trail is heavily used, though only lightly maintained. From the northeast shore of Homer Lake follow the well-defined path along its edge to the lake outlet. Cross, make a very slight ascent, and begin contouring along the north side of Keddie Ridge. Very good views of Mountain Meadows to the north are afforded from here. As the trail works along, note the old stumps from logging operations from previous decades. Descend about four easy switchbacks and continue along through a field of huge boulders before breaking out into a large draw. Cross a small stream and make a moderate ascent up to the **Hidden Lake Trail** intersection. This trail makes about six or so quick switchbacks on the 1/4-mile-or so-long trail to Hidden Lake. Continue on a more or less contour into heavy timber, make two easy switchbacks up to a lodgepole pine and fir basin, pass through this and soon crest above beautiful Deerheart Lake. The trail continues to the lake via three easy switchbacks. Nice lakeside campsites can be found.

HOSSELKUS CREEK TRAIL
Elevation: 4000' to 5200'
Length: +/- 4 miles
Effort: Difficult
Hike Time: About 4 hours
Location: T26N R11E, sections 28,27,22,15
Quadrangle Map: Genesee Valley, Taylorsville **(For map see page 180)**

This is another old miner-built pack trail. It is minimally maintained, apparently by trail-users. The lower end at Genesee Valley is on private land; however, there are several ways to access the trail. I started my hike at the upper end of the trail. For the purpose of this guide I will describe it from the lower end. I am not condoning crossing private land by doing this, though. If possible you should contact the owner(s) for permission. To reach the trailhead from Quincy take **Highway 89** north to **Plumas County A-22,** turn right and proceed to Taylorsville. From Taylorsville continue east through town to the rodeo grounds, bear right, and follow **Plumas County Road 112** about 6 miles to Genesee Valley. Just as the highway begins to cross an arm of the valley to the left is a gated road at the base of a hill. This road, if followed about 2 1/2 miles, will eventually neck down into the **Hosselkus Creek Trail**. Another way is to continue to the Genesee Store where a gated road takes off behind to go the same distance to the trail. There is a residence at the start of the road. You will know you are at the trailhead when the road, which is just right of the creek, begins a moderate ascent with blazed trees. It makes a nice meandering walk in small trees with occasional old growth. There is evidence of old logging, and an old phone line to the Kettle Rock Lookout alternates overhead and on the ground. After a time the trail becomes definite single-track and makes a light ascent to a brushy crossing. Immediately after crossing is what appears to be a fairly recent trail heading left (northwest) up a branch of Hosselkus Creek. Make a gentle-to-moderate ascent along a rocky area with nice creek pools. As the trail enters a shaded glade, begin an ascent across a seasonal creek and wet area, pass a small

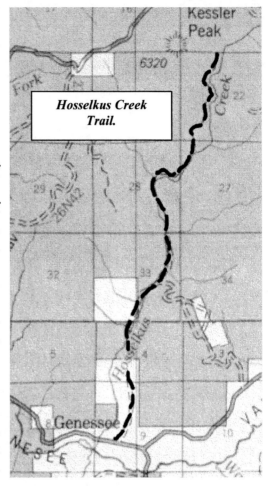

Hosselkus Creek Trail.

water hole, and make a moderate ascent to a switchback. The trail steepens considerably as it passes under the old phone line. Make a sharp right at the end of an old cedar log. As the trail leaves the light cover of trees it makes a moderate ascent, crosses a dry gully, passes under the phone line again, and then tops the ridge back. The trail then makes a light descent and affords a good view of the open, rocky ground across the creek. It enters the trees again, passes under the phone line, crosses a small spring and makes a light ascent. Cross the creek at a rock outcropping, then a dry gulch, and begin making a moderate ascent. The trail steepens as it climbs to cross an old, closed log road. Evidence of old logging is apparent, then the trail crosses over a small ridgeback and drops to a nice level camp area. This is also the last we see of the phone line. Make the easy walk in grass under heavy forest cover to another crossing of the creek. The trail intersects a barely visible skid road, ascends moderately through nice trees to cross over a rock outcrop, while just above is a closed logging road. Make a light descent and contour along the hillside into old logging. From here ascend the ridge back, cross an old road, and continue a short ascent to the end of a logging spur at a log landing. This spur continues uphill about 1 mile to an intersection with another road that connects with **USFS 27N10** at Green Flat. This is the **Beardsley Grade**, which if taken west, will connect with **North Arm Road (Plumas County 214)** in about 6 miles.

HUNGRY CREEK TRAIL
Elevation: 4640' to 5000'
Length: +/- 3/4 mile
Effort: Moderate
Hike Time: About 3/4 hour
Location: T26N R12E, sections 16,17
Quadrangle Map: Genesee Valley **(For map see page 168)**

This trail used to reach into the upper drainages of Hungry Creek. Roads have now made it obsolete, but there is enough of it left for a short jaunt. To access this now abandoned trail use the **Middle Creek Trail** directions and hike up the **Middle Creek Trail** about 1/2 mile or so. The **Hungry Creek Trail** veers northwest at a gentle ascent under old growth ponderosa pine. Evidence of recent helicopter logging is about, and the trail is covered with forest litter. Cross a dry ravine and continue the same grade up through boulders and timber. The **Hungry Creek Road (USFS 27N09)** is visible across the creek. Round the ridge and intersect a very steep skid trail that runs down to the road where it crosses Hungry Creek. The trail continues on a contour above and parallel to the **Hungry Creek Road** until it intersects it at a saddle just a bit further along.

INDIAN FALLS TRAIL
Elevation: 3200' to 3100'
Length: +/- 1/4 mile
Effort: Easy
Hike Time: About 1/4 hour
Location: T25N R9E, section 3
Quadrangle Map: Crescent Mills

Indian Falls Trail.

This quick, though steep walk will take you to a beautiful waterfall on Indian Creek. These falls have significant mythological importance to the Maidu Indian tribe. Reach the trail by taking **State Highway 70 and 89** north from Quincy 10 miles to the Greenville Y. Turn right onto **State Highway 89** and travel north about 2 miles, just past the town of Indian Falls. There is ample parking on the east side of the road at the head of the trail.

INDIAN SPRINGS TRAIL
Elevation: 2300' to 6000'
Length: +/- 6 1/2 miles
Effort: Difficult
Hike Time: About 5 hours
Location: T25N R6E, sections 3,4,10,11,12,13,24
Quadrangle Map: Jonesville **(For map see page 172)**

There is no way that I can find the time to completely rehike each trail after it suffers damage from natural or man-caused events. This trail was another victim of the Storrie

Fire of 2000. I will leave the description as is and hope it will still be of service to you. Reach this trail by taking **State Route 70** 28 miles from Quincy to the Eby Stamp Mill Historical Site opposite Belden. The trail begins just right of the stamp mill and climbs past picnic tables and under some power lines. As you enter a drainage you will pass the small Belden Cemetery to the right. After crossing this dry ravine you leave the live oak canopy and break into the open under large transmission lines. From here you have a good view of Belden and the highway. Make two switchbacks and climb to an abandoned P.G.& E. road where a sign points out the trail. Follow the road about 1/3 mile and note the large reflector above the road. Just past this a sign points out the trail where it makes a sharp switchback up off the road. Make two switchbacks through tall manzanita and climb to the ridge spine where you begin a long, moderate but not unpleasant ascent under a light canopy of black oak. Cross the brow of the ridge, make a slight descent through thick cover, again ascend past a large ponderosa pine with an arrow scar on it pointing out the ***R.M. Greg*** or ***Lazzello Mine Trail***. This mile-long old pack trail is almost completely

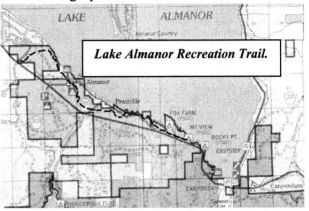

covered with blown down trees and forest debris. Continue ascending and cross the ridge spine. Views of Ben Lomond Peak and the Feather River Canyon are presented here. From here, for quite a distance, the walk alternates between moderate and level. An ascent to the moderate ridge and the west side of the ridge brings the trail to a switchback. About 25 yards ahead (west) is a spring gushing out of the rocks. Eight more switchbacks up the very gentle ridgeback brings the trail to a very wide section with stands of large ponderosa and sugar pine. But for all the fallen trees and forest debris, it is a pleasant walk. Soon the ***Soda Creek Trail*** bears off at a right angle to the trail. Cross a saddle with a small brush field, which the trail passes through the top of, then back into the tall timber. A light ascent levels out on a ridge back, crosses a small stream, then ascends past a National Forest boundary sign and two K-tags. After crossing the head of a small dry ravine and making a moderate ascent to Indian Springs, there are some very nice campsites available.

LAKE ALMANOR RECREATION TRAIL

Elevation: 4519' to 4519'
Length: +/- 8 1/2 miles
Effort: Very Easy
Hike Time: About 4 hours
Location: T27N R7E, sections 3,10,11,12,13 and T27N R8E, sections 18,17
Quadrangle Map: Almanor NW, Canyon Dam **(For map see above)**

This paved, 10-foot-wide path is suitable for hikers, joggers, mountain bikers, rollerbladers, and wheelchairs. Benches and picnic tables are available the entire length.

It meanders through the forest along the west shore of beautiful Lake Almanor. Great views of Mt. Lassen, the lake, and the meadows and forests are plentiful along the whole route. There are a number of sections that are fairly steep, some of which switchbacks mitigate, but for the most part it is an easy trail. It is fun to do it in sections if you do not have the time to follow the entire route.

MIDDLE CREEK TRAIL
Elevation: 4600' to 5800'
Length: +/- 4 1/2 miles
Effort: Easy
Hike Time: About 3 1/2 hours
Location: T26N R12E, sections 16,9,4,5 and T27N R12E, sections 29,32
Quadrangle Map: Kettle Rock, Genesee Valley **(For map see page 168)**

Middle Creek Trail and *Cold Stream Trail* make a great hike if you have transportation at both ends. Both trails are easy walks except for the fallen trees and debris in the trails. It is easiest to hike up the *Cold Stream Trail*, follow *USFS 27N07* around to Middle Creek, and walk down the *Middle Creek Trail*. If you want you can take the new *Antelope Lake-Taylor Lake Trail* from the *Cold Stream Trailhead* to Middle Creek. That trail is above and roughly parallels *USFS 27N07* around to the head of Middle Creek. Reach this trailhead by taking *Plumas County A-22* to Taylorsville 1 mile south of Crescent Mills, or about 15 miles north of Quincy on *Highway 89*. Continue 5 miles through the town of Taylorsville, another 6 miles to the historic Genesee Store, and continue on this road, passing the Beckwourth turnoff. Follow the road up Indian Creek canyon toward Antelope Lake. About 1/4 mile above the left turnoff of *Hungry Creek Road (USFS 27N09)*, and across a large culvert, is the unsigned trailhead. A large parking area with a border of boulders is opposite the trailhead. Walk down an old dirt road about 50 yards to a sign: *Middle Creek Trail*, a register asking for comments but without paper, and a plastic sign saying the trail is easiest. The trail from here for a distance is an old skid road. It then passes through an old logged area, becomes trail again, makes a moderate ascent, rounds the ridge, and runs easily to a crossing of Middle Creek just above its confluence with Hungry Creek. Make a light ascent again on a skid road, passing the old *Hungry Creek Trail* on your left. An old wire fence parallels our route, which now runs above a long, pretty meadow. The road becomes trail again before making a slight ascent back to the road. Follow again, ascending from the road along the hillside just above the meadow. The trail runs along at a fairly level grade to the head of the meadow. There is old evidence of beaver handiwork in this area. Make a light ascent and switchback, pass the K-tag for sections 8 and 9, make another three switchbacks, and a moderate ascent through an area that was recently helicopter logged. The trail is moderate though the creek is making a quick drop. Cross the intermittent draw at the bottom edge of a clearcut visible through the trees and ascend through large trees, past a wet grassy area on the left. The trail now makes a moderate ascent through old growth to a ridge top, crosses to the other side and descends gradually back toward Middle Creek. Cross a wet grassy area and Middle Creek to several blazed aspens, then cross over a small meadow to a blazed pine. Under a thick forest continue to a moderate ascent, cross the creek again, pass a location tag for the 1/4 section of section 4, cross the creek again, and make a fairly steep ascent and two switchbacks to **USFS 26N54**. Go left on and across the road about 100 feet to a closed logging road on the right side of the creek. The trail runs parallel to the closed road and makes a moderate climb. Pass a K-tag for section 32 before entering a meadow. Cross Sage Creek, which runs across the meadow, pass through a group of blazed aspen and cross to a group of large ponderosa pine. There is a nice sized patch of Beargrass here. The trail runs along easily through large pines, though there is evidence of old logging on both sides of the trail. An old road is visible on the opposite side of the creek. Pass the K-tag for sections 29 and 32, and soon reach the edge of a large meadow running up Middle Creek and to the left up a tributary. Cross the tributary and meadow to the trees on the other side. The trail runs between an old road and Middle Creek. Red Tail hawks can be seen perched about the snags in this area. The trail soon connects with the old road, passes a hunter's perch in the trees, and continues straight up the meadow to **USFS 27N07**.

NORTH ARM RICE CREEK TRAIL
Elevation: 6000' to 6400'
Length: +/- 3 miles
Effort: Moderate
Hike Time: About 2 hours
Location: T29N R5E, section 5 and T30N R5E, sections 31,32
Quadrangle Map: Mt. Harkness

Some maps show this trail running along the north side of North Arm Rice Creek. I spent some time there trying to find the trail, but to no avail. Several times I found likely traces but they didn't pan out. I concluded that the trail never existed, or is so old and abandoned that it has disappeared. I find the latter hard to believe, but.... I almost hesitate to include this trail, but it has possibilities and it seems to get some use. Years ago, this trail was a 4WD road someone shoved through, but has since been blocked and is slowly reverting to single track. To reach the trailhead, use the **Blue Lake-Ridge Lake Trail**

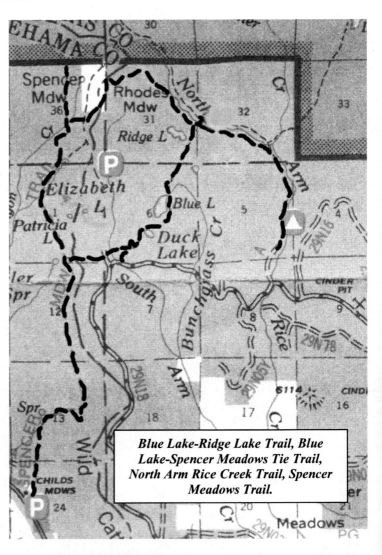

Blue Lake-Ridge Lake Trail, Blue Lake-Spencer Meadows Tie Trail, North Arm Rice Creek Trail, Spencer Meadows Trail.

description and take **USFS 29N18** past the last Upper Rice Creek sign and turnoff. That road will take you to a primitive campground that maps show as a trailhead. Save yourself some boot leather. After crossing North Arm Rice Creek take a right on **USFS spur 29N18A**. Follow this about 1 mile to a berm in a logged area. Follow the road/trail as it meanders along easily on the west side of the creek. There are numerous wet areas. Pass the obscure east end of the **Blue Lake-Ridge Lake Trail** that heads steeply up a draw to Ridge Lake. Note the mountain hemlock that reach good size here. Though there is some maintenance, there are also many large blowdowns across the trail. The trail now veers left and makes a winding, moderate ascent along the hillside, dips across a swale, levels, then makes a mild ascent. Rice Creek is now far below. After cresting, make a moderate, rocky descent, cross a wet area, and ascend bearing right. There is a view of a rock bluff to the right. This bluff is part of the Lassen National Park border. The trail passes through mixed scrub manzanita, lodgepole pine and fir. Make a hard left and enjoy the meadows at the base of the bluffs at right. Descend across a wet area and then make a long, rocky, moderate ascent along the hillside. Hit the ridge top and level, then make a light descent into old logging. Straight ahead is a nice view of Mt. Conard in Lassen Park. Skirt a down wire fence, then descend steeply along the right side of the fence to the base of the hill. You are now at Spencer Meadow which, incidentally, is private property. The old **Spencer Meadow Trail (Child's Meadows Trail)** used to run right through this spot, but has since been rerouted. See that trail description for more information. To get to the **Spencer Meadow Trail** or the end of **USFS spur 29N40**, go left and follow the closed and overgrown logging road along the east side of the meadow to where it breaks over and starts down. By going right, along the base of the meadow you will soon intersect the **Spencer Meadow Trail** near some cabin ruins. If not, you <u>will</u> intersect the creek. The other alternative is to continue down the closed, loose, cobbly road about 3/4 mile to the end of **USFS spur 29N40**. This spur then descends to connect with **USFS 29N18** near the **Blue Lake-Ridge Lake Trail** trailhead.

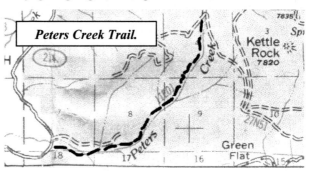
Peters Creek Trail.

PETER'S CREEK TRAIL
Elevation: 3600' to 6777'
Length: +/- 3 miles
Effort: Difficult
Hike Time: About 4 hours
Location: T26N R11E, sections 4,7,8,9,18
Quadrangle Map: Kettle Rock, Greenville NE, Taylorsville **(For map see above)**

This old pack trail has not been maintained for a number of years. Occasionally someone has cut the larger logs out of its path, but the brush and small trees are taking over. My hike was prefaced by a swarm of hornets in a log just behind me, and a large coiled rattlesnake just in front of me. After getting out of that, I was treated to a Golden Eagle swooping down the creek canyon at eye level with me. Later, a bear became vocal, so it's obvious there is still some wildlife out there. The trailhead is located about 1 mile up a dirt road behind the Peter Ranch in the North Arm of Indian Valley. To get there from Quincy, go north on **Highway 89** about 15 miles to **Plumas County A-22.** Turn right and follow it to the town of Taylorsville. Take a left on **Deadfall Lane**, proceed a little over 1 mile to **Plumas County Road 112**, turn left, go a short distance, then go right on **North Arm Road** (**Plumas County 214**). Follow this scenic drive a little over 3 miles to Peter's Creek. Cross the culvert and make an immediate right onto the dirt road. It continues onto national forest as it parallels the Peter Ranch water line. At the end of the road is a sign on a tree pointing out the *Peter's Creek Trail*. Immediately go left at the sign and ascend an old skid trail. The trail makes a moderate ascent in small timber and large rocks, leaves the creek, then drops back again to parallel for a time. There are some nice stream pools and old growth timber through this section. The trail makes light-to-moderate ascents as it crosses a dry gully and enters an area of live oak, then makes a long, winding ascent into a rocky area. After a while it makes a long, moderate-to-steep ascent, then levels into the creek. Old growth cover shades the almost indiscernible trail and the two sets of switchbacks. Another long, moderate-to-steep ascent that is somewhat overgrown and eroded brings us to the creek. Parallel close to the creek on a steep

Peter's Creek Trail sign.

ascent past a rock bluff as you wind through a rocky area with another large bluff on the opposite side of the creek. Cross the creek and make a steep ascent, then cross a wet, grassy area and begin an easy walk through rocks and small white fir. Cross another wet, grassy area and note the recent logging on the other side of the creek. Pass a small pond built with a CAT and follow its overgrown path on a moderate ascent to **USFS 27N51**. This end is unsigned. Another mile of road will take you to the historic Lucky S Mine.

PROVIDENCE HILL-SCHNEIDER RAVINE TRAIL
Elevation: 4400' to 4000'
Length: +/- 1 mile
Effort: Difficult
Hike Time: About 1 hour
Location: T26N R8E, section 35 and T25N R8E, section 2
Quadrangle Map: Twain

Providence Hill-Schneider Ravine Trail.

To access this trail, travel to the Twain-Gray's Flat turnoff on **State Route 70**, about 13 miles west of Quincy. However, instead of turning left into Twain, make a right of dirt **USFS 26N18**. Follow this winding ascent through an old burn about 3 miles, then about 8 more miles of winding road to Providence Hill Mine. A small, somewhat overgrown road breaks away to the left. This will take you down to the unsigned, obscure trailhead. This old trail gradually winds down the hillside, crossing an old ditch and ending at the mouth of Schneider Ravine and an old mine. Some rusting machinery and an old cabin from the 1930s are all that remain. The Rush Creek canyon is very pretty and the trail does afford some decent views.

ROUND VALLEY LAKE NATURE TRAIL
Elevation: 4200' to 4700'
Length: +/- 1 mile
Effort: Very Easy
Hike Time: About 1 hour
Location: T26N R9E, section 15
Quadrangle Map: Crescent Mills

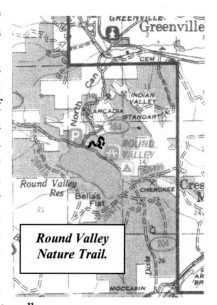

Round Valley Nature Trail.

Take the signed **Greenville-Round Valley Road** up North Canyon from the town of Greenville. In 3 miles you will come to the lake, the dam will be to your right. Parking is available at the trailhead. The trail begins near a trash dumpster and restrooms and has a 500-foot incline to its high point. There are a number of interpretive signs along the trail as it makes about seven easy switchbacks to the top. At that point there is a picnic table and a very obstructed view of Greenville and Indian Valley below. Some of the interpretive signs put up by the Forest Service make some rather interesting statements: Early settlers regarded the white fir as a weed.., when in fact it was the Forest Service who regarded that species of tree as undesirable. The return trip down is a bit steeper and there are no signs, but there are several benches to rest on. After the trail is cleaned up of its heavy debris, it will make a very pleasant walk.

SPENCER MEADOWS NATIONAL RECREATION TRAIL
(Also known as CHILD'S MEADOWS TRAIL)
Elevation: 4900' to 6700'
Length: +/- 6 miles
Effort: Moderate
Hike Time: About 4 hours
Location: T29N R4E, sections 1,12,13,24 and T30N R4E, section 36
Quadrangle Map: Mt. Harkness **(For map see page 184)**

This is posted as a *National Recreation Trail.* To reach the trailhead from the town of Chester, proceed west on **State Highway 36** for 3 miles to its intersection with **State**

Highway 89. The combined roads continue west another 18 1/2 miles, almost to Child's Meadows. There is a wide, paved parking area at the trailhead just before a painted cattle guard on the highway. A covered information board has a sign reading: **Spencer Meadow National Recreation Trail**, Spencer Meadow 5, Lassen Park 5 1/2. Make a short switchback and medium ascent across a new skid trail and recent logging to another switchback, and then a long, gradual ascent under thick cover of young white fir and black oak with occasional larger trees, mostly cedar. The trail makes this same approximate grade, crosses two dry creeks, winds in and out of swales, crosses one more dry creek, and rounds the steep hillside to a section of blasted rock. Though the grade is easy, elevation is gained quickly. The view down to Child's Meadows and *Highway 36-89* is beautiful. Continue this long, almost level ascent to a switchback and a refreshing spring. Ascend a distance to the last switchback, and continue on the easy grade with occasional views of the other side of the canyon. Enter into heavy cover again and make a moderate ascent into old logging. Cross a dry creek and come to an intersection with a sign pointing left and reading: Canyon Route. I did not follow this route, so you will be on your own, or you might check other guides for this trail. As I understand, it is a very scenic alternate route and certainly would make the hike more interesting because you would not be retracing your entire route. The other sign reads: Meadow Route (ahead), *Highway 36*, 2 (back). A light ascent through old logging takes us past a meadow barely visible through the trees on the right. The trail for the next mile or so crosses back and forth over the top of the bench several times. The trees go from bigger and thicker to scrawnier and thinner. At mid-day in summer it can be terribly hot. After awhile make a steep descent into a shaded glen, cross out and into the open again, and hit the signed right trail intersection with the **Blue Lake Trail** (see the **Blue Lake Tie Trail** description). Make a light, winding ascent onto another bench with a nice view of Mt. Conard ahead. Meander in scrub manzanita, then enter the timber and make a light ascent past the unsigned, unmaintained Growler Trail. We are now back in the open on a level walk. After reentering the trees make a short ascent to another level walk and a view of Broke Off Mountain. A light descent into lodgepole pine with a rock bluff on the right leads us to a moderate descent in red fir and a crossing above a small meadow. Cross a grassy area with a lodgepole stand and then a seasonal drainage. Make an ascent along the drainage, switchback, then and a moderate, graveled ascent to another switchback. After topping another bench make a light descent to the base of a small meadow, cross a seasonal outlet and make a level walk in the trees along the left side of

High elevation Sierra Valley in northeastern Plumas County.

Chummy Meadows. You will soon pass a bearing tree with blue paint for the south 1/4 of section 36, on the right. Now make a long, medium ascent onto a forested saddle and the intersection with the **Hanna Trail (4EO7)**, which heads left and down. A sign reads: **Highway 36** (left), Spencer Meadow (ahead). A medium ascent along the hillside brings us to another signed intersection: Lassen National Park 3/4 (left), just yards before a wire fence and Spencer Meadow. Originally the trail continued right and up the east side of the meadow, but has now been relocated along the west side and just out of the private property line. To continue to Lassen Park have your permits in order and your dogs at home. From here, descend across Canyon Creek, which heads out of Spencer Meadow. Parallel a fence line on the right and continue at an almost level walk along the down fence and property line. Gradually the trail climbs the hillside giving glimpses of the pretty meadow below. Cross two seasonal draws and then a wet creek. Soon you will hit a good wire fence and enter private ground for a short way. At a pass-through in the fence is a sign pointing to a horse gate a bit farther on. The rancher's sign implores you to close the gate after use. Nearby are bearing trees for the east 1/16 corner along sections 25 and 36. From here on you will be in Lassen National Park.

STAR LAKE TRAIL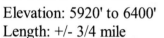

Elevation: 5920' to 6400'
Length: +/- 3/4 mile
Effort: Easy
Hike Time: About 1/2 hour
Location: T30N R7E, sections 35,36
Quadrangle Map: Chester **(For map see page 192, also page 194 for larger map)**

From the town of Chester, travel east 5 miles on **State Highway 36** to Bailey Creek. Turn left at the four-way intersection, pass the garbage transfer station, and turn left on the **T Line**. You will note lettered road signs throughout this region. It is how the private timber companies designate their different roads, and is a practice hailing back to logging railroad days. Cross the old Bailey Creek bridge and turn right at the next intersection. A sign indicates that the Caribou Wilderness is 11 miles and Silver Lake is 18 miles. This is well signed **USFS 10**. Follow it about 9 miles to where the pavement turns to a washboard gravel road. From here continue straight toward Echo Lake for about 1/2 mile or less. The trailhead is unsigned, but is obvious if you proceed slowly. Look for a well-blazed large lodgepole pine on the right (east) side of the road. The road is wide enough for parking here. Once you have located the trailhead, cross a flat and make a moderate ascent on a wide, well-used, well-blazed path. The route also sports white metal diamonds on the trees. In short order it crests the ridge and meanders along a flat before entering a heavy lodgepole stand. Make a very light descent to a flat and a pond on the right. The trail then meanders down to Star Lake, continues along the left side, and passes onto private property and the end of a primitive road. An overgrown arrow has been carved into a large white fir at the trail-road intersection. Star Lake is small but pretty, and in all is a pleasant hike.

SUNFLOWER FLAT-SAUCER LAKE TRAIL

Elevation: 6380' to 6300'
Length: +/- 6 miles
Effort: Difficult
Hike Time: About 4 hours
Location: T26N R5E, sections 35,36 and T25N R6E, section 36
Quadrangle Map: Jonesville

Time constraints would not allow me to check this trail again after the Storrie Fire of 2000, so I do not know if it suffered major damage from that incident. To reach the trailhead to these small lakes, use the description given for the *Sunflower Flat-Soda Creek Trail.* Take that trail to the point where it makes a sharp left down Soda Creek. Cross the stream and make a moderate ascent with three switchbacks to an open ridge top. Enter trees again as the trail meanders along past the very grassy Frog Lake. Green Island Lake sports an all-vegetative island. Cross its outlet and begin a light ascent through a rock field. Just after passing a pond to your right you will round the end of a ridge and see Saucer Lake down below. This is the end of the trail.

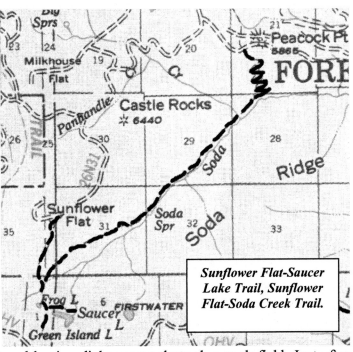

Sunflower Flat-Saucer Lake Trail, Sunflower Flat-Soda Creek Trail.

SUNFLOWER FLAT-SODA CREEK TRAIL (to Peacock Point)

Elevation: 6380' to 5800'
Length: +/- 6 miles
Effort: Difficult
Hike Time: About 4 hours
Location: T26N R6E, sections 21,28,29,31,32 and T26N R5E, sections 35,36
Quadrangle Map: Jonesville **(For map see above)**

This trail also may have suffered fire damage in the summer of 2000. This is a trail that has an uphill finish no matter which end you start at. The preferred way is to start at Sunflower Flat and walk down stream, finishing by climbing out on a series of sixteen switchbacks which, mercifully, are shaded by old growth timber and have a live spring for cooling off on every other one. To reach the *Sunflower Flat Trailhead* take the

Humbug Valley Road about 7 miles south of Chester, or 42 1/2 miles north of Quincy on ***State Route 89.*** Travel this well maintained dirt road through the historic and beautiful Humbug Valley to a five-way intersection. Stay on the road that heads to Humbug Summit. Pass Little Grizzly Campground on the left, and in about 1 mile take a left on ***USFS 26N35*** (red cinder road). Follow this road (it is signed all the way) about 3 miles to a sign pointing to Peacock Point. This is the north end of the ***Soda Creek Trail.*** A sign at that trailhead notes it is 2 miles into Soda Creek. Continue on to Sunflower Flat where there is ample parking. A shot-up sign reads: ***Sunflower Flat Trail 5E22,*** Soda Creek 1, Green Island Lake 2, Saucer Lake 3. The trail makes a moderate descent with about five gradual switchbacks, and a long, easy, winding descent to Soda Creek. Here the trail makes a sharp left to begin down Soda Creek. To go on to Frog, Green Island, and Saucer Lakes, see the description for the ***Sunflower Flat-Saucer Lake Trail.*** A moderate descent through alternating grassy patches and mixed fir and lodgepole pine typifies this trail. After crossing several springs note the gross-looking soda spring on the left. Just past this are aspens with dates carved in the bark dating back to 1900. Ford the creek, ascend a steep bank, and continue meandering downstream. Walk straight across a large meadow, drop through a wet area to the creek, and make the second and last crossing of Soda Creek. Between here and the crossing of LT Creek are several springs and muddy areas, as well as some interesting rock bluffs above the trail. Cross LT Creek (signed) and skirt above a beautiful meadow. This is one of the best and only views along this trail. Very soon the trail begins a gradual ascent into a series of sixteen switchbacks. Although this might sound depressing, they are all very gradual, there is shade and, as noted, water on every other one. As you ascend through the timber, you may note segments of the original trail. It was replaced with the more gradual one you are on. The last pitch to the top is a bit steeper, but soon becomes more gradual till you hit the top and drop over to the signed trailhead. Maps show the trail continuing on to Grizzly Valley, but that segment is now a 4WD and cattle trail.

Morris Lake in the rocky, rugged High Lakes region is a favorite anglers' retreat. It is accessible by the Ben Lomond Trail.

TRAIL LAKE TRAIL (ECHO LAKE to SILVER LAKE TRAIL)
Elevation: 5920' to 5760'
Length: +/- 5 1/2 miles
Effort: Easy
Hike Time: About 3 hours
Location: T30N R7E, sections 1,12,13,23,24,26
Quadrangle Map: Chester **(See also page 194 for larger map)**

This trail is a nice one to use in conjunction with the Caribou Wilderness trails, although it is just outside the wilderness boundary. It works well in a sort of loop arrangement, though you will have to use some roads at both ends. For this trailhead use the directions given for the ***Star Lake Trail***, but pass that trailhead and continue straight toward Echo Lake. Follow ***USFS 30N64*** past the Echo Lake campground turnoff and one more right-hand intersection. Just past the last intersection is the signed trailhead on the left. The sign reads: ***Trail Lake Trail***, Trail Lake 3, Silver Lake 5. As you will see, signed mileages don't add up. The other trailhead option is to take the ***Silver Lake Road (USFS 10)*** just before Echo Lake to the signed trailhead about 1 mile before Silver Lake. The following description is given from that starting point.

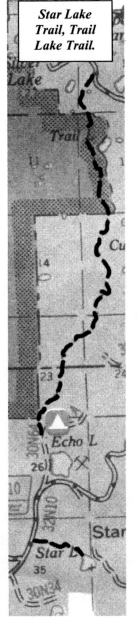

Star Lake Trail, Trail Lake Trail.

Once at the obscure trailhead on ***USFS 10*** you will note a mountain bike sign on the left, or east, side of the road. That part of the trail drops steeply through recent logging and along Cooper Meadow, coming out at the Silver Bowl picnic and boat launch area about 1 mile north. On the west side a sign describes our route: Trail Lake 1/2, Echo Lake 4 1/4, Heckle's Ranch 6. Another mountain bike sign adorns a tree. Incidentally, Heckle's Ranch is named for Forrest Heckle, a Taylorsville native turned Tehama County cattleman. His mother was a pioneer in the Quincy-Taylorsville area in the 1850s. Like many ranchers, Forrest ran his cattle in the high meadows during summer. This trail was no doubt a stock trail originally. Nothing remains of the Heckle Ranch but burned timbers and a fallen-down stock pen. Our well-defined trail makes a moderate ascent onto a bench as it passes through signs of old logging. Blazes and white metal diamonds help mark the way. Pass a small pond on the left and meander at a light descent under a mixed forest cover. The trail soon levels in a lodgepole desert with a meadow at left. The Caribou Wilderness boundary is signed on the right. At shallow, grassy Trail Lake is a sign: Lassen National Forest, Trail Lake, Silver Lake 1 (back), Heckle Ranch 5.5 (ahead), Echo Lake (chunk missing). Pass along the base of a rocky hillslope, cross a basin, and make a moderately winding ascent with two switchbacks under a red fir forest. After cresting the ridge the trail meanders up and down in broken ground for a great distance. As a note, the black rings 6 to 8 feet up some of the trees is paint sprayed over blue paint used to designate cutting for a timber sale. The sale has been scuttled. Make a light, winding descent in manzanita with a nice view of North Caribou Peak to the right. Cross a seasonal drainage, then an old road, and then make a light descent through manzanita that is taking over. Cross another old road and make a medium, bouldery, graveled descent. Near the base of this descent is Cummings Spring, though I did not check for water. Meander through a lodgepole flat and make a graveled, winding ascent to a level walk. Pass an indiscernible K-tag along a very straight, wide section of trail and an aluminum Forest Service survey tag for section 23, then cross a road and pass through old logging. You have also just entered Plumas County. Begin a light ascent on an eroded trail in a small drainage. Ascend more steeply up the left side, all in old logging, to a level walk. Make a light, though somewhat rutted descent to **USFS 30N64** (a red cinder road and the lower trailhead) and the sign mentioned for it. The trail does continue across this road and the next road along, but it is very unmaintained and of no real use anymore.

YELLOW CREEK TRAIL

Elevation: 2300' to 2800'
Length: +/- 1 1/2 miles
Effort: Easy
Hike Time: About 1 hour
Location: T25N R6E, sections 13,24
Quadrangle Map: Caribou **(For map see page)**

Unfortunately, this beautiful walk was also a victim of the 2000 Storrie Fire. However, it can still be a rewarding experience. Reach via **State Route 70**, about 28 miles from Quincy at the Eby Stamp Mill Historical Site opposite Belden. The trailhead is just to the right of the stamp mill and restrooms. This trail runs along this very pretty stream to a dead-end in a box canyon. The hike is extremely easy. A sign notes it is 2 miles and takes 1 hour with no motorized vehicles allowed. A view of the Belden Powerhouse at the trailhead is of passing interest. The trail starts off as an abandoned construction road from the early hydroelectric project days, soon passes through old gold diggings, and begins a slight ascent. There are some nice rock walls as a part of the trail along here. The trail stays about 100-feet above the creek with very steep sides, so be careful. There are several spur trails dropping down to mining claims, but signs point out the main trail. Live oak and Douglas fir predominate here, with beautiful blue and green pools in the stream. Near trail's end is a now defunct cable car once used for crossing the creek to some old gold diggings. The trail ends in heavy second growth timber at a modern miner's camp. By scrambling along a deteriorated trace, you may get a nice view of the box canyon just above the end of the trail.

CARIBOU WILDERNESS TRAILS
No Motorized Vehicles

The following text is excerpted from the Caribou Wilderness guide produced by the U.S. Forest Service:

The Caribou Wilderness is a gentle, rolling, forested plateau with many forest fringed lakes. Reminders of volcanic and glacial origin can be seen throughout these wildlands. Crater peaks, cinder cones and numerous large and small depressions have become beautiful, timber-edged lakes and are scattered throughout this plateau region. The land itself is rough and broken. Caribou Peaks, Black Cinder Rock, and Red Cinder are points of interest. The average elevation is 6,900 feet. The highest point, Red Cinder, is 8,370 feet. Located on the eastern slopes of what was once Mt. Tehama, this area is surrounded by the volcanic peaks of Swain Mountain, Bogard Buttes, Prospect Peak, Ash Butte, Red Cinder Cone and Mt. Harkness

The forest cover is mostly lodgepole pine with a mixture of Jeffrey pine, white and red fir, western white pine, and hemlock. In early summer, wildflowers brighten the trail and water lilies cluster in ponds.

The headwaters of the Susan River originate in the Caribou. This water percolates up through the porous volcanic aquifer and is a major year around water source for the east slope of the Cascades. The larger lakes that are deep enough to support fish are home to brook and rainbow trout. The water here should also be considered as having Giardia. Pack animals are used here frequently and it does get heavy human use at certain times of the year. Practice the usual safe water treatment methods and you should be fine.

For more information contact the Almanor Ranger District in Chester, CA at 530-

Caribou Lake-Black Lake Trail, Caribou Lake-North Divide Lake Trail, Cypress Lake Trail, Hay Meadow-Cone Lake Trail, Hay Meadow-Long Lake Trail via Beauty Lake, Hay Meadow-Long Lake Trail via Hidden Lakes, Indian Meadows-Hidden Lake Trail, Triangle Lake Loop Trail.

258-2141. Remember, this is a wilderness and no motorized or mechanized vehicles are allowed.

Although there are at least three trailheads I will use only two, Hay Meadow and Silver Lake. To reach the Hay Meadow trailhead from the town of Chester, travel east 5 miles on **State Highway 36** to Bailey Creek. Turn left at the four-way intersection, pass the garbage transfer station and turn left on the **T Line.** You will note lettered road signs throughout this region. It is how the private timber companies designate their different roads and is a practice hailing back to logging railroad days. Cross the old Bailey Creek bridge and turn right at the next intersection. A sign indicates that the Caribou Wilderness is 11 miles and Silver Lake is 18 miles. This is well signed **USFS 10**. Follow it about 9 miles to where the pavement turns to a washboard gravel road. Take the signed left turn and follow to the trailhead where there is ample parking, a horse loading ramp and trailhead bulletin board. Though the last 2 miles are rough, the road is suitable for low-clearance autos.

The trails are listed alphabetically within this subsection.

CARIBOU LAKE-BLACK LAKE TRAIL
Elevation: 6520' to 6620'
Length: +/- 3 1/2 miles
Effort: Moderate
Hike Time: About 2 hours
Location: T31N R7E, sections 32,33,34,35
Quadrangle Map: Harvey Mtn. **(For map see page 194)**

To reach this trailhead, continue past the left turnoff to the Hay Meadow trailhead near Echo Lake and follow **USFS 10** to Silver Lake. Pass the east shore turnoff and Silver Beach Picnic area. A signed left indicates the trailhead. Older maps show a route that is now closed. A lower parking area has a sign pointing to the trailhead which is north and just above. It reads: Wilderness Parking, Caribou Lake Trailhead (right), Caribou Wilderness 1 (right). Restrooms and an information board are available, as are garbage cans that are a favorite of the bears. A light descent takes the trail along a meander on the right side of this good-sized lake. As we leave the lake pass a pond and meadow at right and make a light ascent to the wilderness register. After registering continue the ascent and round a point with a pond on the left. Pass through a flat and then contour along the hillside to the **Caribou Lake-North Divide Lake Trail** intersection and three signs: Cone Lake 6 (ahead); Caribou Lake (back), Hay Meadow (left); Jewel Lake, Eleanor Lake, Triangle Lake (ahead). Continue right and pass along the edge of Cowboy Lake, cross the outlet and make a short, winding ascent over a knob, descend and make a number of small ups and downs and meanders to the Caribou Wilderness sign. Cross a rocky draw, make a mild ascent to a switchback, then a steep, loose switchback, then another switchback, recross the rocky draw and make a long, mild ascent to another switchback. Ascend past gnarled old junipers to the last switchback, then a short ascent to signed Jewel Lake. I was lucky enough to see a beautiful Great Blue Heron while passing by. Pass this lake and a small pond on the right. Eleanor Lake is off to the right. Make a short, steep ascent past another access trail to Jewel Lake and begin an undulating walk along a bench with glaciated rock. On the right are two ponds, then an ascent into a lodgepole pine basin. A light winding ascent in a narrow drainage takes us past a pond at left and onto the top of a saddle. From here it is a very mild, sandy descent to the intersection with the *Hay Meadow-Cone Lake Trail* and Black Lake. Two signs read: Caribou Lake (back); Hay Meadow (left), Cone Lake (right).

CARIBOU LAKE-NORTH DIVIDE LAKE TRAIL
(Including Gem Lake Trail, 7000', 1/4 mile)
Elevation: 6520' to 7000'
Length: +/- 3 miles
Effort: Moderate
Hike Time: About 2 hours
Location: T30N R7E, sections 3,4 and T31N R7E, sections 33,34,35
Quadrangle Map: Chester, Harvey Mtn. **(For map see page 194)**

Use the directions given for the *Caribou Lake-Black Lake Trail* to reach this trail intersection about 1 mile or so from the trailhead. Once there, pass along the left side of Cowboy Lake under large firs to a gentle switchback. Just before this a trail breaks left to a small pond just out of sight. Meander a distance to the base of a steep rock slope and bear right, gently ascending to a switchback, then a moderate ascent to another switchback at the top of the slope. Wind up with a view of Caribou Lake and come to the Caribou Wilderness sign (down at this writing). Cross a flat with big red fir, then make a light, ascending switchback to the intersection with signed *Cypress Lake Trail*. Meander up and down in bouldery ground, cross the outlet to a dry pond ahead and skirt the left side. A rocky bluff makes a backdrop on the other side. In a short while the *Gem Lake Trail* heads uphill at a moderate, but eroded grade to the right. It is about 1/4 mile to the lake, and though the map shows the trail continuing along the lake shore, it doesn't. Gem Lake is very pretty though. Make a light ascent over a knoll and descend past a pond on the left. A meandering walk parallels the base of a rocky hillslope, then twice crosses the dry outlet to North Divide Lake. Continue in lodgepole pine along the north side of North Divide Lake to a signed intersection with the *Hay Meadow-Cone Lake Trail.*

CYPRESS LAKE TRAIL
Elevation: 6960' to 7120'
Length: +/- 1 1/2 miles
Effort: Moderate
Hike Time: About 1 1/2 hours
Location: T30N R7E, section 3
Quadrangle Map: Chester **(For map see page 194)**

Take the *Caribou Lake-North Divide Lake Trail* about 1 mile to this signed intersection. Go left up a short incline in scrub manzanita to a flat, and pretty Emerald Lake. This lake has several nice campsites. Bear left along the lake, cross the outlet and begin an easy ascent across glaciated rock. The trail continues to wind along in a rocky, dry lodgepole desert, veers east to skirt a rocky bluff, and meanders down to the base of a rocky knob. Cross the outlet to the grassy pond at right and contour along the right side of the knob. Make two short, light ascending switchbacks and come to a good view of Caribou Lake and Silver Lake. You might also note the grizzled juniper trees. Wind along in the open past a pond way off to the left. The trail is faint so bear right and uphill. Ducks mark the light, winding ascent near the edge of the rocky bluff we just skirted. Shortly the trail ascends to Rim Lake, a small jewel of a lake. From the bluff north of Rim Lake is a glimpse of Emerald Lake. Continue meandering up, noting the ducks. There are some ducks that obviously mark a route headed down to the left. These indicate the old **Silver Lake-Cypress Lake Trail** that is no longer used or maintained. The Rocky Peak ahead and left is North Caribou. A level meander and crossing of a dry wash brings us to two short switchbacks that descend under a rocky bluff. Meander on the level parallel to the bluff at right and soon encounter a pretty pond on the right. After winding around the end of the pond, make a few ups and downs to beautiful Cypress Lake and the end of the trail.

HAY MEADOW-CONE LAKE TRAIL
Elevation: 6400' to 6720'
Length: +/- 10 miles
Effort: Easy
Hike Time: About 5 hours
Location: T30N R7E, sections 4,9,16,21,27,28 and T31N R7E, sections 16,20, 21,29,32,33
Quadrangle Map: Chester, Harvey Mtn. **(For map see page 194)**

This trail could be considered the main trail for the Caribou Wilderness because it runs right up the center of the wilderness area with a number of side trails branching off. Fine views of the various peaks are had from this route. Beginning at the Hay Meadow trailhead, the trail skirts left of that lush, large meadow as it enters the trees. Along a mild ascent, sign the self-registration forms provided for maintaining wilderness usage figures. The trail soon reaches Indian Meadows, the Caribou Wilderness sign, and a fork in the trail. **Indian Meadows-Hidden Lakes Trail** goes right, our trail left. One sign points back to Hay Meadow and ahead to Beauty Lake, the other points right to Hidden Lakes. Continue left, crossing a rocky outlet to the meadow's pond. Make a light ascent at the top of which is a wet draw to the right. Meander, then make another light ascent onto a bench with a K-tag for our location between sections 21 and 28. After light ascents and descents, intersect the unsigned **Hay Meadow-Long Lake via Hidden Lakes Trail** on the right. Continue straight on a moderate ascent to another bench and in a short distance hit the signed intersection with the **Hay Meadow-Long Lake via Beauty Lake Trail**. The sign indicates Beauty Lake is left and Long Lake ahead. Meander with a seasonal creek at right, make a light ascent up the ridge side, cross over the top and note a pond at right. Pass another pond at left with a rocky backdrop, pass a dry basin, work along a seasonal stream bed, ascend to a bench and Long Lake is visible ahead and to the right. Soon the trail hits a signed intersection: Cone Lake (ahead), Hidden Lakes (right). Continuing ahead is another intersection: Hay Meadow (back), Caribou Lake, Cone Lake (ahead) and Posey Lake (left). A sign also indicates the body of water here is Long Lake. This is a

Vintage trail sign in the Caribou Lakes Wilderness.

shallow lake, but has nice campsites. Meander through a lodgepole desert on the left (west) side of the lake. As the trail passes the north end, cross a muddy area between the lake and a pond. The trail makes a nice meander past meadows and ponds in alternating and combined grass and lodgepole pine. This trail was marked by a blaze-happy crew. Not only do many trees have two blazes on the same side, some have three! Make slight ascents past a large pond, small pond, basins and grassy areas to South Divide Lake and, shortly, North Divide Lake. At the west end is another signed intersection: Caribou Lake 3 (right), Hay Meadow (back), Cone Lake (ahead). Continuing ahead, the trail meanders along on the level in heavy lodgepole, crosses, then works along the left side of a dry creek to Black Lake. Skirt along the right side past a sign proclaiming its name and enter a lodgepole thicket. Soon another intersection is encountered: Hay Meadow (back), Cone Lake (ahead) and Caribou Lake (right). Meander ahead in open, pine studded ground to Turnaround Lake. The trail meanders past nice campsites, one on rocks about eight feet above the water. As the trail reaches the north side, a short spur continues along the lakeshore to some secluded campsites at the base of a rocky slope. Our trail makes a hard right up the short ridge side to a level walk, then a light descent to Twin Lakes. Pass along the right side through heavy lodgepole cover with numerous dead and down trees. An unsigned trail intersection is at the north end of the lake. This is the south end of the **Triangle Lake Loop Trail.** Continuing straight we soon come to the south end of Triangle Lake (Polhemus Lake on 1894 quads), the largest in the Caribou Wilderness. Red Cinder makes a nice backdrop as the trail runs along the east side of the lake. Contour along under large Jeffrey pine before making a light descent to a signed trail intersection: Caribou Lake (back), Cone Lake (ahead). The unsigned fork going left is the north end of the *Triangle Lake Loop Trail*. To reach Cone Lake continue ahead at a mild descent for about 1 1/2 miles.

HAY MEADOW-LONG LAKE TRAIL via Beauty Lake

Elevation: 6400' to 6760'
Length: +/- 4 miles
Effort: Easy
Hike Time: About 2 hours
Location: T30N R7E, sections 16,17,20,21,27,28
Quadrangle Map: Chester **(For map see page 194)**

About 1 1/2 miles up the *Hay Meadow-Long Lake Trail* take the signed left trail. Make a light, winding ascent to Beauty Lake and a sign: Beauty Lake, Long Lake 2, Posey Lake 1.3, Evelyn Lake .5 (all ahead), Heckle Ranch 3.5 (back). The trail descends lightly to the northwest end of the lake past nice campsites with trails leading to them. Make a mild ascent and meander along past a lily pad pond on the left to Evelyn Lake on the right. There is a nice campsite near the trail and some small rock bluffs on the west side of the water. Pass a small lake on the left and begin a long, light ascent to signed Posey Lake and nice campsites. Meander through an open area, make a light ascent, then descent, pass a pond on the left and a short descent to Long Lake and the *Hay Meadow-Cone Lake Trail* intersection and a sign: Posey Lake (back).

HAY MEADOW-LONG LAKE TRAIL via Hidden Lakes

Elevation: 6400' to 6760'
Length: +/- 3 miles
Effort: Moderate
Hike Time: About 1 1/2 hours
Location: T30N R7E, sections 16,21,22,27,28
Quadrangle Map: Chester **(For map see page 194)**

About 1 1/4 miles up the *Hay Meadow-Cone Lake Trail* make a right at an unsigned trail intersection. A slight descent will soon cross a seasonal drainage and flat to the base of a hillslope. Make a long moderate ascent to a switchback and ascend around the ridge, meandering to a pond (at left) and an intersection with the *Indian Meadows-Hidden Lakes Trail*. A sign points back to Hay Meadow. Another sign reads: Hidden Lakes, while shortly you will see that this sign and the other signage to come is incorrect. Pass along the right side of the lake and in a short distance is another of the Hidden Lakes on the left. A sign reads: Hidden Lake No.2, (actually No.1) Hidden Lake No.1 .2 (back), Hidden Lake No.3 .2 (ahead). At the sign begin a short, winding ascent over a knoll to a pond on the left. Cross a bouldery wash and make a winding ascent to Hidden Lake No.2 on the right. The trail ascends to a bench above the lake, affording a nice view, then drops past a nice campsite and meanders to Hidden Lake No.3. Meander past the lake, pass a pond at left, make a moderate descent to another pond on the left, and a winding ascent to a bench. A large rock formation is on the right. A level walk through heavy lodgepole past a pond on the left makes a short, easy descent to a flat and the intersection with the *Hay Meadow-Cone Lake Trail*. A sign indicates Cone Lake to be ahead and Hidden Lakes, back.

INDIAN MEADOWS-HIDDEN LAKES TRAIL

Elevation: 6480' to 6760'
Length: +/- 1 mile
Effort: Moderate
Hike Time: About 1 hour
Location: T30N R7E, sections 21,22,27
Quadrangle Map: Chester **(For map see page 194)**

This trail is not shown on the Forest Service handout, but it is a popular and well used trail. About 1 mile up the *Hay Meadow-Cone Lake Trail* you will come to pretty Indian Meadows. The Caribou Wilderness sign is also here. A sign points right to Hidden Lakes. This is our trail. Skirt the edge of the meadow, pass through many blowdowns (all cleared), and a K-tag for our location between sections 22 and 27. The trail crosses the head of the meadow and a seasonal draw at the same time as it heads under heavy cover. Meander a distance and then begin a moderate ascent that quickly becomes steeper with four sorta sweeping switchbacks. The moderately steep, winding ascent levels, then makes a short, steep pitch to the intersection with the *Hay Meadow-Cone Lake via Hidden Lakes Trail*. From here follow the description for that trail.

TRIANGLE LAKE LOOP TRAIL

Elevation: 7040' to 7040'
Length: +/- 1 mile
Effort: Easy
Hike Time: About 1 hour
Location: T31N R7E, sections 20,29
Quadrangle Map: Harvey Mtn. **(For map see page 194)**

Starting at the north end of pretty, blue Triangle Lake, take the westerly-headed trail along the lake's edge. This level path passes nice campsites as it rounds the end of the lake. A signed trail intersection points the way west to Widow Lake in Lassen National Park. Continue straight and cross a dry creek. This side of the lake has a rockier shore and so the trail climbs to a fair height above the water. A short, rocky but easy descent brings the trail back to shore level. Pass along the very southern end of the lake, crest the small ridge and meander past one of the Twin Lakes at right. Cross the lake outlet and soon connect with the *Hay Meadow-Cone Lake Trail*.

LASSEN NATIONAL PARK
No Motorized Vehicles

Lassen National Park is one of the most beautiful and interesting places to visit in California. Until 1980, it was the most recent and active volcano in the United States. There is so much to see and do here that one could spend days, even weeks. However, because of the large amount of printed material already available on it, the plethora of rules and regulations, permits and fees, I have decided not to hike and describe its trails, but rather to reproduce trail material provided by the park. Those trails are listed alphabetically in this subsection. For information regarding park usage call or write Lassen National Park, P.O. Box 100, Mineral, CA 96063-0100. Phone (530) 595-4444.

BOILING SPRINGS LAKE TRAIL
Length: +/- 1 1/2 miles
Hike Time: 1 hour
Features: Easy 200' climb, mudpot, flowers, forest, trail leaflet.

BUMPASS HELL TRAIL
Length: +/- 1 1/2 miles
Hike Time: 1 1/2 hours
Features: Gradual 500' climb first mile, 250' descent into thermal area, largest thermal area, hot springs, steam vents, mudpots, trail leaflet, stay on established trail.

CINDER CONE TRAIL
Length: +/- 2 miles (2 1/2 if the trail is followed down the south side of the cone)
Hike Time: 1 1/2 hours (2 1/4 hours if south side trail is followed)
Features: 800' climb, fairly steep with loose cinders, forest scenic, wear high shoes or boots, for geologists and photographers, trail leaflet.

FOREST LAKE & BROKEOFF MOUNTAIN TRAIL
Length: +/- 1 1/2 miles to Forest Lake, 3 3/4 to Brokeoff summit
Hike Time: About 1 1/4 hours to Forest Lake, 2 1/2 hours to Brokeoff summit
Features: Uphill, steady climb 700' to Forest Lake, 2,600' to Brokeoff summit, scenic, flowers, streams

KINGS CREEK FALLS TRAIL
Length: +/- 1 1/2 miles
Hike Time: 1 1/4 hours
Features: 700' descent, cascades, forest, flowers, photography.

LASSEN PEAK TRAIL
Length: +/- 2 1/2 miles
Hike Time: 2 1/4 hours
Features: 2,000' uphill on steady, steep grade (15%). Begins at 8,500', recent volcanic activity, timberline trees, trail leaflet, bring water and jacket, watch out for lightning.

LILY POND NATURE TRAIL
Length: +/- 1/2 mile
Hike Time: 1/2 hour
Features: Easy walk, lakeshores, forest, trail leaflet.

MANZANITA LAKE TRAIL
Length: +/- 1 1/4 miles
Hike Time: 1 hour
Features: Level, pleasant walk, lake, flowers, wildlife, trees, shrubs, scenic.

MILL CREEK FALLS TRAIL
Length: +/- 2 1/4 miles
Hike Time: 1 1/4 hours
Features: Downhill about 300', uphill about same, highest waterfall, forest, flowers.

MT. HARKNESS TRAIL
Length: +/- 2 miles
Hike Time: 2 hours
Features: Enjoyable 1,300' climb, scenic, flowers, historic fire lookout.

SUMMIT LAKE TO ECHO LAKE & TWIN LAKES TRAIL
Length: +/- 4 miles
Hike Time: 3 hours
Features: 500' uphill first mile, descend 500' to Lower Twin Lake, forest, lakes, flowers, summer swimming, good for overnighters.

TERRACE SHADOW & CLIFF LAKES TRAIL
Length: +/- 1 1/2 miles
Hike Time: 1 1/2 hours
Features: Downhill 300' to Terrace, 350' to Shadow, 650' to Cliff Lake. Forest, lakes.

Lassen National Forest:
Almanor Ranger District, P.O. Box 767, Chester, CA 96020. Phone (530)258-2141
Eagle Lake Ranger District, 477-050 Eagle Lake Road, Susanville, CA 96130. Phone (530) 257-4188

Lassen National Park: P.O. Box 100, Mineral, CA 96063-0100. Phone (530) 595-4444.

UNEXPLORED TRAILS

Due to time and other constraints, these trails were not personally hiked. I have tried to describe them from maps, interviews, and other sources as well as I can. Remember that most may be extremely difficult trails and the user should exercise every precaution. In fact, some of these trails may no longer exist. I do not recommend you hike these trails, but if you do, please be very careful.

EASTERN YUBA COUNTY

CHEROKEE CREEK TRAIL
Elevation: 2300' to 3700'
Length: +/- 2 miles
Effort: Extremely Difficult
Hike Time: About 4 hours
Location: T19N R8E, sections 12,13,1
Quadrangle Map: Strawberry Valley

This wide trail was once utilized by wagon traffic as part of the Young's Hill to Brandy City Trail. Historical references indicate it was the major route from the south side of the North Yuba River into the northern section of Sierra County and the southern section of Plumas County. As of 1995, it was extremely brushy and grown over. From what I could see though, it would make a first-class hiking and riding trail if it were restored.

COUNCIL HILL-BRANDY CITY TRAIL 9E132 (via Canyon Creek)
Elevation: 4000' to 3800'
Length: +/-2 1/2 miles
Effort: Extremely Difficult
Hike Time: About 4 hours
Location: T20N R9E, section 30 and T20N R8E, sections 25,36 and T19N R8E, section 1
Quadrangle Map: Strawberry Valley

Quads show it ending in Canyon Creek. Charles Hendel shows it continuing to Brandy City about 1890. Seems it would hit a road on the Canyon Creek rim.

GOPHNER RAVINE-WAMBO BAR TRAIL
Elevation: 3844' to 2000'
Length: +/- 2 miles
Effort: Extremely Difficult
Hike Time: About 4 hours
Location: T19N R8E, sections 5,8,9
Quadrangle Map: Strawberry Valley

To reach this trailhead take *USFS 20N14* off the *Marysville-La Porte Road (USFS 120)* about 2 1/2 miles south of the town of Strawberry Valley. Proceed south along this road about 1 1/2 miles to an intersection with *USFS 20N04*. Make a left and stay on this road about 1 mile to a 4-way intersection where you proceed straight ahead on *USFS 20N81* about 1/8 mile. The trail appears to run down along Gophner Ravine for over a mile to a crossing of Deadwood Creek and Wambo Bar. From here the trail continues along the North Yuba River 1/2 mile to the mouth of Slate Creek and *USFS 20N16*. The trail has been logged-over on the private ground and, for the most part, is not maintained and quite brushy.

KELLY BAR TRAIL
Elevation: 3400' to 2100'
Length: +/- 1 1/2 miles
Effort: Difficult
Hike Time: About 3 hours
Location: T19N R8E, sections 14 See also T20N R8E, section 25
Quadrangle Map: Strawberry Valley

Reach the trailhead by taking the *Pendola Extension Road* about 3 miles to a sign reading *Kelly Bar Trail* 1 mile and *Slate Range Bar Trail* 1 mile. There is a pine plantation on the right of the road. Pass the *Slate Range Bar Road* and continue ahead on the good gravel road. After about 2 miles take a left at the sign reading *Kelly Bar Trail* 1/2 mile. Because of the steepness and looseness, passenger cars are discouraged. After about 1/2 mile there are camping and parking sites along the road. The trail begins on the right side of the parking area at the end of the road. It is quite steep with winding switchbacks and heavy OHV use.

OAK FLAT-RACE TRACK POINT TRAIL
Elevation: 3600' to 2200'
Length: +/- 3 1/2 miles
Effort: Extremely Difficult
Hike Time: About 4 hours
Location: T19N R8E, sections 2,3,10,9
Quadrangle Map: Strawberry Valley

For this trail leave the *Marysville-La Porte Road (USFS 120)* about 1 mile north of Strawberry Valley at the Strawberry Valley Ranger Station. Take *USFS 20N30* on its winding route about 7 miles to an intersection with the *Oak Flat Road (USFS 20N68)*. Follow that road about 2 1/2 miles to a dead end where the trail takes off. It runs along the top of the ridge, occasionally going up and down before dropping the last 1 1/2 miles down to Race Track Point at the end of *USFS 20N16*. This is an unmaintained trail that gets very brushy and very hot in summer. Oak and brush predominate over the area once you begin to get lower in elevation.

SLATE RANGE BAR TRAIL
Elevation: 3400' to 2100'
Length: +/- 1 1/2 miles

Effort: Difficult
Hike Time: About 3 hours
Location: T19N R8E, section 15
Quadrangle Map: Strawberry Valley

Reach the trailhead by taking the **Pendola Extension Road** 3 miles to a sign reading **Kelly Bar Trail** 1 mile, and **Slate Range Bar Trail** 1 mile. There is a pine plantation on the right of the road. Make a left onto the good gravel road, pass through an open gate, and descend about 1 mile to a large turnaround and parking area. The trail drops off on the left or west side of the parking area. As I recall, an OHV trail splits off to the west also. The foot trail winds through madrone and oaks, is very brushy and, according to one source, there is not much to see.

Gold panning was the earliest and simplest method of retrieving gold from the Feather River region's streams. Later, miners with giant water cannons replaced this type of mining.

SIERRA COUNTY

BEE RANCH TRAIL
Elevation: 3400' to 6300'
Length: +/- 2 miles
Effort: Very Difficult
Hike Time: About 3 hours
Location: T20N R11E, sections 22,27
Quadrangle Map: Sierra City

According to maps, this trail begins on private land and steeply ascends the mountain to the ridge top. Gus Poggi of Downieville indicated that at one time it was a good trail. However, the entire hillside looked very brushy when I scouted it from the ridge top on the **Packer Saddle-Union Flat Road (USFS 93)** in 1997 and I was not able to locate the actual trail.

CRAYCROFT RIDGE TRAIL
Elevation: 6800' to 6600'
Length: +/- 1/4 miles
Effort: Moderate
Hike Time: About 1/2 hour
Location: T21N R11E, section 18
Quadrangle Map: Mt. Fillmore

From the **Chimney Rock Trail** on the shoulder of Needle Point this old trail heads south. Overgrown blazes mark part of the route. According to one source, in about 400 yards it is converted to a 4WD road. At the time I was there I was not able to follow it out to confirm this information.

SMITH LAKE TRAIL (Smith Lake to Lavezolla Creek Trail)
Elevation: 6100' to 4600'
Length: +/- 2 miles
Effort: Very Difficult
Hike Time: About 3 hours
Location: T21N R11E, sections 28,27
Quadrangle Map: Gold Lake

This somewhat steep old trail runs down from Smith Lake to Lavezolla Creek. There are overgrown blazes at the bottom end of the trail. It appears to run along a dry ravine.

BUTTE COUNTY

CHINA GULCH TRAIL
Elevation: 3200' to 990'
Length: +/- 3 miles
Effort: Extremely Difficult
Hike Time: About 3 hours
Location: T22N R5E, sections 29,31,32
Quadrangle: Berry Creek

The map shows the trailhead as being off of a dead-end spur of *USFS 22N84*, which is a spur of *USFS 28*. These roads are accessible from the *Oroville-Bucks Lake Road (USFS 119)*. The trail appears to drop via many switchbacks into private property and onto *USFS 22N70X* along the North Fork of the Feather River near Big Bend.

FALL RIVER TRAIL
Elevation: 3100' to 2400'
Length: +/- 2 1/2 miles
Effort: Extremely Difficult
Hike Time: About 3 hours
Location: T21N R7E, sections 19,20 and T21N R6E, section 24
Quadrangle Map: Cascade

Reach the trailhead via *USFS 21N25* a little over one mile off *USFS 22N94*. The turn off is about one mile north of what was the town of Fall River. The trailhead is at Nelson's Crossing, and according to a U.S.F.S. ranger is a good trail. It stays along the water until the river makes a sharp bend to the south where the trail climbs onto the side of the canyon above the river. Almost 2 miles below Nelson's Crossing, and on the north side of the river, is a ¾-mile-long trail full of switchbacks that will supposedly take you quickly up to *USFS 22N25* spur in section 24.

FRENCH CREEK TRAIL
Elevation: 2000' to 1000'
Length: +/- 1 1/2 miles
Effort: Extremely Difficult
Hike Time: About 2 hours
Location: T21N R5E, sections 11,12

The trail runs up French Creek from state land at tip of an arm of Lake Oroville. Access appears to be via *USFS 28 and 34*. The first mile is on private property, and all may be on private land.

JACKSON RANCH TRAIL
Elevation: 3700' to 2000'
Length: +/- 1 1/2 miles
Effort: Very Difficult

Hike Time: About 2 hours
Location: T21N R6E, sections 25,26
Quadrangle Map: Brush Creek

Reach the trailhead via the **Jackson Ranch Road** about 7 miles off the **Camp One-Rogerville Road (Butte County 40805A)** east of the now non-existent town of Feather Falls. This trails switchbacks steeply down to Feather Falls where it connects with the **Watson Trail**. This was a motorcycle trail that has been closed to that use. Very steep, it is best as a route down, but not back up.

SKYHIGH-LITTLE NORTH FORK FEATHER RIVER TRAIL
Elevation: 3500' to 2800'
Length: +/- 1 mile
Effort: Extremely Difficult
Hike Time: About 2 hours
Location: T22N R6E, section 26
Quadrangle Map: Brush Creek

Sky High, the peak, is actually across the Little North Fork from our trailhead. Reach the trailhead by driving east on the **Oroville-Bucks Lake Road** about 26 miles or west 32 miles from Quincy on the **Oroville-Quincy Road** to **USFS 23N60**. Take that road about 1 mile to a spur to the right. Follow the spur about 3/4 mile to the trailhead. This trail switchbacks quickly to the river.

The Middle Fork Feather River's rugged canyon trails provide strenuous hiking.

PLUMAS COUNTY

BARKER'S CABIN-ONION VALLEY CREEK TRAIL
Elevation: 5200' to 4000'
Length: +/- 1 1/2 miles
Effort: Extremely Difficult
Hike Time: About 2 hours
Location: T23N R9E, section 33 and T22N R9E, section 4
Quadrangle Map: Onion Valley

Reach the trailhead by taking the **Cleghorn Bar Road** from Onion Valley on the **Quincy-La Porte Road** about 9 miles to Barker's Cabin site which, incidentally, is very difficult to find. The map indicates the trail makes a moderate descent to a seasonal creek, crosses, and climbs out to **USFS 22N67Y**.

HARTMAN BAR RIDGE-SOUTH BRANCH MIDDLE FORK FEATHER RIVER TRAIL
Elevation: 4600' to 4000'
Length: +/- 1/2 mile
Effort: Extremely Difficult
Hike Time: About 1 hour
Location: T22N R7E, sections 26,35
Quadrangle Map: Cascade

I made several attempts to locate this trail with the end result being that I found absolutely no sign of it. In all likelihood, heavy logging in the area in years past probably destroyed it. Another possibility is that a road has been laid down over it. There are several in this area with like circumstances.

HIGH RIDGE TRAIL
Elevation: 2800' to 3100'
Length: +/- 3 miles
Effort: Extremely Difficult
Hike Time: About 4 hours
Location: T22N R8E, sections 3,2,1,35
Quadrangle Map: Dogwood Peak

Supposedly connects the bottom end of the Stagg Point 4WD road with the PCT. Forest Service sources say it is unmaintained and hard to find.

HOPKINS CREEK-WEST NELSON CREEK TRAIL
Elevation: 5500' to 4900'
Length: +/- 3 1/2 miles
Effort: Extremely Difficult
Hike Time: About 4 hours
Location: T22N R10E, sections 14,11,12 and T22N R11E, section 7
Quadrangle Map: Blue Nose Mountain

This old pack trail starts near Blue Nose Ravine on a spur road off the ***Sloat-Gibsonville Road (USFS 23N10,)*** about 20 miles south of Sloat. It follows an abandoned mining ditch for about 1/2 mile before skirting the shoulder of Blue Nose Mountain. A large plateau is crossed just before beginning an ascent of about 1/2 mile to another flat area on a ridge back. Here the trail begins a steep descent along the right side of a seasonal creek, about 1/4 mile to a 4WD road into West Nelson Creek.

HOTTENTOT CREEK–WINTERS CREEK TRAIL
Elevation: 4400' to 4200'
Length: +/- 2 miles
Effort: Very Difficult
Hike Time: About 3 hours
Location: T23N R10E, sections 19,20
Quadrangle Map: Onion Valley

This is a trail made from an abandoned mining ditch by present-day miners and fishermen. It is not a particularly pleasant trail. Reach the trailhead via the ***Hottentot Creek Road*** off the ***Quincy-La Porte Road***. The trailhead is shared with the ***Hottentot Creek Trail***. Descend on the ***Hottentot Bar Trail*** through a small glade to a mining ditch. Leave the trail and follow the mining ditch west to Hottentot Creek, where you cross and continue on north shortly before again heading west. Several scramble trails dive off this rough, brushy ditch-trail to the Middle Fork of the Feather River. All are steep, loose, and rough, and are not recommended unless you are well suited for that type of travel. The ditch-trail continues along the canyon wall toward Winters Creek. This hike is a good one for canyon views but is rough and hot in summer.

MONTGOMERY CREEK TRAIL
Elevation: 5100' to 3600'
Length: +/- 2 miles
Effort: Very Difficult
Hike Time: About 3 hours
Location: T25N R10E, sections 10,11
Quadrangle Map: Taylorsville

To reach this trail, take ***Highway 89*** north from Quincy about 15 miles, or south from Crescent Mills 1 mile. Turn right on ***Plumas County A-22*** toward Taylorsville. About halfway there take a right on the ***Emigrant Road (USFS 26N21)***. Follow this graveled road about 4 miles up to its intersection with the ***Mt. Hough Road***. Almost immediately bear left onto ***USFS 25N29 A***. Follow this road about 1/2 mile around the ridge point. The trail descends from here along a seasonal stream to Montgomery Creek, where it gets lost for about 1 mile to private property and Indian Creek. The ***Genesee Valley-Taylorsville Road (Plumas County Road 112)*** is just across Indian Creek. There are great views of Montgomery Creek canyon and the north side of Grizzly Peak from the head of this trail.

WEBER BAR TRAIL

Elevation: 4500' to 2200' (approximately)
Length: +/- 2 miles (approximately)
Effort: Very Difficult
Hike Time: About 4 hours (approximately)
Location: T22N R8E (approximately)
Quadrangle Map: Bucks Lake, Dogwood Peak?

According to one informant, this trail drops into the Middle Fork of the Feather River from somewhere near Bucks Lake.

U.S. Forest Service signs being made around 1910 at the Quincy ranger office on Oddie Way.

"DEAD" TRAILS

Unlike the unexplored trails, for various reasons these trails no longer exist, or in some instances, never did! I have listed them only because they do appear on present-day maps or they were once historically significant. Some of them still are partially intact but not enough to use.

BACH CREEK RIDGE TRAIL (Plumas County)
Location: T23N R10E, sections 6,7,8
Quadrangle Map: Quincy

Past logging activity has obliterated it.

CABLE CROSSING TRAIL (Butte County)
Location: T22N R6E, section 36
Quadrangle Map: Brush Creek

Now a 4WD road to the river.

CLIPPERSHIP MINE-GARDINER'S POINT RESERVOIR TRAIL (Sierra County)
Location: T21N R10E, sections 7,12
Quadrangle Map: La Porte

This trail is actually an old wagon road once used to supply several mines in the area. Both ends of this trail are on private land. To compound matters, both pieces of property have been heavily logged, obscuring the trailheads.

COLD SPRINGS-CLAREMONT TRAIL (Plumas County)
Location: T23N R9E, sections 10,15
Quadrangle Map: Onion Valley, Quincy

Obliterated by past logging activity, part of it is now a road.

FIDDLE CREEK TRAIL (Sierra County)
Location: T19N R9E, sections 8,9,10,3
Quadrangle Map: Goodyears Bar

May never have existed, although there seem to be plans underway to build it. See <u>Yuba Trails</u> by Meals & Lamella.

H&G MINE TRAIL (Plumas County)
Location: T23N R9E, sections 23,24,26
Quadrangle Map: Onion Valley

What shows on the map is now a closed, overgrown logging spur. As for the H&G Mine, it is merely a trench cut in the hill by a tractor.

HARTMAN BAR RIDGE-HUNTER'S RAVINE TRAIL 7E26 (Plumas County)
Location: T22N R7E, sections 26,27,22
Quadrangle Map: Cascade, Haskins Valley

This trail seems to exist only in an old mapmaker's mind and on paper. Extensive on-the-ground research failed to turn up a trace of it, and individuals very familiar with the exact area cannot recall any trail there. It also happens to be some of the steepest, most rugged ground along the Middle Fork, and it is doubtful a trail would have been built there, but....

HOG GULCH TRAIL (Sierra County)
Location: T22N R10E, section 35
Quadrangle Map: Mt. Fillmore

Actually, this is an old water ditch running right down the ridge back to old diggings on the West Branch of Canyon Creek. At the top of the ditch it is extremely brush-choked.

HOPKINS CREEK-PEAK 6908' (Plumas County)
Location: T22N R10E, sections 13,24
Quadrangle Map: Blue Nose Mountain and Mt. Fillmore

There was no sign of the trail despite intensive on-the-ground research. A road and heavy logging since the late 1970s may have obliterated it.

LITTLE GRIZZLY VALLEY-PEACOCK POINT TRAIL (Plumas County)
Location: T26N R6E, sections 8,17,21
Quadrangle Map: Jonesville

Originally part of the **Soda Creek Trail**, it is now a 4WD/cattle trail, though not an unpleasant walk. The landowners at Little Grizzly Valley do not mind hikers using it as long as they don't camp on or disturb their property.

MOUNTAIN HOUSE-12 MILE BAR TRAIL (Plumas County)
Location: T25N R8E, sections 18,19,30
Quadrangle Map: Meadow Valley, Caribou, Twain

I hate to call this one dead, but for all practical purposes logging has obliterated most of it. This is another old pack trail, utilized heavily during the 1850s-1870s by miners going from Spanish Ranch via Mountain House to Rush Creek and 12 Mile Bar on the East Branch of the North Fork of the Feather River. It is steep for the most part and difficult to follow in a number of places due to logging, erosion, and roads. A careful eye must be kept out for ducks, overgrown blazes and the meandering ditch-like groove from heavy usage. Just for interest's sake, I have left in my notes from my efforts to follow the trail. To reach the trailhead, travel 18 miles northwest of Quincy on **State Route 70** to Virgilia.

Take the winding dirt *Virgilia-Mountain House Road* about 4 miles to a five-way intersection on top of the ridge. Take the right-hand fork that follows west along the very top of the ridge for about 2 miles to the site of the old Naas Cabin. This spot is about 250 yards north of the site of Mountain House. From Naas Cabin site follow the trail northwest through a heavy brush field about 1/8 mile to where the trail is discernible in timber, and where the hill slope drops slightly west. Smashed, rusted parts of an old auto can be seen in the trail. From here the trail basically follows the ridge down to a crossing of the *Virgilia-Mountain House Road* coming up. However, logging over the years has obliterated most of the trail the rest of the way down the mountain until near the river and Twelve Mile Bar.

MT. ALMA TRAIL (Sierra County)
Location: T21N R10E, section 28
Quadrangle Map: Mt. Fillmore

Extensive logging has ruined this old trail. A small part is used for 4WD. Apparently this was one of the old ridge-top trails used to travel from one mining section to another.

MT. ETNA via HOPKINS CREEK TRAIL (Plumas County)
Location: T22N R10E, section 23
Quadrangle Map: Blue Nose Mountain

Now a logging road.

NELSON CREEK TRAIL (Plumas County)
Location: T23N R10E, sections 26,35,36
Quadrangle Map: Blue Nose Mountain

A collection of short trails from creek bar to creek bar that a Forest Service mapmaker connected on paper only. It does not exist as shown, and according to early diaries and journals never did.

ONION VALLEY-RICHMOND HILL TRAIL (Plumas County)
Location: T22N R7E, sections 5,6
Quadrangle Map: Onion Valley

This trail is actually one of the first mining water ditches built in the region. It and two others took water from Onion Valley to Saw Pit Flat and Richmond Hill placer diggings. The ditch is quite overgrown now.

ROCK CREEK TO ROCK CREEK CROSSING TRAIL (Plumas County)
Location: T24N R6E, sections 17,18,19,20,30
Quadrangle Map: Storrie

U.S. Forest Service maps show a trail running roughly up Rock Creek to Rock Creek Crossing. From my experience it appears this is a road now. As for a small trail right on the creek, it goes about 1/8 mile before ending in the creek.

YELLOW CREEK TRAIL (PARALLEL TO CO. RD. 307) (Plumas County)
Location: T27N R5E, sections 34,35,36 and T26N R6E, sections 28,29,31,32
Quadrangle Map: Jonesville

I could not find it along the road, but it may exist.

Sometimes a sign is all that indicates a trail.

GLOSSARY

adit: A tunnel constructed by miners to obtain gold or other minerals from the earth. Adits can be very dangerous due to their age and the shifting and compressing of the earth. Always stay out of them, and away from their openings, where the ground tends to fall the most. Gas and poisonous air is also a hazard.

bar: A gravel bank, usually at water level along a stream. These were where the early California miners found gold, not a drink!

bench: Flat ridgetop extending a certain distance.

BLM: Bureau of Land Management. A federal agency charged with managing federal lands not administered by the Forest Service or other agency.

blaze: Two shallow notches, the smaller square one above the larger rectangular vertical one, cut into the bark of a tree along a trail to indicate its direction. A set of blazes is generally cut into opposite sides of the tree. If a trail makes an abrupt turn, one set of blaze marks faces the direction of the turn and is generally at 90 degrees to the other blazes facing the trail. This practice is now discouraged as damaging to the trees. Also, as the tree grows the blazes become grown over and are sometimes hard to discern.

brook: A small, natural stream of fresh water.

cairn: Sometimes called ducks. These are stacks of rock of various size and style to indicate the route of a trail across a meadow, rock field, or other area where the tread is not discernible.

CAT trail: Usually a skid trail for pulling logs to a landing, sometimes a fire trail used to make a break in the fuel to stop a forest fire from progressing. Named for Caterpillar-brand tractors.

CDF: California Department of Forestry. This is the state's forest
service. They administer timber and other forest-related activities on private and state lands.

compass: A device with a needle that points to magnetic north and is used for determining direction or location.

contour: A line joining points that are on the same height above sea level. Topographic maps include this feature. In this guide, to contour is to walk basically on a level plane.

creek: A small stream or part of a river.

diggings: A term that originated during the Gold Rush to describe a gold producing spot miners were working in. Later bastardized to diggin's.

ditch: A hand dug canal used by early miners to divert water from a stream to the area they were mining in. Many of these still make great walks because the grade is almost level. Unfortunately, many have also been converted to logging roads.

drainage: All that area shedding water into one stream or river.

duck: A small stack of rocks, usually only two or three high, to indicate the direction of a trail through a meadow or other open area. Sometimes called a cairn.

elevation: The number of feet of a location above sea level; the altitude.

fire trail: See CAT trail.

4WD road: Generally a very steep, rough road suitable only for the use of walkers, equestrians, OHV's, or four-wheel drive vehicles. Two-wheel drive vehicles should never attempt these roads.

grade: Term to describe the elevation loss or gain of a trail in general terms, i.e.: follow

the grade up.
hogback: A very narrow or sharp ridgeback that drops steeply to each side.
hydraulic mining: The application of water, under pressure, against a natural bank of gravel. This method of mining, though one of the most economically feasible and profitable forms of placer mining, was also one of the most destructive overall. Technically still legal, in California it is all but defunct today.
K-Tag: A yellow tin or aluminum tag, generally found along roads and sometimes trails, that gives reference to the location of section corners and quarter corners. On the tag is a grid divided into thirty-six squares, each representing one square mile. The thirty-six squares together represent a township and range. A nail or tack within the grid will give your approximate location on a map. Along roads they are generally shot up so it can be very hard to tell where the nail is (was).
landing: An open area for the collection of logs waiting to be loaded onto trucks during a logging operation. It is usually an area about 100 feet by 100 feet.
legend: Key or explanation of symbols used on a map.
log deck: Stack of logs waiting to be loaded on a truck, or in the case of cull decks, stacked to be out of the way and later burned (sometimes).
mining claim: A piece of land, usually twenty to forty acres, that has been claimed by an individual or a group for the minerals thereon. A mining claim gives the tax-paying owner certain rights, but also allows for other uses provided they do not interfere with that owner's rights.
OHV trail: Off Highway Vehicle trail. A trail or road set-aside for the use and enjoyment of dirt bikes, quad runners, and other motorized vehicles.
overstory: Large, old-growth timber that overshadows the younger second growth, or understory, beneath it.
riparian: Pertaining to, or situated on the bank of a river or other body of water.
river: A large, natural stream of water.
saddle: An area between two higher points, generally on a ridgeback.
scale: To represent in smaller measurements the size of the original. On maps it is to show the relationship of the distance on the map to the distance on the ground, i.e.: 1= 1 mile.
shut-in: A part of a canyon where the walls come straight down to the water on both sides, usually necessitating a hike over and around, or a swim through.
skid trail: See CAT trail.
snag: A dead tree, usually of a fairly large size.
stream: A brook or river.
switchback: A part of the trail that cuts back and forth above (or below) itself to provide a gentler elevation gain or loss, especially in steep terrain.
topographic map: A map showing land features, elevation intervals, and contours by use of lines. These are the most useful maps for hikers and generally come in two scales, 7.5 minute (2 1/2 = 1 mile) and 15 minute (1= 1 mile).
trail: A route of travel used for foot and animal traffic.
tread: That portion of the trail that you walk on.
understory: Commonly known as second growth timber. Younger trees, usually of a different species, that grow up beneath the overstory or old-growth timber.
U.S.F.S.: United States Forest Service. Federal agency charged with managing the

national forests. In this area it is the Plumas National Forest, Tahoe National Forest, and Lassen National Forest.

watershed: A portion of the drainage of a given area.

Hydraulic mining (right) was a major, though very destructive form of mining in the Feather River region during the late 1800s. In this photo the monitor or water cannon is attacking a huge tertiary gravel deposit. The mud, water, and gold matrix was washed down the hill into sluice boxes where the heavier gold was recovered, while the worthless mud and silt ran into the rivers.

Drift mining (left), utilizing tunnels dug into the mountains, was also a major gold production mining method for many years. Shown here is an ore car with the tunnel entrance behind and a sluice box for recovering the gold in the foreground.

INFORMATION CENTERS

Chester-Lake Almanor Chamber of Commerce, 529 Main St., P.O. Box 1198, Chester, CA 96020, (530) 258-2426 / (800) 350-4838, almanor@psln.com

Eastern Plumas Chamber of Commerce, 73136 Highway 70, P.O. Box 1379, Portola, CA 96122, (530) 832-5444 / (800) 995-6057, www.psln.com/epluchmb

Indian Valley Chamber of Commerce, 208 Main St., P.O. Box 1198, Greenville, CA 95947, (530) 284-6633, PSLN1.psln.com/ivchmbr

Lassen National Forest, Almanor Ranger District, Highway 36, Chester, P.O. Box 767, Chester, CA 96020, (530) 258-2141

Lassen National Forest, Eagle Lake Ranger District, 477-050 Eagle Lake Road, Susanville, CA 96130, (530) 257-4188

Lassen National Forest Headquarters, 55 S. Sacramento St., Susanville, CA 96130, (530) 257-2151

Plumas County Museum, behind the courthouse, 500 Jackson St., Quincy, CA 95971, (530) 283-6320, www.countyofplumas.com, pcmuseum@psln.com

Plumas County Visitors Bureau, 550 Crescent St., 1/2 mile west of Quincy. P.O. Box 4120, Quincy, CA 95971, (530) 283-6345 / (800) 326-2247, www.plumas.ca.us, or pcvb@psln.com

Plumas National Forest, Beckwourth Ranger District, 23 Mohawk Highway Road off Highway 70, west of Blairsden, CA 96103, (530) 836-2575

Plumas National Forest, Feather River Ranger District, 875 Mitchell Avenue, Oroville, CA 95966, (530) 534-6500

Plumas National Forest, Greenville Work Center, 128 Hot Springs Road, Greenville, CA 95947, (530) 284-7126

Plumas National Forest Headquarters, 159 Lawrence St., P.O. Box 11500, Quincy, CA 95971, (530) 283-2050

Plumas National Forest-Mt. Hough Ranger District, 39696 Highway 70, west of Quincy, Quincy, CA 95971, (530) 283-0555

Quincy Chamber of Commerce, 464 W. Main St., P.O. Box 3829, Quincy, CA 95971, (530) 283-0188, PSLN1.psln.com/qchamber

Sierra County Visitors Bureau, P.O. Box 206, Loyalton, CA 96118, (800) 200-4949

Tahoe National Forest, Downieville Ranger District, 15924 Highway 49, Camptonville, CA 95922, (530) 288-3231

Tahoe National Forest, Sierraville Ranger District, Highway 89, Sierraville, CA 96126, (530) 994-3401

HIKING INFORMATION & CLUBS

American Hiking Society
633 Los Palos Drive
Washington, DC 20041-2160

California Greenways Foundation
P.O. Box 20160
Lafayette, CA 94549

California Trails Foundation
P.O. Box 183
Los Altos, CA 94023

Rails to Trails Conservancy
1400 Sixteenth St., NW
Washington, D.C. 20036

Pacific Crest Trail Association
5325 Elkhorn Boulevard
Sacramento, CA 95842

Tread Lightly!
298 24th Street, Suite 325
Ogden, Utah 84401

MAP SOURCES

Plumas County Museum
500 Jackson Street
Quincy, CA 95971
(530) 283-6320

Plumas County Visitors Bureau
Plumas County maps
P.O. Box 4120
Quincy, CA 95971
(800) 326-2247

U.S. Geological Survey
P.O. Box 25286 Federal Center
Denver, CO 80225

SUGGESTED READING

The Chinese in Northern California, Barbara Pricer
Feather River Adventure Country Trails, Tom DeMund
Geologic History of the Feather River Country, Cordell Durrell
Gold Ghosts & Skis, The Lost Sierra, Bill Berry & Chapman Wentworth
History of Plumas, Lassen & Sierra Counties, 1882, Fariss & Smith
History of Rich Bar, James Young
History of Sierra County (5 vols.), James J. Sinnott
How to Shit In the Woods, Kathleen Meyer
Indians of the Feather River, Tales of Concow Maidu, Donald P. Jewell
La Porte Scrapbook, Helen Gould
Nelson Point, David Matuszak
The Northern Maidu, Marie Potts
Plumas National Forest Anglers Guide, Andrew Harris
The Shirley Letters From the California Mines, Louise Amelia Knapp Smith Clappe, aka Dame Shirley
Sierra Nevada Natural History, Tracy Storer & Robert Usinger
Tails & Trails, Interview with Packer Gus Poggi, Hank Meals
Wild & Free, Good Things to Eat from Plumas County Fields & Forests, Barbara Pricer
Wildflower Walking in the Lakes Basin, Toni Fauver
Yuba Trails, Susan Lamella & Hank Meals

For a list of local history books, write to Plumas County Museum, 500 Jackson Street, Quincy, CA 95971, or call (530) 283-6320.

SOURCES CONSULTED IN WRITING THIS GUIDE.

Brown, Orville. Personal conversation, various dates 1990-1999.
Chandler, Seth. Letters, 11/6/1854. Plumas County Museum.
Edwards, William H. Diary, 1853-1859. Plumas County Museum.
Gold Mountain Record, Yuba-Feather Historical Society, Forbestown, January 1997.
Illustrated History of Plumas, Lassen & Sierra Counties. Fariss & Smith, San Francisco, 1882.
Mountain Messenger, Downieville, CA. Various issues.
Pack Trains & Tails of Sierra County, The Trails and Tails of a Downieville Packer, An Oral Interview with Gus Poggi. Hank Meals, Tahoe National Forest, 1992.
Plumas County Museum, Quincy, CA. Various archival files.
Plumas National-Bulletin, Quincy. 1/4/1917, various issues.
Poggi, Gus. Personal conversation at Downieville, June 27, 1999.
Recollections of Early Days in Sierra and Nevada Counties, Interview with Mrs. Irene Rowley. Richard Markley, Tahoe National Forest, 1988.
The Shirley Letters from the California Mines, Louise A.K.S. Clappe. Ed. by Carl I. Wheat. Alfred A. Knopf, NY 1949.
Sierra City and Goodyears Bar. Sinnott, James J., The California Traveler, Inc., Volcano, CA 1973.
The Sierran, Sierra County Historical Society, various issues.
Up and Down California In 1860-1864. The Journal of William H. Brewer, Professor. Ed. by Francis Farquhar. 3rd edition: U.C. Berkeley, Berkeley, CA.

INDEX OF TRAILS

Abandoned Feather Falls Trail	103
Antelope Lake Nature Trail	167
Antelope Lake-Taylor Lake Trail	167
Bach Creek Ridge Trail	212
Badenaugh Canyon Trail 17E01	43
Barker's Cabin-Onion Valley Creek Trail	209
Bear Lakes Trail	81
Bee Ranch Trail	206
Belden-Soda Creek Trail	171
Belfrin Mine Extension Trail (Seymour Trail)	104
Bellevue Mine Flume Trail	44
Bellevue Mine-Howland Flat Wagon Road Trail	45
Bellevue Mine-Wallace Creek Trail	46
Ben Lomond Trail	173
Berger Creek-Saxonia Lake Trail	82
Big Bald Rock Trail	134
Bizz Johnson Trail	173
Blue Lake-Ridge Lake Trail	174
Blue Lake-Spencer Meadows Tie Trail	175
Boiling Springs Lake Trail	201
Brandy City Trail	46
Brandy City Pond Trail	48
Buckhorn Mine Trail	135
Bucks Creek Trail	135
Bullard's Bar-Dark Day Trail	48
Bullard's Bar Trail 8E07 (Sunset Vista to Schoolhouse)	48
Bullard's Bar Trail 8E10 (Schoolhouse Trail)	50
Bumpass Hell Trail	201
Butcher Ranch Trail	50
Butte Bar Trail	105
Buzzard's Roost Ridge Trail	105
Cable Crossing Trail	212
Camp Rodgers Saddle Trail	136
Canyon Creek Trail	51
Caribou Lake-Black Lake Trail	195
Caribou Lake-North Divide Lake Trail	196
Cascades Trail	137
Castle Rock Trail	52
Chambers Creek Trail	175
Chapman Creek Trail	52
Cherokee Creek Trail	203
Chimney Rock Trail	53
China Gulch Trail	207
Cinder Cone Trail	201

Clippership Mine-Gardiner's Point Reservoir Trail	212
Cold Springs-Claremont Trail	212
Cold Stream Trail	177
Council Hill-Brandy City Trail 9E132 (via Canyon Creek)	203
Craig's Flat Trail	54
Craycroft Ridge Trail	206
Cut-Eye Foster's Bar Trail	55
Cypress Lake Trail	196
Deadman Springs Trail	138
Deer Lake Trail	83
Dixie Mountain Trail	178
Dixon Creek-Union Creek Trail	106
Dome Trail	139
Downie River Trail	55
East Branch Canyon Creek Trail	56
Empire Creek Trail	57
Eureka Diggings-Little Canyon Creek Trail	58
Eureka Peak Trail	107
Fall River Trail	207
Feather Falls National Recreation Trail	108
Fern Falls Overlook Trail	83
Fiddle Creek Trail	212
Fiddle Creek Ridge Trail	60
Fingerboard Trail (Minerva Bar Trail)	110
Fish Creek-McRae Meadows Trail	110
Five Bear Mine-Bach Creek Trail 10E16	140
Forest Lake & Brokeoff Mountain Trail	201
Frazier Falls Overlook Trail	83
French Creek Trail	207
Gem Lake Trail	196
Gophner Ravine-Wambo Bar Trail	203
Granite Gap Trail 7E12	160
Grass Valley Bald Mountain Trail and PCT Tie Trail	112
Grassy Lake Trail	84
Graves Cabin-Kennedy Cabin Trail	113
Gray Eagle Creek Trail	84
Grizzly Forebay Gauging Station Trail	141
Grizzly Forebay Trail	141
H&G Mine Trail	212
Hall's Ranch Trail	61
Hanson's Bar Trail	114
Hartman Bar National Recreation Trail (South)	115
Hartman Bar Ridge-Hunter's Ravine Trail 7E26	213
Hartman Bar Ridge-South Branch MFFR Trail	209
Hartman Bar Trail (North)	142
Haskell Peak Trail	61

Hay Meadow-Cone Lake Trail	197
Hay Meadow-Long Lake Trail (via Beauty Lake)	199
Hay Meadow-Long Lake Trail (via Hidden Lakes)	199
Heinz Creek Trail	143
Hewitt Mine-Hopkins Creek Trail	116
High Ridge Trail	209
Hog Gulch Trail	213
Homer Lake-Deerheart Lake Trail	178
Hopkins Creek-Peak 6908'	213
Hopkins Creek-West Nelson Creek Trail	209
Hosselkus Creek Trail	179
Hottentot Bar Trail	116
Hottentot Creek-Winters Creek Trail	210
Hungry Creek Trail	181
Hunter's Ravine Trail	144
Illinois Creek Trail	62
Illinois Ridge-China Bar Trail	117
Indian Falls Trail	181
Indian Meadows-Hidden Lakes Trail	200
Indian Springs Trail	181
Jackson Creek-Middle Fork Feather River Trail	144
Jackson Ranch Trail	207
Joe Taylor Trail	117
Kelly Bar Trail	204
Kennedy Butte Trail 7E27	118
Kings Creek Falls Trail	201
Lake Almanor Recreation Trail	182
Lassen Peak Trail	201
Lavezzola Creek Trail	63
Lily Lake Trail	85
Lily Pond Nature Trail	202
Little California Mine Trail	145
Little Grass Valley Lakeshore Trail	119
Little Grizzly Creek Trail	64
Little Grizzly Valley-Peacock Point Trail	213
Little Jamison Creek Trail	85
Little North Fork Trail	145
Long Lake Dam Trail	87
Long Lake Trail	87
Long Lake Trail (from Gray Eagle Lodge)	88
Long Valley Trail	146
Lost Cabin Springs-Sugar Pine Mine Trail	148
Madora Lake Nature Trail	119
Manzanita Lake Trail	202
Marble Creek Trail	148
McCarthy Bar Trail	150

Trail	Page
Middle Branch Mill Creek Trail	150
Middle Creek Trail	183
Mill Creek Falls Trail	202
Mill Creek Trail	160
Mill Creek Ditch Trail	151
Minerva Bar Trail (Wilson Gomez Route)	120
Montgomery Creek Trail	210
Morristown-Canyon Creek Trail	65
Mount Elwell Trail	88
Mount Elwell Trail (Smith Lake Trailhead)	88
Mountain Boy-Pat's Gulch Trail	65
Mountain House Creek Trail	151
Mountain House-12 Mile Bar Trail	213
Mt. Alma Trail	214
Mt. Etna via Hopkins Creek Trail	214
Mt. Fillmore Trail	66
Mt. Harkness Trail	202
Mt. Lola Trail	66
Mt. Washington Trail	90
Mud Lake Trail	90
Nelson Creek Bridge-Union Creek Trail	121
Nelson Creek Trail	214
Nelson Point-La Porte Road Trail	121
Nelson Point-Turntable Trail	122
No Ear Bar Trail	152
North Arm Rice Creek Trail	184
Oak Flat-Race Track Point Trail	204
Oddie Bar Trail	153
Old Poker Flat Trail	67
Onion Valley Creek Mine Trail	122
Onion Valley Creek Trail	123
Onion Valley-Richmond Hill Trail	214
Overmeyer Trail	124
Pacific Crest Tie Trail (Upper Salmon Lake)	91
Pacific Mine-Canyon Creek Trail	68
Pauley Creek Trail	68
Peter's Creek Trail	185
Poormans Creek Road-Hopkins Creek Trail	125
Port Wine Trail	69
Port Wine Ridge Trail	70
Providence Hill-Schneider Ravine Trail	186
Ramshorn Trail	70
Rattlesnake Creek Trail	72
Red Fir Nature Trail	92
Richmond Hill-Berg Creek Trail	125
Right Hand Branch Mill Creek Trail	161

Trail	Page
Rock Creek to Rock Creek Crossing Trail	214
Round Lake Trail	92
Round Valley Lake Nature Trail	187
Sand Pond Interpretive Trail	94
Sardine Lakes Overlook Trail	94
Sawmill Tom Trail	126
Sawpit Flat Trail	127
Sawpit Flat Wagon Road Trail	128
Second Divide Trail	73
Seven Falls Trail	128
Shake Cabin Trail	129
Sierra Buttes Trail	95
Silver Lake-Gold Lake Trail 8E04	162
Silver Lake Trail	95
Silver Star Mine-Baker Creek Trail	153
Skyhigh-Little North Fork Feather River Trail	208
Slate Range Bar Trail	204
Smith Creek Trail	96
Smith Lake Trail (from Gray Eagle Lodge)	97
Smith Lake Trail (via Little Jamison Creek Trail)	97
Smith Lake Trail (Smith Lake to Lavezolla Creek Trail)	206
Spanish Ranch-Rich Bar Trail	163
Spencer Lakes Trail (via Spencer Creek)	74
Spencer Lakes Trail (via the PCT)	74
Spencer Meadows National Recreation Trail	187
St. Charles Hill Trail (Brown Bear Mine Trail)	75
Stafford Mountain-West Branch Canyon Creek Trail	76
Star Lake Trail	189
Summit Lake to Echo Lake & Twin Lakes Trail	202
Summit Trail (Bucks Lake)	154
Summit Trail (Lakes Basin Recreation Area)	98
Sunflower Flat-Saucer Lake Trail	190
Sunflower Flat-Soda Creek Trail (to Peacock Point)	190
Tamarack Connection Trail	99
Terrace Shadow & Cliff Lakes Trail	202
Third Divide Trail	76
Three Lakes-PCT Tie Trail	164
Three Lakes-Rich Bar Trail (via Kellogg Lake)	164
Three Lakes Trail	166
Tobin Trail	154
Trail Lake Trail (Echo Lake to Silver Lake Trail)	192
Triangle Lake Loop Trail	200
Upper Nelson Creek Trail	130
Upper Salmon Lake-Deer Lake Trail	100
Wades Lake Trail	101
Watson Cabin-Abandoned Feather Falls Trail	130

Watson Ridge Trail	131
Weber Bar Trail	211
West Branch Canyon Creek Trail	77
West Branch Mill Creek Trail	156
West Branch Nelson Creek Trail	132
West Coast Mine-Canyon Creek Trail	78
Wildcat Creek Trail	156
Yellow Creek Trail	193
Yellow Creek Trail (Parallel to County Road 307)	215
Zumwalt Flat-Nelson Creek Trail	133

ABOUT THE AUTHOR

Scott Lawson, a fifth-generation Plumas County native, was born in Greenville, and raised in Quincy, Meadow Valley, and Butterfly Valley, where early on he developed a passion for hiking. An avid outdoorsman, he has canvassed all areas of the Feather River region, developing an extensive knowledge of the land and its features. He is the Director of the Plumas County Museum in Quincy, California. When not hiking he is reading, working in the garden, or traveling. Scott's interest in local and California history couples well with hiking, bringing a unique historical insight to the trails in this guide. He lives with his family in Graeagle, California.

Photo by Sarah J. Lawson.